MW00782073

Rescue Me

A Powerful Memoir by an Olympian.

Katherine Starr

Rescue Me

A Powerful Memoir by an Olympian.

Katherine Starr

Published by:
KS Enterprises

Text Design: marianne.angelo@bgr8r.com

Cover Design: marianne.angelo@bgr8r.com

A CIP record for this book is available from the Library of Congress Cataloging-in-Publication Data

ISBN: 978-0-578-35650-1

Printed in USA

To my dad, Eddie, and Mary

Contents

Contents (continued)

Introduction

I was born Annabelle Cripps in the USA, to two British parents who immigrated to the States with my oldest brother. My family settled in Madison, Wisconsin, where my father, a doctor, was head of the dermatology department, as well as an accomplished athlete in his youth. I moved from Madison to Great Britain at 11 years old to pursue my Olympic dreams and follow in my father's footsteps or surpass the accomplishments that he had made in swimming for himself. I competed on two Olympic teams for Great Britain. During the course of my career I returned to the States to attend the University of Texas at Austin, where we earned three NCAA team championships and a second place finish title my senior year.

After the end of my athletic career, I followed a path of self-destruction, losing all connection to life in a meaningful way. At 14 years old I was raped by my coach and held that secret pain inside of me, not telling a soul. I had given up on life and saw no reason to live; I was just barely showing up at times because I didn't have the courage to kill myself. I was so disconnected and so afraid to find joy in my life again. I had given my spirit away as a young girl when I started swimming competitively; I gave my power to my coaches while losing my ability to speak up.

I would spend almost ten years in dark despair, until I found my way to sobriety. And that was just the beginning of my healing process; I was so broken that I spent many years in suicidal ideation from the pain and shame of the past. But I kept searching and seeking the truth. Why had God placed so much misery into my life? There had to be a reason and a purpose. I was about to find out. After going on a spiritual trip to India I had an awakening when I rolled my car, just skirting death. I was needed and wanted. I became aware and conscious of my responsibility. After that almost fatal accident I thought hard and deep about my life, my choices, and many sublime moments where I knew I was experiencing God, although I still didn't know exactly what my path and purpose was.

I felt drawn to change my name and become the person I was meant to be. It was then that I became Katherine Starr. While the pain of Annabelle has never left me, my mission in life is to speak for those who are suffering in silence. I now advocate for athletes to have a voice and I have spoken around the world to address the issue of coach-athlete sexual abuse.

However, there was something missing in my journey, and that was me. The joint that held my reconstructed shoulder fell apart and it wasn't until I started training with elite trainer Peter Park, that I realized my body could be strong again. My body is strong and yet I'd been hiding it under layers of weight because I kept saying to myself that's what sexual abuse victims do. Soon after working with Peter. I had the ability to break the praise, attention, and recognition cycle that had driven me and plagued me my whole life. I didn't need to be married to misery and victimhood. I could live in integrity and truth. I could rescue myself.

It's when I look back that I see so many people who came into my life to guide me, heal me, and help me find my way to a higher-self, and that I disconnected from them when I took wrongful ownership of my talents and gifts in life. Only when I was able to see a different story from what I was telling myself did I understand the path that I created and wanted to heal from. I didn't need to win a medal, perform in an event, or have anyone cheer me on. I could just be.

I'm writing this book for everyone searching to find themselves. For everyone who is struggling to find meaning and purpose after trauma, tragedy, and disappointment. Perhaps you will be moved to forgive that old enemy like I did or perhaps you will open up your heart and listen to what you've known to be true all along. And maybe you'll be entertained too. I've lived a pretty amazing fucking life. Thank you for giving me the opportunity to share it with you.

CHAPTER 1

Pure Passion

The kids were jumping in and out of the pool, splashing each other, giggling, laughing, and doing everything else that makes the swimming pool the happiest place on earth, a place of worship for children. What kid doesn't like to play in the pool?

My earliest memories start around age three, when I distinctly remember lying in the kiddie pool viewing the main pool about 20 feet away. With my belly scratching the bottom, creating knots in the Lycra from rubbing against the bottom of the pool, my eyes skimmed the top of the water, blowing bubbles, intently watching the older kids in the main pool who appeared to be having so much fun. Like an alligator watching its prey, I was waiting for my moment to act. The clouds came and went, and the joyful noise of the kids also dipped in and out as I pondered whether I was brave enough to jump into the big pool unnoticed. It was heaven and a pot of gold at the end of the rainbow all wrapped up in one.

My mother walked around the pool deck at the country club with my one-year-old sister in her arms. My brothers swam in the big pool, playing with their friends, while I waited and waited. Six weeks of summer had already flown by. At this point my only friend was the broken mermaid statue sitting in the middle of the kiddie pool and the big oak tree that shaded me from the bright sun when I spied on the big kids' pool. Now was the right time with the lifeguards busy with some of the kids horsing around at the deep end, while my mother was in deep conversation with my little sister on her side, while the kids in the shallow end played Marco Polo.

It was like my Siren song. I heard "Marco" and then there was a silence as the swimmer swam under the water to another part of the pool to yell "Polo." In those moments of pure silence I so wanted to share their experience. I heard their "Marco" one more time and pushed up off the bottom of my 12-inch deep pool as the water rolled off my back. I took that cautious but calculated step across the baby pool, being mindful to not slip, because time was precious, and I had very little of it. Now at the edge of the big pool's shallow end, I saw that the lifeguard was still engaged with the other kids' misbehaving. I had to take my chance, and so I gulped in a big breath and swung my arms in the air as I hurled myself into the pool with all the force I could muster.

The game ended when the young swimmer saw me jumping into the pool—at that moment the lifeguard stopped yelling at the kids. I sank to the bottom of the pool. The silence, the comfort of being fully submerged was overwhelming because there wasn't enough room inside of me to hold onto the excitement. Then my feet touched the bottom, and my eyes opened to a blurry vision of bodies moving toward me in slow motion. I let out a bubble of air that propelled me to the surface. I knew I had arrived since my head was above water again, immersed in this mass of water. I was free for a moment. I was in my own personal heaven.

That feeling was short-lived when the young swimmer quickly grabbed me and plopped me back on the side of the pool. The lifeguard dashed over to make sure I was removed safely from the big pool and I was returned to where they thought I belonged: the baby pool. Then my mother ran over, sister in tow, asking what was going on. The lifeguards informed my mother that I was not allowed in the big pool until I knew how to swim a lap.

My mother, in her defense, asked when I could take swimming lessons because obviously I was bursting at the seams to learn. The life-guards explained that it was too late in the season to register for lessons and that I would have to wait until next year. *How could they do that to me?*

Did they not understand I had discovered my newfound freedom? How could they deny me the joy that I so coveted all summer?

As you can imagine with any child who doesn't get their way, they scream like they're burning the place down. And I had a set of lungs that gave out such a primal cry, where I couldn't breathe, but tried to talk at the same time. I screamed to anyone who would listen that, "I know how to swim!" I swore with such confidence that I could swim a lap like they told my mother I needed to do. Of course up to this point I had not had one swimming lesson and all that anyone knew about me was that I was the kid from the baby pool.

I screamed so loud that my mother had to get my father off the golf course, just to calm me down. All I could repeat was that, "I can swim, I know how to swim!" However, I had no proof to back this statement up other than what I knew in my heart and mind. All the screaming in the world wasn't going to change anyone's mind until I could prove to all of them I could indeed swim the required lap.

My tired red eyes resisted and persisted until my father made his way to the pool, mad that my stubbornness (or was it my confidence in myself?) pulled him away from his weekly golf game with his friends. Yet, what father could deny his little girl, who expressed excitement for the very same thing that he himself loved so much and continued to do every day?

My father reached down to put his hand on my shoulder and asked, "What's wrong?" There was a magic in his touch and a twinkle in his eye. In that moment I knew he was my advocate and I would do anything to please him and gain his love, which was now being shared four ways with my brothers and sister.

I squeaked out in my high-pitched and panicked voice, "They won't let me swim in the big pool." At that point the lifeguard cut in and said that I needed to have swimming lessons in order to be able to swim in the main pool. My father was quick enough to ask if I could swim one lap, would I be allowed in the pool? The lifeguard paused for a moment, which seemed like a lifetime to me, but responded with a nod and a mumbled "yes."

I sighed with relief, as well as with the fear of what I needed to do. The panic and fear was still there, but I released it with the biggest breath I could muster.

My dad said he would buy me a plate of french fries if I made it across the pool. The distraction of food, combined with the joy of knowing I was at the end of the rainbow, eased the pressure I had found myself under.

I quickly jumped in the pool and swam a few strokes to immediately make my way to the side of the pool. The lifeguard stood over me larger than life to tell me I couldn't do it, and with a touch. of disdain continued to say that I wasn't ready for the big pool. Before he could finish speaking, I pushed off the wall and put one stroke in front of the other.

I looked down at the blurred black lane line at the bottom of the pool. I moved my body like a snake in the water, swiveling my hips side to side to propel my body forward. Only knowing when to breathe when my eyes bulged out of the sockets, I brought my head up to the surface, capturing a snapshot of my brothers at the other end, who laughed and taunted me, but for the sake of the moment we'll say they were cheering me on. I was halfway there.

Everything stood still as I swam over the noticeable edge that delineated the drop off in the deep end of the pool. I was doing it. It was the moment that my courage became pride. I put my head down and pushed over the deep water, not sinking at all, but moving steadily across the water. All that I envisioned and taught myself in the baby pool was happening. I was in another world. I made it.

I touched the wall and my father leaned down and put his hand on my head to shake it in a term of endearment. My father's smile meant the world to me. I had made him proud. I too was proud. At that moment, I became Daddy's little girl.

Wow, I'm a swimmer now, I thought with a big grin on my face. My dad was so proud, and my brothers had their first of many conversations about "Little Annabelle" and her ability to swim. The excitement ran so deep that I went to sleep that night with my swimsuit on. It literally became a part of me. The next morning came and I woke up to an itchy scratchy swimsuit, with indents in my bright white delicate skin, but it was worth it.

Every day for the rest of summer we would wait for what seemed a lifetime for our mother to be ready to take us to the country club to hang out at the pool all day. I asked my mother a million times, "Are you ready yet? Can we go swimming? Can we go?" I doubt that I took a breath between all those questions and spoke as quickly as I could. I guess it's like pressing that elevator button a bunch of times, like it will get you there quicker. *You don't understand. I'm a swimmer and I need to go experience my newfound freedom.*

Eventually, my mother packed us all in the car and we drove up to the Maple Bluff Country Club, a small community, in Madison, Wisconsin, where I grew up. My mother dropped my brothers and me right outside the pool entrance, as she parked the car with my baby sister.

The day after I qualified for the "big" pool I walked into the pool and it was different; something had changed inside of me. I could feel my eyes twinkle as I studied where I wanted to enter the big pool. *I'm a real swimmer now.* I could try the diving board as my first point of entry. Although that was exciting in its own right, I wanted to save that experience for another time. My piercing three-year-old eyes scanned the entire pool and chose the closest spot, right in front of me. I whipped off my clothes and dropped them right there on the pool deck.

I stood on the side of the pool, almost like I was paying my respects before I became submerged in the magic of the water. It was truly magical when you jumped in and it just held you. It was like being wrapped in unconditional love. The perfect touch on your body, it laid right up next to you. Nothing was quite like it.

I couldn't wait to repeat my lap and show off to everyone that it wasn't a fluke. I saw my mom walk by with my sister and waved to her, so she could see. "Look at me!" I put my head down and rotated my arms around like a windmill hoping to skate quickly toward the wall. I saw the blur of the black "T" on the walls, which seemed to not be coming much closer; I frequently crested the surface to see if I made any progress. I put my head back down and kept trying until I made it. After that lap, I quickly pushed off the wall to repeat my accomplishment over and over again. I was determined to swim like the big kids. I was a big kid now.

My mother walked to the side of the pool after speaking with someone and asked me if I wanted to join the swim team. I couldn't believe my ears! *Yesterday I was in the kiddie pool and today I'm on the swim team!* I took a split second to say "yes." I pushed off the wall and my excitement was so great that I let out a scream under the water. I naturally didn't want my pure joy to be revealed.

The country club swim team had never won a swim meet all summer, and in fact they had never won a swim meet ever. On that swim team there would turn out to be five Olympians (four of them gold medalists in their sports), a Stanley Cup winner, and the famous actor Chris Farley and the Farley family. What a team of talent and we never won one swim meet, not one!

The country club needed a fourth swimmer in the Girls 8 & Under relay, and I was it for the big final city meet. How exciting—I had reached the pinnacle of success! I wonder how many other Pre-K kids made the team.

I didn't really care about the other kids; all I really cared about was telling my dad. The love that my dad showed me was nothing like I had experienced before. The delight in his voice and now how easy it was to get to sit on his lap after dinner. I just seemed to move right up the ranks to Daddy's little girl, and was close to being his favorite, not that our parents meant to have any. If I could have captured and held that look in his eye when I told him that I was on the swim team and competing in a real swim meet, my life would have been filled with love to last many lifetimes. I didn't know what any of this really meant—it was how my dad responded to me. It was a look and feeling that I would spend the rest of my life chasing.

The minutes, hours, and days were endless waiting for the swim meet. In the summer, the nights in the Midwest stay light until after 10 p.m. and my bedtime was around eightish, so while I lay awake, I had a lot of time for my mind to race in wonder. I would practice over and over in my mind, moving my arms around and around getting ready for the big day.

Morning finally came; the swim meet was really here! My brothers and I got ready because they were competing too. I'm fairly certain I was waiting in the car way ahead of time and before anyone else was anywhere near ready to go.

We arrived at the meet and there were lots of people screaming really loud. It scared me. I would hear "Go!" over and over in some sort of rhythm, and then suddenly it stopped with all the other cheers.

I went from excitement to scared in a split second and then back to excitement. I wasn't sure what I had to do. We walked onto the pool deck and I didn't just see the kids swimming; they were diving in from the starting blocks that stood about three feet high from the edge of the pool. Not only had I not seen these starting blocks before, I wasn't much taller than they were. I hadn't practiced this part of the race in my mind. What was I to do?

I tugged on my mother and told her that I didn't want to do this. I started to cry. My excitement had tipped the other way; oh what to do. My mother found the coach to tell him I wasn't going to be able to swim. Then my father arrived to see how upset I was. My dad lowered himself to my level and asked me what was wrong. I pointed at the high blocks. I had tears of disappointment. I was so devastated.

My dad grabbed my arms and swung them up over my head together, to demonstrate how to dive in. He patted me on the head and said, "Little Annabelle, you'll do great." I took a deep breath and started practicing, putting my hands above my head over and over. I watched, without anyone seeing me, while I studied the other swimmers diving in for their races. I could feel the rhythm and movement in me gain confidence as every race went by. Little by little my fear started to fade away.

My relay race came around and the other three girls, who were all eight years old, held my hand as we walked over to the blocks. I was instructed that I needed to wait until my teammate touched the wall and then I could go. They put me in fourth position, which typically was saved for the fastest swimmer, but in this case, they didn't want to be too far behind by the time I went.

The three girls swam before me, and while the third was in the water my two teammates stood beside me and told me when I was to step on the starting blocks. I watched with such concentration as these big girls, who were more than twice my size, swam next to me. My time was coming up so fast.

I had my dad's confidence in me and that was all I needed. After the girl touched the wall I peeked over the top of the blocks to see my dad. My attention zoned in on his voice as he yelled, "GO, Annabelle, go!" That was the only voice I heard among a mirage of screaming parents and kids.

I took my cue and threw my hands above my head, but I forgot to push off with my legs and fell off the starting blocks, doing a half belly flop that propelled me toward the bottom of the pool. As I submerged, my father's voice of confidence faded off into the distance. I knew I couldn't touch the bottom because we would have been disqualified. My eyes popped open and I let out a gasp of air that immediately launched me up to the surface. I skimmed right on up and saw my dad's big grin, as bright as a Christmas tree. I moved my arms as fast I could, keeping my head down until I really needed a breath. It was like time just stopped and air wasn't necessary in my world of peace and joy.

That was so much fun. I got out of the pool and ran over to my dad and hugged him all wet, leaving an imprint of my body on his pants. I touched my father's heart. That was the day I felt safe and protected from everything.

During that summer I had the thrill of seeing my dad every day after work when he would come up to the country club and swim laps. I got to swim with my father by holding on to his neck and resting on his back. He would pull me across the pool like I was the grand marshal in a parade, passing all the other kids with such happiness across the pool. As he swam with me on his back, I would submerge my head with his, valiantly not letting the swirl of water push me off his back as he swam breaststroke. I practiced closing my eyes and holding my breath with his. I was determined to guess the rhythm of my father's swimming, hoping to be in perfect harmony as we would move up, down, and forward in the pool. It was like I was constantly trying to have our hearts and minds beat as one. This became a common thread in my life.

As the summer wound down, those joyous moments with my father were coming to an end. I felt an immense sadness for the loss of my time with both of my everythings: my father and swimming. This weighed heavily on me. It was my first understanding of loss. The emptiness of not being in the mysticism of the water and cherishing the moments with my father, doing something that we both loved. A dark cloud hung over me. As I fell asleep at night it seemed like all I could think about was: How could you take away my best friend, my companion, the only place where my heart was truly full, and the one place that I felt safe and where I belonged? I never wanted summer to end.

I started first grade and I could feel myself becoming lost. The long nights in the water were quickly becoming just a distant memory. The pride of the children in the streets and the malaise of noise from the pool had died down to utter silence. The seriousness of life and the order of school was staring me in the face.

I went to a school called Edgewood, a private Catholic grade school situated across town. While my family isn't Catholic, it was the only local private school. Since I started school in preschool there, the school wasn't new to me, but having a full day of school was. Also what was new to me was my height. That summer I seemed to have grown a lot, and stood noticeably taller than my peers and almost as tall as my younger brother who was 18 months older than me. I was in this awkward body that I hadn't adjusted to the space that was allocated to me.

The new me, or the developing me, was challenged on the first day of school, because I couldn't quite fit underneath the desk; it just rested on my legs. I had these nervous legs, or restless legs, or something that would make my desk move up and down all day in class. The smacking of the desk on the ground seemed to annoy my teacher so much that I was constantly being sent to the principal's office.

I sat there in the principal's office waiting. The kid next to me had feet that didn't even touch the ground. They swung back and forth, happy as all get out. I yearned for the water in that moment, as I kept making myself smaller and smaller both inside and out just to fit into the chair. Finally, after many visits to Principal Sister Mary Kate's office over the first month of school, the nuns had had enough. They weren't sure what they'd had enough of, but it seemed to work to my benefit.

My mother was called to the nuns' office and informed of the problem; I was disturbing the rest of the class and they needed to do something about it. The details of the conversation are fuzzy to me, but their solution was to have my mother take me swimming every day after school, and I would also need to run around the school every morning at least three times or so until I could sit still in class, whichever came first.

My punishment was to swim every day?! I couldn't wait to go home and sit on my dad's lap at dinner and share with him my good fortune: I would get to swim every day after school because I was disturbing the class. Something came alive inside me. The shame of not fitting in, and not being like the other kids seemed to be all okay. I was going to be okay.

Let the games begin. I was off and running, well swimming anyway. The daily swimming quickly became part of my routine. I learned that feeling of doing your best time or winning a race was a high like no other. I learned that if I did my best, my father would cherish me with his love and give me more of his attention than my brothers and sisters.

The transition from summer to school that year was a success, although the sadness of anticipating Labor Day would be a pattern that would continue to have its challenges with me for many years to come.

CHAPTER 2

The American Dream

Over the next few years, I started swimming six days a week and my identity was changing: I was not just Annabelle anymore; I was Annabelle the swimmer or just "the swimmer." My love was growing for being a swimmer, a competitive swimmer. It was like my love for the long summer nights marked a time when my heart was full with joy. As the winter drifted away and we moved past the lull of spring, it was summer swimming season again—the funnest part of swimming. I got to swim outdoors, the swim meets seemed like they happened every weekend, and in my free time I got to swim some more. I was in heaven. For a cherry on top, during the summer of '76, the Bicentennial year, I was at the top of my age group. I was eight and competing in my final year as an 8 & Under.

There were so many great changes happening that summer, with one of those being my parents moving into a new house on the other side of Maple Bluff, the biggest house in the neighborhood, besides the governor's mansion, and next to the Oscar Meyer mansion (Yes, that Oscar Meyer! The brand name is now spelled Oscar Mayer). My sister and I shared a bedroom that overlooked the water with a clear shot of the beautiful capitol across the lake that lit up every night like my heart did about swimming. My life was quickly becoming a dream in so many ways: swimming in the lake every day, swimming in practice every day, and being in a swimsuit all day every day. Really, could my dreams get any bigger?

Well, my dreams could get bigger it seemed. There was something missing in my life, a puppy. Puppies were fun and exciting, but my parents hadn't let us have a dog up to this point. They were strict in many ways and this was one example. Like any little girl who wants something bad enough, I learned to beg and plead, and with that tactic you need to have a bargaining chip. What I did have was a love for swimming, a love for my connection to my father, and a desire to win that allowed this pattern to repeat itself. My dad gave me a bet or a reward, you decide what you want to call it, or maybe we should say a carrot. If I won the state meet and broke the state record, then they would get me a dog. Therein lies the chase.

My heart started to chase the puppy and my mind started to focus on swimming and more importantly, winning. My father and I shared a common goal: my own success—it wasn't just a talking point and a way to connect with me. He was vested in my outcome. He was before, but now the stakes were greater and they went deeper, attaching to my passion that ran through me like Class V rapids. It was a force of passion and love that I can't explain other than I felt it as a young girl. Harnessing it and pointing it towards the love of my father made it flow even more. Besides, it felt good. I felt alive, and I had something special to share with my dad that my siblings did not have.

As July Fourth approached, so did one of my swim meets. It wasn't the state meet, but it was still competitive and important, and the last qualifying meet before the state meet later in the summer. The Fourth was on a Sunday that year and it was a big celebration, so I didn't swim on Sunday, just Saturday. At this point in my life I didn't have time to play with other kids my age, and certainly had no time for TV because I was swimming every night. The idea of celebrating the Fourth of July in a country that I loved and respected meant the world to me. I wish I could trap all that excitement in a bottle.

The night before that race I had this dream I can still remember it as clear as day. It was so weird; I could hear God telling me my life was being recorded and that one day it would be played back for others to see. I had this idea about what my life would turn out to be. The way my eight-year-old self translated that dream was that I was going to be famous one day because I was a great swimmer and the whole world was going to know what a great swimmer I was.

I woke up from that dream ready to swim, ready to win, ready to be the best. I was given this confidence about myself like I was on steroids or something. It was a subtle strength I could feel running inside of me. I never said anything to anyone about it and carried myself around like I had a secret from the world. I was special.

The walk downstairs from my bedroom to the kitchen was quite a walk; it seemed like it was far away, so I imagined it like I was walking on water. My mother had the cereal out that I liked and a grapefruit that I hated. I needed to put the entire bowl of sugar on the grapefruit so I didn't actually taste it. When my mother noticed, she would take the sugar away. It was never enough. After I winced my way through the grapefruit and ate my cereal, my dad came down the stairs and said that he would be at my swim meet later. My mother was going to take me and my dad would arrive by the time I swam. There was a lot of "sitting around time" at a swim meet and my father wasn't particularly good at that.

With this enhanced confidence and my father coming to see me swim with a potential puppy on the way, life was good. We packed up the car and off we went to the swim meet.

The one thing about swim meets is that they are loud, well, on and off loud. They are all full of cheers and then when the race starts there is silence so the swimmers have a fair chance to react to the starter. The name of the game is focus, focus your mind. It was like that focus was implanted in me with my dream from the night before. It didn't mean that I wasn't also wondering if my dad was going to be there as my head turned towards the door waiting for this prominent person that I was so proud to have as a dad come watch me swim. The idea of that made me feel special.

As my race drew closer, I kept checking the heat sheet to see where we were and when I was up. It got closer to the race and butterflies started to swirl in my stomach. I walked behind the blocks where you wait patiently for your turn, but still no sign of my dad. He wasn't one to be late or miss anything, but I wanted to see him; I wanted to know that he was there, like all the chess pieces needed to be in their place. As the final heat before me stepped up to the blocks, in walked my dad. A surge of joy filled my little body and I am sure I pushed out my already protruding stomach.

I was a little nervous; there was some performance anxiety, not that I knew what that was, but I had a jittery feeling that I would come to know well. As the loud cheers stopped and we stepped on the blocks, all my ears could hear was my father yelling, "Go, little Annabelle!" He might as well have been the only one there. That was all I needed to hear, my dad, that was it.

This time when I dove in I was in a time warp of sorts. I moved through the water with ease, there wasn't an ounce of pain, it was all power and grace. My stroke was perfect, and my rhythm was smooth. I could feel it both on the inside and out. I couldn't see a single person in my view and I wasn't sure where anyone went, but I kept going. I did have a thought there was a false start and I didn't know it; my heart skipped a beat and then I moved my mind right along to the finish. I touched the wall, looked around, and I was more than a body length from the next swimmer. I had broken the state record! I looked at my dad, a man of few words, who just smiled, it really was a twinkle. I was his little girl. I got out of the water and dripping wet determined to ask or maybe beg or really bargain for the puppy, wanting whatever extra affection I could get out of my dad in that moment.

That wasn't the only celebration because tomorrow was July Fourth. I had the day off and my dreams were already coming true. That year's July Fourth started with a parade in the village with us kids decorating our bikes with ribbons and riding them with the other kids along the neighborhood street escorted by the local police. I had a skip in my step, as there was an internal pride meeting going off, not that I knew what was going on. I could see a difference between me and the other kids. It wasn't just in the way that I was treated; it was how I responded to life around me.

I felt like I was in the dream. I had found the dream for me or at least part of the dream. My father, when he moved to America, was to pursue his dream of becoming a world famous and renowned doctor. I too wanted what my dad wanted, but for me, my version of that. He dreamed big and so could I. I still wanted to be able to blend in with friends my own age, at least I thought that until I learned I had this ability to dream big for something in my life. I wasn't witnessing that with the other kids, not that they didn't dream, but their focus seemed in the moment and mine was in the future, and I knew this moment was going to be a reflection of the outcome of my future.

All this didn't mean that I wasn't dreaming to get my dad's attention. I was enamored with my Dad. It was always a premium to get any time and attention with him. Every moment was special, even when my dad came home from the hospital following his open heart surgery; all I wanted to do was crawl on the bed and cuddle with him. I knew he was wincing in pain having just had his chest cut open, but he let me crawl right on. It was his sacrifice to love me despite the pain that he was in. It wasn't just me, it was all of us. He held in his pain so we could feel loved.

Later on that July Fourth, there was lots of partying with my parents' friends all along the lakeshore in Maple Bluff. This year, since we moved to the wealthier part of the bluff, the parties were bigger as well. At least that was the way it seemed, combined with the special occasion of this particular Fourth. I too was a bigger person, not just in size in relation to my parents' friends children, but now in relevance to my accomplishments compared with the other children. The other parents could include me in their conversations, a common reference point. I was starting to be seen and heard. I grew up with that statement that children should be seen and not heard, but I had conquered that.

As the evening wound down, I felt my passion for my love of America as the fireworks lit up the night sky. I also became "Annabelle the swimmer," and my father became "Annabelle's father." I watched how my dad changed at those parties, how he was so proud of me. He was before, but now he could tell everyone else about that pride that he had for me. The glee in the people's eyes became addicting and desired by me.

Yet I wasn't exactly the most accomplished person in my neighborhood. I grew up in a place of greatness, with so much talent, some we knew about at this point and others were successes waiting to happen. Connie Carpenter, one of our neighbors, participated in the '72 Winter Olympics at the age of 14. I was only six years away from that. Then there was my neighbor, Jim Montgomery, who made the USA Olympic Team for the upcoming Olympics. Jim was introduced to me after I had just broken many state records and he thought I could be a potential Olympian one day too. There was a fire in my belly that lit up like the fireworks outside. I could believe in my Olympic dream without much hesitation or resistance. I was also shy and coy—all the emotions I was going to hide in that moment.

My dad and I were excited to watch our neighbor Jim compete in the upcoming Olympics. All that meant for me was time with my dad and watching what I loved: swimming. Waiting for the Olympics to come on the air in a few weeks seemed like light years to me. What was even more amazing was that my dad would leave work a little earlier to make sure he got his swim in and then we could watch the Games together. My siblings were welcome to join us, but they didn't seem as interested unless America was winning something. My father, on the other hand, held a strong allegiance to the strength of Great Britain. This would be where I had my first internal conflict with my father. I had just come off the high of loving my country a few weeks ago celebrating the Fourth, to my father now having a vested interest in the British Olympians. The only time my father and I weren't conflicted and at odds was when we cheered on our neighbor Jim.

When my father arrived home from the pool he needed to lie down and would read his book until it was time for dinner or, in this case, to watch the Olympics. He didn't waste any time when it came to the flow of life and was often multi-tasking with a book and something else. I constantly badgered him to pay attention to me. I needed his full attention. When the swimming came on and it was time to watch Jim, I wanted to be swimming right alongside him. The races aired and I got into the starting position and held the pose until the beep went off and then jumped up in excitement. I was never a very animated kid but rather always quite reserved. I studied other people as I did in this case of watching Jim swim his race. I was interested in the rhythm and the cadence of his swim and wanted to emulate him in my actions as well.

The swimming events were always held the first week of the Olympics, so I had a whole week of joy with my father. A few days into the Olympics we watched David Wilke compete for Great Britain in the men's 200 meter Breaststroke. So far all I knew was how great all the American swimmers were and I didn't know anything about any British swimmers. Every summer my parents would take us to Europe with a stop in England to see my British grandparents. I had swum in swimming pools in London and they weren't as nice, clean, or modern as the ones that I trained in back in Wisconsin. I figured, how could there also be a good swimmer from Great Britain?

As I watched his event with my dad, I saw a change in my dad's personality and demeanor. Usually reserved, all of a sudden he became animated and vocal when David Wilke touched the wall for the gold. My father was so proud to be British. I wasn't quite feeling the same way, but I didn't let him know that. My heart was torn in that moment; I wanted my neighbor and everything American to win. Was it the underdog that my father was cheering for? It didn't seem like it; it seemed like he was cheering for his love of being British. I went along with his love because I loved my dad. I figured I had the best of both worlds. Yet I knew my father's pride in being British was greater than his love for being in America and being part of the American Dream and the land of opportunity. I saw for the first time we were different that way.

Then my dad started to tell me about his experience as a young man. He said that he should have gone to the Olympics, but it was during the Cold War and they only took eight swimmers. I hadn't ever seen my dad disappointed or sad; angry and short, but not disappointed and sad. I wanted to give my dad the gift of him being an Olympian. I wanted to take away his sadness. All I heard was the world was wrong and that shouldn't have happened to my dad. I was determined from that point on that I was not going to let that happen to me.

That moment didn't stop my dad from sharing the rest of his stories about representing Great Britain. He told his stories every night after I raced him in the pool, which by this point, hands down, he was in my wake and couldn't keep up with his speedy daughter, the fish that I had become. It didn't stop me wanting to keep asking my dad for more stories about what it was like to represent your country. I would pepper him with questions, mostly about the stroke he swam, which oddly enough was a combination of swimming butterfly and breaststroke, an actual stroke back in the day and he still swam it. It was always funny for me to watch and a little embarrassing, but it also made my dad stand out and I liked that too. Swimming at the club and then watching the Olympics became our ritual over the next week. I was having the best summer yet.

The wonders of the summer weren't over; I still had the end-of-summer state meet with records to break and a puppy to earn. I'm sure my parents were sick of me asking about the puppy all this time, but I needed to make sure that there was a puppy at the end of this rainbow. I wanted the records, let's be honest. My father was all about legacy and excelling, leaving the world a better place and being the best version of yourself wherever you go. I was going to be that too. My goal was to break records that would stand the test of time. I didn't want to just win, I wanted to be special. After all, I was chasing my father's love and approval. One thing for sure was that it didn't matter what country I was from as long as my dad was proud of me, or at least I was going to make my dad proud of me even more when I broke all the records.

When it came time for me to compete, I was a seasoned professional for an eight-year-old; after all, I had been doing this for the past five years, unlike some of my peers who had just started that summer or the year before. I had already developed my pre-race ritual of arriving to the blocks early, not too early, but with enough time to get organized without being tired on my feet. I needed to preserve my legs before I swam, it was how I felt rested. That or I was lazy and wanted to preserve my energy for my race.

As we stepped up onto the blocks, I learned to tune out the noise. When we take our marks, the force of energy to perform shifted to a nothingness, like I was floating. As the beep went off there was a natural movement and reaction to jump through the air. When I entered the water

I could feel the water roll down my back. There became no separation between the water and me, we moved together to defy time and space. When I raced I had no distraction of planning for the next set or another person in my lane; it was me in the pool and the race against time. I just swam; I couldn't see anyone, but I could hear my dad, well, I could feel the drive of my dad inside of me. I could feel the determination of energy flow through me. I wanted to be the best, and more importantly, when I swam that race I knew that I was going to be an Olympian one day. It was plausible because I knew it was inside of me; my dad also knew it was too. I loved the praise, I loved being Daddy's little girl, I loved the way that my dad was proud of me.

It wasn't only about the puppy now, that was a reward along the way. I needed the next thing; I needed to know where I was going. I had earned my puppy, but it didn't reward me like I thought it would. I had to share it with my siblings; it wasn't going to be just mine. It wasn't like I wasn't going to love my dog, but rather that my brothers and sister would share in the result of my hard work, and that seemed unfair and unrewarding. At least that's what I thought at the time.

At the end of the summer there was always a banquet at the country club and because I won everything in my age group, it would be extra special this summer. It was common at the country club to have such great swimmers, but winning wasn't something that Maple Bluff was known for when it came to team success.

I was also going to meet Jim Montgomery who would share his medal haul with us at our banquet. *Wow,* is all I could say. I would get to share the spotlight with Jim, my success and his. I doubt that Jim thought of that, seeing as I had broken every state record possible in my age group and he was the best in the world, but to me we were both from Maple Bluff and we both had won something and that was all the bond I needed. One could say that we both held tremendous pride in our individual success.

At the end of the banquet, Jim wore his medals and I was first in line, standing alone with Jim touching those medals like they were my own. I could feel them around my neck. I wanted them. The surge of desire moved through me in that moment not unlike the moment that I got up the courage to run across the pool deck and swim in the big pool at age three. I knew I could swim and now I knew I was going to be an Olympian one day. My eyes glossed over with conviction; there was never a doubt in my being. I saw a real-life Olympian and now I was going to become one.

I arrived home after the banquet filled with more joy than I could handle with a head full of dreams to keep me busy for the rest of my life, or at least the rest of my youth. As I headed towards bed, my father called out my name, "Little Annabelle." He always added the word "little," and I was far from that. He said, "One day you'll represent Great Britain in the Olympics." My dad patted me on my back like he believed in me too. I knew that was my dad's way of saying I love you.

I rested my head on my pillow with dreams of going to the Olympics, but I felt one major conflict that I wasn't sure what to do with, the idea of being British. My parents were British, my grandparents were British, the cousins were British, even my oldest brother was British. I loved America, I'm an American. I hadn't thought this through. I wanted to be like my dad and follow in his footsteps. I wanted to be better than my dad, and he wanted me to be better than what he achieved.

As the summer faded away so did the excitement. What I gained from that summer was that I was going be an Olympian one day. I also learned about how much I loved greatness and I wanted that for myself. It felt good to pursue it; it made me feel special, and it also made me feel like I was like my dad and loved by my dad. What little girl wouldn't want that? I did have this internal conflict that was starting to percolate inside of me, of *who am I? Am I British or American?* This question would plague me going forward.

CHAPTER 3

Worlds Divide

After a summer filled with joy and excitement it was time to get back to work. Yes, get back to work. My mindset had changed that summer from swimming to going to work towards my dreams. I had turned my life into a singular focus that required all of my attention morning, noon, and night. I matured into this mindset, one that my father taught me and one that was also part of my own internal makeup of who I am as a person. I was driven while also being honed for success and greatness.

This drive and success was rewarded with me being moved up to the highest training group. Here I was eight years old and moving up to train with the high school team. I had officially left all the kids my age which also meant that I was no longer the fastest person at practice, especially when there were high school boys in my group. I had a new ladder to climb. My father always felt that you should be in pursuit rather than be pursued when you're a champion. At least that was the way I understood it at the time.

The new training group came with a new coach, Fred, who was gruff and not particularly friendly. Swimming was all business when you got to practice without any warm or fuzzy conversations. The fun chatter with your friends before and after practice seemed to be less of a thing when you got older; that or I was so young no one knew how to talk to me because I wasn't even close to anyone else's age. Or maybe everyone was too focused to have anything to say at practice.

My training was usually six days a week including four mornings, but I remember some Sunday practices. Sundays my family generally went to the Episcopal Church on the square where the magnificent, dynamic, and structurally stunning state capitol stood. The capitol was also in direct view from my bedroom every night. I enjoyed passing by the building because it filled my soul with an energy I craved. The church itself was as old but not quite as stunning. All that beauty and grandness didn't bring me to liking church. Maybe it seemed more like school. When we were in the church for the service it was another environment for me to feel awkward and out of place with my restless energy and uncontrollable movements that stuck out like a sore thumb. When it came time to leave Sunday school and join your parents in the service, which was probably for about ten minutes, it was also the same time they put the donuts out in the hall. My mind became obsessed: when was I going to get a fresh hot donut? It felt like the closing remarks lasted forever and the praying became all about getting to the donuts faster and me scheming how I could get more donuts than what was allotted for everyone else.

However, all that focus on the donuts wasn't going to make me go to church over swim practice. I don't know if it was my decision to swim or if it was required by the coach, but either way it got me out of church and into the pool. They all knew me at church as this star swimmer in the making. Even the priest would bless me on the way out. I was special there. That specialness is what gave me permission to move my attention away from God and towards me.

It was here where I started to drift away from the idea that God lived within. I had had the dream and God told me where I was going. I got my marching orders and it was time to put my mind to work towards the path and direction in my life. I missed the donuts, but who wouldn't? They were hot and gooey in my hands when I picked them up, and after placing that first bite in my mouth, I was filled with utter euphoria. But they weren't enough to keep me wanting to come back to church. I had work to do.

While my life started to change with being removed from my peers in the pool, it also started to change at home as well. This would be the beginning of my family starting to go its separate ways, as my older brothers moved to England to attend boarding school. It appeared that was a tradition in our family, at least for my dad. He wasn't shy about telling us that he was sent to boarding school when he was six so his mother could play golf all the time. It was funny that was his story because my dad grew up with multiple nannies when most wealthy people just had one.

I saw a different story. I saw how the younger of my two brothers got into frequent verbal sparring bouts with my mother. They would have a match of wits and intelligence and both were determined to win. It was a battle that I never liked and would avoid at all costs. As the arguments intensified, it seemed like the only solution to the problem was to send my brothers away.

I had my own experience with my mother. It wasn't packaged like my brother's fights with her, but it came in a way that allowed me to produce the same amount of anger to show her how I was being wronged.

After school I had to wait on my own for an hour and half before practice started at school. That was always lonely, but I seemed to figure out how to manage and deal with it. I channeled that loneliness into a visualization exercise, making my mind super-prepped for practice. My dad had taught me to do that, how to focus on my swimming, like being able to hone this energy flow that we all have.

When I wasn't able to do that, I was meandering around looking for a store to find food, because, I seemed to always be hungry. On occasion, okay on many occasions, I would spend my bus money on candy that wasn't even very good knowing that I was going to have to beg the bus driver to let me on the bus to get home without getting in trouble. Trouble came in the form of Mother hitting me with the belt. I was motivated to not invite further pain into my life, but sometimes buying the candy over having bus fare was worth it. All this because my mother played bridge and resented my dad for having to take all of us kids around town without something else to do in her life.

My mother's obsession with bridge and mine with swimming didn't gel in perfect harmony. This was compounded by the fact that me saying how I truly felt wasn't something you freely did with my parents. I had learned early on in my family that you don't express yourself with what you want or what your dreams are. You can chase a puppy or a financial reward, but sharing a dream was not okay. It seemed to fall into the category of boasting or highlighting your siblings' lack of drive or desire. When you shared a dream you lit a fire that became your responsibility to put out. At least that was the way I experienced dreaming, especially with my brothers, and even more so with my dad.

When it came time for my brothers to leave for the UK, I was okay with it, because maybe I would get more time with my dad and could publicly dream and talk about the life that I saw for myself and wanted to create.

When my brothers left, I thought, *Great, it's just my sister and myself at home. I am the star.* I was, after all, Annabelle the swimmer. It became easy for me to win everything except my dad's attention now. My brothers' leaving created the opposite effect that I thought was going to happen. My mother became more involved with her bridge and my dad changed his expectations of me.

It also meant that my mother's rage would be focused on me and my little sister. Swimming gave me an oasis away from my mother when everything was painful about life and living in my family. When I was in the water, the touch of the water on my body was the only form of unconditional love I knew. The better I swam, the more I fell in love with the water and how it touched my body. The sting of the belt hitting my body was washed away in the pool.

As I continued to excel in the pool, the challenges and the accumulating number of wins diminished in value. So did my dreams, it seemed. It was like my dad had upgraded my dreams, meaning that I had to work harder to get his attention. However, the more attention I got from him the better protection I got from my mother's rage. Winning became twofold: less rage from my mother and more attention and love from my father.

My father was all about greatness and excelling. At this point in my father's career, he had invented the SPF system for sunscreen along with other impressive accomplishments. The drive to be worthy and accomplished became my bond with my father. Yet I was needing to expand that beyond the empty wins; they were too easy. My parents subscribed to *The Daily Telegraph,* a conservative British newspaper that arrived every day along with the British swimming association magazines that announced the British rankings. It was the rankings that became my next pursuit, with first place the only place worth having.

As the magazines arrived they became the goal and focus of my dream. Although at this point I had dropped the word "dream" and started focusing on being an Olympic gold medalist. That was the only benchmark and goal that one could have; everything else was considered a waste of time. My dad was very clear about not wasting his time. He communicated the importance of time and winning with a story he often liked to repeat. He once owned a MG7 or something like that, and only seven people ever passed him in that car. Maybe that is why I have a propensity for driving fast today.

I needed to be more impressive and do something I hadn't done before in order for my father to lift his head from his book and learn about some part of my swimming. His unspoken message to me was: Only come back when you are better than last time. Last time I was the best in the state; MVP at the swim meet. It turned out that this swim meet wasn't competitive enough or I didn't swim fast enough despite all my wins. There was something "not enough" about what I had accomplished.

When I would bring home the next trophy and the British swimming magazines later came in the mail reporting my win, I would open them with excitement to see where I was in their rankings. But the age groups were divided up differently so it gave me a false sense of accomplishment. Was I as good as I was in America? It gave me a way to talk to my dad because he seemed to be more engaged with me when I included how I ranked among my British peers.

I started to learn about comparing myself with others, probably something we naturally do when we have siblings, since there was a lot of comparing about who got what and how much. Those comparisons started to compound on each other and gave me a sense of importance. The higher my rank, the more important I was. As I started to think about my importance, I also started to separate myself from my siblings thinking I was more valuable or more something. This mindset started to trickle to my teammates, especially since I was several years younger than anyone I trained with. I took my age difference as something unique and special.

As I divided myself from others with my uniqueness, I also divided myself from God or my relationship with God. When training fell on Sundays I chose training because it was more important than God, although it was really a question of training versus donuts when you think of it that way, it became a little more challenging to make that decision. It was really about me choosing my self-importance.

My self-importance got bigger and so did my demands and temper. I was in practice one day and we were given a set of 5 x 200 fly. I was in the lane with the big guys swimming at the back of the lane with several swimmers in each lane. When the boys would swim past me, they made a huge wave and when I came up to breathe, I was met with a mouthful of water. I wasn't able to push myself over the waves to clear the water, so I kept choking. I also didn't want to do that set because it was hard and uncomfortable and being uncomfortable was not something I welcomed and often took action to correct. At some point in that set, pretty early on, I just got out of the pool and threw my cap and goggles onto the pool deck and said that I wasn't doing that anymore. I was quitting. I was walking away. And I did. I just walked away.

I was also filled with fear and guilt. How was I going to explain this? Once I got out of practice I decided I wasn't going back. I started to think about how I was going to hide this from my mother. I didn't have my brothers around to take the attention off of me. My self-importance was not working in my favor. What was I going to say to my dad? I knew I couldn't entirely hide since my hair would be dry by the time my mother picked me up from practice.

When my mother arrived to pick me up, late of course, she learned about my choice to quit the workout and my failure had become her failure somehow. I wasn't allowed to leave the pool until I went back in there and apologized to my coach. I thought he was out of line with even giving me that set and making me do that with older guys. I also knew this coach. He had a temper himself and went as far as throwing stuff at us in the pool like chairs and other potentially harmful items. To go ask for mercy from someone who wasn't treating you right was par for the course. But I was still scared. I wanted my mother to stand up for me.

When I got home that night and sat down for dinner it was only my sister and me with my parents. The tone of the conversation became serious. My father was not happy with my decision to get out of practice that night. While I defended myself with a long "but D-a-a-a-d" explaining what I had to deal with, I'm sure I added in some drama of the difficulty that I had breathing during that practice. My mother just sat there deferring to my dad. It was like she brought the prisoner home and I was to hear the punishment from my master.

All this led to my dad thinking we should consider finding another swim program. My father starting to think out loud about me going to England to train. "Maybe Little Annabelle would be better served in the British system," he told us at the table. It wasn't something that I was immediately wanting to pursue. I also knew I needed to be willing, but I was braced with this idea that I didn't want to upset my dad. I also didn't like where I was swimming. I was torn by this.

I went to bed that night feeling conflicted and lost about what to do. I held one focus in my mind and that was to be an Olympian. Yet I was lost about how all that was going to come together. I was here and still had to go back to practice tomorrow with my tail between my legs and ask for mercy. Of course I had to make a claim that I wasn't going to act like that again. I was going to have to find a new way to figure out how to deal with practice when it got hard and unmanageable.

Now that I had this idea that I could be going to England, I felt something unraveling inside of me. At school I started to not apply myself knowing there was a way out. Let's be honest here: I wasn't a fan of school. I wasn't even in class half the time because my mother thought that education was too slow in the US; it was not challenging enough or teaching us the right stuff. My learning was a combo of attending class and library schooling, meaning when I was pulled out of those "dumb-according-to-my-mother" classes, I had to go to the library and do whatever my mother supposedly gave me to do. I don't really remember much of that time other than sitting in that hard library chair when all I wanted to do was move. I found moving around relaxing; it was like me stepping into myself and not being blocked by this uncontrollable amount of energy that passed through me on a daily basis.

Waiting for practice to start after school got old and laborious. I got sick of waiting for my mother in the cold and having to figure out how to get on the bus because no one was coming to pick me up. My tolerance for my life was weighing on me. I had already won everything and broken every state record there was for me to break. Soon I would be moving up in age and start at the bottom of the age group, meaning I would be one of the younger ones. It also meant that I was going to get to do longer races which played to my strengths.

During this time my new coach, Fred. My dad was excited to have me swim longer races because that's where I shined. I could go and go when it came to freestyle, but butterfly was another story. At this point in my swimming career, it was clear that I was a freestyler and more of a distance swimmer than a sprinter, not that I wasn't the fastest in that as well. I showed a clear dominance in the longer races. My coach Fred was very much into me training for those longer races which also came with boredom and monotony.

While I had at the back of mind this idea of swimming in England and following in my dad's footsteps, I also desperately wanted to be winning again. My new age group created this lull because when you are at the bottom of your age group, it comes with less praise and less immediate self-importance. It also meant that getting my dad's attention was more challenging as well. My dad had no sympathy and felt that I should rise to the occasion because that was what champions did.

I appreciated his drive but it also frustrated me. I didn't know how to get what I knew was possible. I could get the best times and be impressive, but when compared with the other older kids I wasn't as impressive. The only saving grace with my age was that in England my age group was 11 & Under. My parents thought maybe they should take me to England to swim some races over there and see how I could do, and so, they entered me into some races and off we went. We also could see my brothers and have the family back together again for a couple of weeks. In those days taking a couple weeks off was acceptable, especially when it involved travel.

When I arrived at my first UK swim meet, it was different because the pool wasn't as inviting as the ones I was used to and I heard different noises in the pool; the cheering was not the same. These were all reserved British people politely watching without a whole lot of cheering going on. I kind of liked that because I am noise sensitive. The blocks were also different and not as nice. It was like a 3-Star hotel compared to the 5-Star I was accustomed to. I also watched the kids swim: they were good but not great. I assumed that I would win every race.

When it came time to compete, they didn't use a gun but a whistle and they held you differently on the blocks. I picked it up quickly but it still threw me off. I started swimming and felt like the water was different in this pool. It felt colder, harder, and not as smooth. I know that sounds weird because how could water be different? But it was. Not to mention that the distance of the pool was different as well. It was in meters and I mostly swam in yards. The lighting in the pool was also different as well; it was lighter and harder to precisely see the wall and where to turn. All things that I had never considered.

As I swam my first race I was a cocky and proud swimmer that ended up coming in second: a place I was unfamiliar with. How could anyone beat me? I hadn't lost a race in forever, like ever, well maybe breaststroke, but that's another sport as far as I'm concerned. I was beaten by a young woman named Sarah Hardcastle, who by the way was also younger than me. I justified coming up short in this race by saying I wasn't used to swimming in England and that everything was different. It wasn't like she beat me at everything: I did win the 200 meter Freestyle which was quickly becoming my signature event.

I wanted a redo. I wanted the comforts of my own bed, and to not feel jet lagged. If all the variables were in my favor what would have been the outcome? Since I lost this race in England, where thankfully they swim in meters year round and we swim in yards, maybe I could work the number to my advantage. My dad was happy with my results, however. I wasn't sure why I didn't win. My mother wasn't mad at me either. It was very odd. They gave all the excuses in the book why I didn't win.

I was good with this version of support and it made the rest of the trip more comfortable when I visited all my parents' family. We also visited three schools in the event I stayed in England: Cheltenham Ladies' College, Millfield School, and Kelly College. I was choosing between an all-girls school; a co-ed, sport-focused and very expensive school; and, an all-boys school except for 6th form (junior/senior year) where they allowed girls to attend. Kelly College had some of the best swimmers in Great Britain, including Olympian Sharon Davies who was 13 in her first Olympics and was one of the fastest women in the world. I was starstruck and wanted to be just like her.

After I visited all three schools, I took Cheltenham off the list when I found out the last person to get up in the morning did everyone's laundry and I sure didn't want to do that every week. Millfield's pool was crappy, yet I liked everything else including all the swimmers. I was most impressed with Kelly College because of who went there.

When I got home to Madison it was back to swimming with Fred, being at the bottom of my age group, and feeling the emptiness of having no brothers at home. I missed them fighting with me, hitting me, and us coordinating our efforts to defeat my mother's demands. Now I was left to do that all alone. My sister was no fun; she was too young and busy telling on me when I didn't wear a skirt to school. During this time I never owned a pair of pants because I was always dressed in formal clothes. I knew I needed to quickly change this situation.

I feared my coach Fred and never wanted to talk to him after a swim. I actually feared him in the same way that I feared my mother. He would yell and be demanding in ways that would make my body hurt. I felt like I had no protection from him, no way to stop the anger that he showed us in the pool. The angrier Fred got, the more I wanted to go to England.

When I came home at night and my dad asked me about how practice went, I was always managing the ideas and my future possibilities in the back of my mind. All I really wanted was to see my dad's twinkle back. He was happy with how I swam in England, but it wasn't twinkle happy. I saw only his "good happy" and I knew he could be happier.

A few weeks after returning from England, my school was closed for spring break. I thought I would get a break from Fred and practice. I wanted a break. I wanted to have a moment where I could just go play and be with other friends my age and wear my new cords that I earned for getting a AAA time (the fastest qualifying time for State) in my new race, 500 freestyle.

It turned out Fred had different plans for me. I was the best kid on the team, but he treated me like I was the worst. He felt he needed to apply more pressure on me because I had the most potential. That was another word that started to enter my world: potential. I became someone who had a lot of potential. I was being credited for success that I hadn't earned but no doubt would someday. I became a slave to praise, potential, and recognition. If any of those were threatened I became submissive to the dream.

My mother picked me up at practice the last day before the spring break school closure. I was happy to have a moment of relief from swimming and just be a kid. I craved it, wanted it, and it was a treat when it came along. I was leaving the pool, with wet uncombed hair, because I didn't have time to make it neat. Besides, it was only going to get wet again soon. Then Fred called my mother over. Like any child I stayed where I was while I watched their body language trying to figure out the conversation. *Did I not swim hard enough? Did I not perform to some level that was expected of me?* Whatever it was, doubt and guilt started to seep into my being; a feeling I didn't like and tried to avoid. My mother walked back towards me and told me there was practice next week. My head dropped and my feet dragged even more than usual as we left the pool area.

My break wasn't going to happen. I had a goal of being an Olympian one day, but I also wanted moments where I could remember just being an 11-year-old girl. The news didn't stop me from complaining all the way home. Most of my complaints involved me threatening my mother that I was going to tell Dad about something she wasn't doing for me.

My attitude and sense of importance was growing exponentially because I was constantly filled with importance from all those around me, especially when it came to my dad. Since our trip to England, the topic at every one of our dinners centered around if I was going to go there or not. I was hesitant to make any commitments about anything. I loved America and didn't want to leave, but then again the idea of leaving my mother and following in my dad's footsteps was also appealing. It wasn't that I liked swimming for Fred; swimming was giving me the praise and became the drug I needed. I was like an electric battery that needed to be charged in order to go full throttle.

The following week, during spring break, I returned to practice, and when I arrived at the pool all the lights were out and it appeared no one was there. I was scared at first because it was dark. What little girl, albeit I was an easy 5' 7" at this point in my growth cycle, is comfortable in the dark? After all, I had a teddy bear at home that went with me everywhere but Bear couldn't get wet so taking him to the pool was out of the question and I didn't want anyone to know that I was scared.

I was sitting there with nowhere to go and in walked Fred. I could see his shadow as he came clearer into view and the darkness become lighter. I asked him, "Where is everyone?" He said, "It's just you." My heart dropped to my feet. I was going to be alone with him; it was bad enough when there were not other swimmers there. I could feel myself well up on the inside and I wanted to start crying. Fred raised his voice like there were fifty kids in there and it echoed through my body, rattling my tears. "Get in!" I wasn't even ready with my cap and goggles, which I put on so fast and then jumped in the pool. There were still no lights on. I asked if he could turn the lights on. He said, "No. You have to swim without them today." There was a little light from the walls, but for the most part it was just so dark. When I took a breath it was all darkness plus I had smoked-up goggles and that didn't make it any easier.

As I came into the wall for the 10 x 500 free set, I didn't even look up. I listened for the set and looked for the clock. I was trying so hard to keep myself together and not fall apart inside. This was a challenging set for anyone because it was certainly boring and in the dark it challenged every emotional structure in my being. I pushed over the wall, knowing

I had to do this set. I knew what happened last time when I stormed out of the pool and I didn't want to do that again. My goggles were now full with my tears. I could no longer see the wall to judge my turns. I was in a quandary: Do I stop and fix my goggles, which would get me yelled at and punished, or do I just swim blind? I tried on my next flip turn to see if I could empty my goggles of tears so I could gain some vision and not burn my eyes from the chlorine in the pool.

I tried that method of swimming for a couple of 500's but I couldn't take it. I couldn't take all aspects of this: the boredom, the loneliness, and being alone with this crazy coach I couldn't stand. I tried to keep going but my thoughts slowed me down. I couldn't push off one more wall without hyperventilating from the type of crying I was doing. I needed to concentrate, I needed to stop; I couldn't take it anymore. What was I going to do? Then something just snapped in me. I stopped in the middle of a 500, got out of the pool and said, "I'm leaving and going to England. I'm no longer ever going to swim for you!" I picked up my stuff and ran into the unlit locker room. I could hear the echo of my cries vibrating off the metal locker doors as I shook in fear.

When my mother came to pick me up I was crying and so upset about the whole practice. I told her I quit and I was never going to swim for Fred again. My mother needed to sort out the mess I created both with the coach and with my dad, but she needed to deal with the coach first. I watched my mother just fold to my coach's wishes; she accepted whatever he said. I knew I had no chance. I knew she wasn't going to protect me; she couldn't. My mother basically just threw me under the bus. All this wasn't going well for me and now I was going to have to deal with my dad.

We arrived home and of course I needed to be the first one to tell my story since my mother wasn't there to see what really happened and I needed to make sure I was heard. I also knew that going to England was now my only option because there was no going back to Fred after today. The one thing I will own about myself is that I'm stubborn and strong-willed. When I want something I'm going to get it. I had so much guilt and shame there was no way I could face Fred again, and my mother was of no use to me. Instead of telling my dad I didn't want to face Fred again, I told my dad that I wanted to go to England and train. "I want to be like you, Dad." I heard the nervousness and hurriedness in my voice and sought out my dad's comfort, but I really needed him to let me know that I was still loveable even though I had just screwed up.

My dad and I didn't rehash the events of that day at all. He started to dictate to my mother that he would ask Jack, the men's coach at the University of Wisconsin, if I could train there until I started school in England in the fall. My dad was very demanding with my mother; he was mad at her that this happened to me, that this happened to his precious prized possession child. I didn't get the happy twinkle from him in that moment but I got what I wanted: a knowingness that my dad was going to protect me even from my mother.

CHAPTER 4

Across the Pond

The whims of my temper had set me on a path of moving to England to train, and there was no turning back now. I had one direction to go and that was forward. I couldn't have any regrets or say anything. I had made my bed and now I needed to lie in it. It was that or stay with my mother not knowing when she would feel the urge to hit me for something that appeared minor at the time. Who knows? I was a kid and probably entitled at this point.

In the days of no wheels on suitcases and light packing wasn't a thing, I packed up two hardcase suitcases, a swim duffle bag, a backpack, and of course my teddy bear, called Bear. I had a hard time closing the suitcases, which I then had to carry downstairs, leaning to one side with the cases hitting my legs as I pushed them along trying not to show any sign of struggle. Essentially my trip started when I left my bedroom; at least that is where one could pinpoint the beginning of the hardship I was about to endure.

In my formal family, I was taught to dress up for travel, so I put on my nice clothes for my first solo trip across the pond to England. It wasn't my first trip; I was actually a seasoned traveler at this point in my life, with our frequent trips to Greece, my favorite country, and of course the trips to visit our relatives in England every year.

After I organized myself and had all my luggage ready to go, my parents drove me across town to the university campus where a bus awaited to take me to Chicago O'Hare Airport, a three-hour bus ride. My dad got my stuff out of the car and the bus driver loaded it on the bus. I took my backpack with my ticket and passport in my bag and had Bear dangling by the side of my leg holding him by his arm.

I stood waiting to get on the bus, obsessing on the thought that I was going to be a champion. This thought gave me a determination that I hadn't seen in anyone else; it was mine and a special part of me. I looked at my dad as I desperately wanted him to see me in that moment. Then he patted me on the back and said, "Make me a champion, will you?" I nodded. I wasn't even sure what he meant by "me" in that statement because I was mostly focused on the pat on the back as it always felt protective and loving. I wanted to hang on to that feeling like a piece of candy.

Bear and I began our journey together. The first thing I did was change into a pair of pants. I was at least free to make my own decisions about myself—that was one benefit of traveling alone, not having to answer to anyone. I managed to remain happy on the bus holding onto my newfound independence. It also helped that I carried some candy I'd packed along for the trip.

What I didn't know was that my life was going to change the instant I arrived in Chicago. I got off the bus and the driver took all my luggage off the bus and set it on the sidewalk. I looked at it all and wasn't sure how I was going to move my mass of stuff to the check-in counter. I had Bear in one hand, a backpack, a swim bag and two heavy hardcases to move all at once. *How was I going to do this?* I knew tears weren't an option. I knew that I had to figure it out because my mother would be so mad if I missed that flight. I had to make it work.

I love how Bear took priority, like how was I going to do this without harming Bear? I put the swim bag across my body, put on the backpack from a squat position; and lifted the suitcases. I had already started lifting at this point so I knew how to pick up heavy things without hurting my back. I would make it a few feet and then would need to rest. I did this all the way to the counter with Bear taking the safest, most protective center spot under the strap on my swim bag across my chest.

All I had to do now was wait around the airport. Back in those days, the airport was wide open without security and the Hare Krishnas wandered about. They were all so fascinating to me. I remember walking by them and they offered me a book. They said it would bring me something seemingly desirable and they wanted me to have it. I liked gifts and was always curious about books. But when I walked away they wanted money for it. It was no longer a gift. I remember my feeling of being fooled and the icky feeling inside. I immediately had this distrust of strangers from that moment, that they aren't what they appear. I soon learned to keep to myself and focus on the task at hand.

The flight to London was long and tiring. I was tall and cramped in my seat and tried moving around to find some comfort, but I doubt any came. Upon landing I was mostly dreading having to deal with my luggage again, because I had to travel from London Heathrow to Euston station. I was going to have to go on the Tube and that involved a change of Tube lines. I learned to dread the idea of the challenge looming in front of me. I'm not sure if I was just mentally preparing myself for a workout and it seemed dread was a common go-to when it came to knowing something hard to do was approaching.

I gathered my multiple bags, gritted my teeth while ignoring the daze in my mind from the no real sleep and the jet lag, as I pushed myself towards the goal of arriving at Euston. With everything I did I set a mental goal, a time to get there, and a number of steps before I could put my luggage down. To manage everything I set an objective that I had to achieve before I could I move to the next level of what...who knows? It was my own video game I was living in to keep life interesting and entertaining; it wasn't like I had anyone to talk to, let alone complain to.

After many struggles, I arrived at Euston in relatively good condition with all my belongings in tow, albeit exhausted and tired. All I had to do now was buy a ticket and wait for the train and I would have accomplished my objective. I had a vision and a plan and I was going to see it through. The only problem with this plan was that it involved sitting and waiting for the train and platform to be announced.

I sat there in the station watching the trains get listed. There was something mesmerizing and rhythmic about it. There was a click,

click, click as they rotated the platform information and the train stops. I stared and stared and eventually my eyelids became too heavy. I could lift a heavy suitcase but didn't have the same strength to keep my eyes open, and I eventually dozed off only to awaken to the train listing rotating to a black screen. I had missed my train.

This internal failure started to well up inside of me. I had felt this only so slightly one time before when I got second in the 400 meter freestyle in my first ever race in England. I was able to shrug that off to some degree because of all my many excuses. But this time was different. It was me feeling like I had failed myself. I was setting off on this journey and I was going to be a gold medalist and I had failed. I hated this feeling; I wanted to run from it. I also had to call my mother because I needed more money to buy another train ticket. I feared having to ask her and hear her lecture me. I didn't want to feel her force and anger from one of her typical lectures. A tear squeaked out of my eye. Just one. It sat on the edge of my eyelid and slowly rolled down the side of my cheek as my tired and exhausted mind tried to cope with my failure.

I eventually got picked up at the train station by my new swim coach, Terry Davies, and his daughter, Sharon Davies, the most famous swimmer in England. They lived in Plymouth, about a 45-minute drive from Kelly College in Tavistock in Devon. I wanted to be excited but I was also shy and trained to not express myself. I was mostly excited to meet Sharon, Great Britain's darling. Sharon was in the 1976 Olympics when she was thirteen; I was not sure how she did then but she was now one of the best in the world.

I arrived at their house to have tea and tried to stay awake and be polite. Sharon was kind, bubbly, and chatty. She was enamored with my Americanness and she made me feel lucky I was from America. There was a pride in being British, but it was also a put down and was characterized by being one of the underdog hardworking folk. That was who Sharon essentially was: a hardworking underdog but also one of the best in the world. Knowing I was going to be training with Sharon gave me a fire in my belly.

After tea, I was tired and told them I needed to go to sleep, it was 3 p.m. and I just couldn't take it anymore. Terry got up and said, "Let me prepare your room." He left for a few minutes and went outside. I heard some things banging around out there and then he came back in. He asked if he could help me carry out my luggage, mostly because he didn't want me to hit the walls of the house as he escorted me outside. I wasn't really sure where I was going and then he stopped outside the garden shed to open the door and wave me in. "Welcome to your new place."

I entered the garden shed where I could barely stand up without hitting my head. I noticed tools in the corner propped up against a makeshift dresser. There was a cot and a little side table with a lamp. The lamp was plugged into an extension cord that ran through the window into the house. There was also an electric heater in the shed. I got in the shed like I was getting on a boat while Terry loaded my luggage at the entrance. He looked at me and said if I needed anything they would keep the kitchen door open until 9 p.m. "Make sure you go to the loo before then and we'll turn the heat off when we go to bed. We leave at 5:15 a.m. to go to practice, so make sure to set your alarm and be waiting at the car by then." I stood there taking in the instructions so tired and exhausted that they didn't faze me at the time. Terry closed the door that only locked from the outside. While it was afternoon, I just said goodnight as the door closed in my face.

I fell into the cot, crashed really, not knowing what had just happened other than I knew I needed some sleep, hoping I was in a dream and this would all end soon. I curled up with Bear. I was too tired to be mad, angry, sad or anything.

When I woke up in the middle of the night, I wasn't exactly refreshed, but more importantly I had to go to the bathroom. Now what was I going to do? It wasn't like I was in a swimming pool and I could just go there; yes, we all do it. I had to pee outside and then return to a cold shed with no heat. This was a far cry from the 9,000-square-foot house I grew up in with a view of one of the most stunning buildings in the world. I had no one around but Bear and a suitcase full of American junk food. However, there was one thing left for me to do: binge and get through the night. It was the only way I could find all of this tolerable. I was not in America anymore. That was clear...was I British now?

I numbed out my current state of misery—this was not what I signed up for when I stormed out of practice that fateful day or was it? I had this alarm clock that when you opened it, it rested in its case. The click of the second hand became louder as it moved through time. My fear synchronized with the sound as I lay in darkness wide awake with nowhere to go for a few hours until it was time to head to practice.

When it was time to go to practice, Sharon, Terry and I got in the car for the long drive through the Devon moors. The darkness of the night dissipated into the morning dew. This was also during the time when there was a rapist on the loose. I would stare out the window in a tired gaze expecting a monster to appear at any moment. This became my morning ritual with Terry, and occasionally with Sharon, when she was not busy being famous and traveling the world.

After practice I would walk through the village and stop to get breakfast because the school food I was supposed to be eating was a little too unpleasant for me. It was cafeteria-type food that wasn't fun or appetizing. I started to create my morning ritual of stopping by the café. Sometimes I would have the urge to call my parents to let them know about a good practice I had and then make my way to Kelly College.

I arrived at school right when the bell went off or a couple minutes after. I tried to time it right but wasn't always successful, mostly because I already didn't like this new school and wanted to be there as little as possible. I became known as "the American;" something that I was proud of turned out to make me the target of bullying and quite frankly, physical outrage seemed to be okay for some people when they caught sight of me. It unleashed something in them that needed to violently attack me. I took the beatings a few times and then figured out a different path to my classes. It wasn't like I could hide; I stuck out like a sore thumb because of my stature.

I would carry on with this schedule, trying to find my way and settle into my new life. There were so many things that weren't right for me or comfortable, but I was making leaps and bounds and strides in the pool. When I first arrived at Kelly College I was swimming in the slow lane and Sharon, of course, was in the fast lane across the six-lane pool. Now I was the one in the fast lane.

It didn't take long for my success to become a topic of media interest. Shortly after my first swim meet, I found out the *Daily Mail* wanted to do a cover story on me. One day during practice after school, a reporter arrived who would have normally talked to Sharon, but this time they were there to interview me. I arrived at the pool ready for training which also included dryland exercises that day. I dressed in my workout clothes and headed to the weight room where the reporter and the photographer started to follow me around. It was a weird feeling of stepping into a dream while also being me. After all, this was part of being famous and an Olympic gold medalist.

As my workout continued, I could feel a sense of self-consciousness flow through my body. I wasn't much for having my picture taken in general, and now I had to be okay with the captured moments. I basically pushed down any negative feelings and told myself that I wasn't allowed to boast or have an inflated ego, not that I used those words at the time. It was like my innocence was being taken away every time the news photographer took my picture.

I completed my workout and then it was time to do the actual interview—it wasn't like I had any training in this area. The question put me on the spot to answer was, "Why did you leave America, where the facilities are grand and the opportunity is plentiful? Why are you in Britain, basically training in a more challenging environment when you could have had it better by staying in the US?" I explained about my dad and following in his footsteps and that I was British on the inside. I needed to hide being an American at school and now I needed to hide my Americanness while in pursuit of my dream. I was learning that it couldn't co-exist inside of me. At least not if I wanted to go to the Olympics and my dad to love me.

A few days later, the article came out and I was exposed in Britain as this young rising star with aspirations of being the next Sharon Davies. My sense of self changed that day, I had a fire and a drive that I knew too well: the need for praise and attention. It was certainly not something that I was getting at home in my new living situation, the garden shed. I had to pursue it elsewhere.

As the school bullying continued, so did my need to protect myself and my body from harm. It was clear the physical gifts of my body were my most important asset. I started to skip school with a classmate who mostly wanted to skip so she could smoke. I tried smoking and remember that first drag and the head rush. I felt a little sick as well. The head rush swirled my thoughts around in my mind in a way that I couldn't figure out what they were telling me; it was a moment of freedom from me and my thoughts. I also knew it was wrong, but the idea of breaking the rules and saying "FU" to the system seemed to be a good outlet from what I was truly feeling about my life, a life that I wasn't sharing with anyone.

I was learning how to have a secret and how to quietly survive. I carried on living the life that I was forced to do and the one where I loved swimming. It was the idea that you have to be bad in order to experience the good. So I focused my attention on training and winning.

When winter arrived I had been in England almost six months and it was time for the 1980 Winter Olympics, held in Lake Placid, New York. It just so happened they started on my birthday. I got to celebrate my birthday and the Olympics together, although this time it was while I lived in Great Britain. I didn't have my dad to share those special moments with me, but I did have Sharon and her family. After all, this time I was watching the Olympics with an actual Olympian who was one of the fastest swimmers in the world.

Every night during the Games I was able to take a break from the loneliness of the garden shed for warmth and feel connected to my dream of being an Olympian one day. While British pride was everywhere no matter where you looked, I was secretly able to cheer on another hometown Olympian, or two or three, with Madison's Eric Heiden taking home five gold medals in speedskating. I loved speedskating, it was my back-up sport, but speedskating didn't have the same training facilities or ease of training that swimming did.

I got used to being inside and warm, and celebrating with a family for two weeks and knew it was going to be hard to go back outside to the cold shed. I had forgotten the intensity of the loneliness but at least I had Bear to keep me company.

The cycle of swimming started to develop into "how could I shut off the world?" I had an outlet to avoid whatever plagued me. I didn't have to tell anyone what was going on with me, no one asked, and

I wasn't going to freely share. At this point I don't even know that I had any words to describe what was really going on. I knew I was hurting. I also knew that I was swimming faster pretty much every time I entered a swim meet. Every time I swam with success it was rewarded either through public attention by being written up in the newspaper, coaching praise, or if I was really lucky, I got to have a conversation with my dad. I didn't have any restrictions on making reverse charge calls and did so frequently. That wasn't the problem. The problem was that no one in England really cared about Annabelle.

Over the course of the next few months, I found a rhythm, not one that I liked per se, but one that kept me from questioning the path I was on. I got up to swim, sort of went to school, swam again, and then returned to the garden shed. When Saturday afternoon came, it was the lull in my week where I was totally alone, without any friends or family; just me and the shed, and of course, Bear.

Weekends became very difficult for me. If I was at a swim meet, I was showered with praise and attention, but if I wasn't, I was in a shed staring off into space, dreaming about something other than this horrible, cold, and miserable place. I had no one to talk to about it because everyone knew where I was living and staying. What was I going to say? My parents heard my complaints and even saw the place during one of their visits. Where do you go from there?

As the effects of the misery and the loneliness compounded inside of me, I started to skip school and hang out with some of my school friends who encouraged me to join them one day, so I did. We went to this hotel, to the top floor, and out the roof exit. We hung out there and watched the people move around the town, while my friends smoked. I would take a drag from them on occasion. I knew it was hurting me, but I couldn't help myself.

Skipping school and smoking didn't stop the positive trajectory of my swimming. I was swimming faster just about every time I got in the pool and had quickly moved up to swimming in the senior meets. There was a swim meet coming up in London. I always found relief in the business of a swim meet, the lead-up and the actual competition itself. I loved the goals that I would secretly create for myself.

After the Winter Olympics that year, the Soviet-Afghan War started to create doubt around what was going to happen to the upcoming Olympics in Moscow, Russia. I saw the powerlessness of the athletes first-hand while also being aware of the complete disregard for people who were putting their heart and soul into their craft. I could feel this anguish and anger inside of me. I didn't feel affected by it myself, but it created a fear that my passion, dream, and goals could be stripped away by a government or other controlling power. That didn't sit right with me, but what did I know—I was a kid.

That summer I returned to Madison, and I was so happy to sleep in a very comfortable, large American home and go to swim practice where you could smell fresh-made bagels from the bagel store that sat atop of the hill behind the pool. It was both a tease and joy of knowing that practice was half done, but you wanted those amazing-smelling bagels now.

The summer flew by and all I did was set every state record, get praise and glory from my coach, teammates, and friends. I was back in heaven. The problem with this success was that it was falsely attributed to the training I was doing in England. Living in England seemed to have become a good thing. I was actually swimming fast because I was happy to be home. As the summer wound down so did my spirit because I had to return to the shed. It was so hard to muscle up my energy to do that. I asked my parents to not return, but they first said I couldn't quit now and then said this was what I wanted to do and I had to return. It was the "you made your bed, you need to lie in it" train of thought.

My dad wasn't forceful either way. He would have talks with me about being an Olympian and that I was so close to my goal. I only needed to focus and stick with it. I knew that. I just didn't want to stick with it where I was at. I missed America. I was so desperate that I missed my mother hitting me with the slipper, well not really, but it was familiar and it was attention, not good attention, but attention nonetheless.

I returned to England only to suffer the same struggles with my travels as last time, except that I knew what was coming and I became strategic in my own mind so I could defeat the challenge. It became all about rising to the occasion. I was tasked with defeating my opponent, and that opponent was me, the negative me, the concerned me, the scared me, all those things that got in my way of being the best.

When I arrived back at school, it was more or less the usual suspects: school was the same, the garden shed hadn't been demolished, and the feeling of loneliness was alive and well. Especially the first night when I was jet lagged and I woke up in the middle of the night with nowhere to go, with everyone asleep and not a stir in the streets.

The only thing that wasn't the same was the higher level and more competitive swim meets that I was now qualifying for in Great Britain. As the swim meets changed so did the destinations.

This time I was headed to London with my teammates who were mostly boys, and a few women. At this point, I was extremely shy with my body. When I changed in the locker room, I would keep my body protected with the way I was bent over, and by leaving some of my clothes on while I put my suit on; I was never fully naked. While many of the swimmers were uninhibited, I became very conscientious of my body. It became another emotional charge that I wasn't sure how to handle.

I was also easily swayed towards the boys who showed me any kind of attention. I was so desperate to connect with other human beings. A couple of the boys a few years older than me started to show interest in me and wanted to see me in between prelims and finals. I thought they liked me because of how fast I was swimming; I thought they wanted to spend more time with me. I hadn't made finals, and additional rest wasn't really something that I needed to do, so I hung out with these boys. One of the coaches came out of his room, ask what I was doing in there and told me to stop going to the boys' room. I liked the attention they were giving me. I knew it was wrong, but it also fed the dark side of me.

It wasn't until the last night when one of the older boys, who was seventeen and I was twelve, almost thirteen, knocked on my door and I let my drunk teammate into my room. It wasn't that I let him but rather that I couldn't say no. I really couldn't say anything. He entered my room and started making out with me. I liked the kissing and the attention. I felt connected to something and someone and told myself that this person must like me and care about me because they wanted to make out with me. I was still a child in every way; I hadn't even started my period or fully grown my breasts.

The next morning, I woke up full of remorse, I had never felt this way. We all had to get on a bus for the four- or five-hour bus ride back to Devon. Whatever it was it was longer than I wanted to be in the presence of my teammate that I just made out with. I also knew that I needed to keep secret what had happened. It wasn't like anyone told me to; it was that I judged the consequences of my actions, and I knew they were not acceptable for the person that I thought I was. My actions didn't line up with my own integrity that I held for myself. It was like I was falling out of the social class I was striving to become a part of. That was also part of the pursuit of being an Olympian; it was a pursuit to be in the highest class of society, not just be the fastest person in the world.

The darkness of the secret returned with me back to the garden shed. It wasn't that it festered in my mind, it festered in my actions and choices.

At the same time that this happened there was also a masked person who was out terrorizing women on the street late at night. I knew this from getting in the car every morning with the paper on the front seat. I would look at the news and think that I saw that person but couldn't be sure. It was dark and the amber streetlights on the corner lit up the street and when I would hear a noise, I would look out the window and see shadows. I wasn't sure if that was my imagination or if it was real. Either way it scared me. It was more fodder for me to add to all the emotions and experiences that left me feeling helpless and alone.

As these experiences began to build up, I started to gather food, candy, and anything that I could eat later like a squirrel getting ready for winter. I needed to know that I had enough food to pass out and make it through the night. Whatever it was, I needed something. This became my pattern and became a part of me. In today's language we might say this was my survival mechanism. It didn't appear I had a disorder because I was swimming and thus hungry all the time, so to have enough food was just something that I told myself I needed in order to swim and survive, not just to survive emotionally as I was doing.

The weekend after the London trip I was back in the cold and miserable garden shed. I did, however, have music to entertain me; it wasn't like I could binge watch or even watch any TV at all. But I got to listen to the radio, and if I was lucky I could tune into the pirate radio station that was broadcast from the Channel Islands. It became even more exciting with the signal going in and out. I remember looking around the shed not being happy with my collection of food. Needing something to do, I decided I would pack up my bag and go to the candy store. For some odd reason, I decided I needed company and that I was going to bring Bear with me. The two of us left the shed without saying where we were going, not that it was my habit to do that.

When the door shut behind me I had this nervous energy in my stomach, like I was about to compete. I wasn't sure what it was, but could feel it deep inside in my belly. I walked hastily towards the store, wanting something different from my usual choices while not knowing what. I thought for a moment that maybe I would call my mother but then remembered she was already in England visiting my grandfather. She had no plans to visit me because there wasn't a swim meet. At least not an important swim meet that was worth coming to. I could have called my dad but he always needed the buffer of my mother, or he needed a few drinks in him to share more freely, if you will. My only real option to entertain myself was to find a really good candy store so that was what I set out to do.

I just started walking and meandering, and after a little while I wasn't really anywhere that I had been before, and then I suddenly saw this really nice candy store. I had an American Express card, my bank book, (it's how they did it at the time, like a savings book that stated how much money was in your account) and some cash with me. I didn't have any financial restrictions placed on me, albeit I was told to only use the American Express card in case of emergencies. I stood at the counter and ordered so much candy, biscuits, crisps, everything that brought me the slightest amount of pleasure, and even a few things that I was hoping would bring me pleasure, being stuck in the garden shed.

I walked out of the store with my backpack filled to the brim, so much so that Bear's head couldn't quite fit all the way in, but that was okay, as I would eat everything soon enough once I found a place to go. I stood in front of the store and a bus pulled up, and without another thought I just got on the double-decker, went upstairs and decided to just sit there and eat my candy. I had no idea where the bus was going, but I was going to take it and go wherever it went. I sat on the bus eating, watching people come and go while I stuffed my face with candy.

As the day turned to night, I was becoming more and more fearful and didn't want to return to the garden shed. I couldn't take that life anymore; I didn't have the fight in me to go back there for another night. I had this American Express card and some cash, but where could I go? I started to look for the nicest hotel I could find. After a little while I saw what appeared to be a suitably lit up hotel in the near distance. I got off the bus with my bag of food and Bear and stood across the street deciding what to do.

I had backed myself into a corner. I couldn't go back and couldn't go forward and it was dark. I needed to find some place to sleep and it wasn't going to be worse than the shed. I started doing what I knew how to do best: just do it, just go for it, no time to think this through or you will fail. I was faced with being strategic with my next decision. I had everything I needed to execute this plan.

I soon walked into this very posh hotel and said that I would like a room for a couple of nights. I knew I wasn't going anywhere the next day because I had a full day off from practice. I was in hiding and needed time to figure out my next steps. As I asked for a room, I pulled out my American Express card and handed it to the person checking me in as he was about to ask my age. Since the card had my name on it, not my parents' name, he accepted it, ran the card, or took a carbon copy of the card to keep on file, and then handed me the key. Since I didn't have any luggage with me, they just escorted me to this amazing room with a four-poster bed with a red velvet canopy on top, surrounded by dark wood furniture beautifully placed throughout. There were lights from the village square glissading the room with a rainbow reflection along the white walls. I was handed a menu for room service and then the bellman left.

I went through my backpack on the bed, dumped out all the candy, placed Bear next to me, and we had a party. I ordered room service, watched TV and cranked up the heat. I didn't have a change of clothes, but who cares? I had on a T-shirt and I was good. I stayed in that room not wanting to go anywhere. I could look out the window when I wanted and watch the people in the village move around. I felt like Rapunzel in the tower without the long hair, high up in the castle, because the hotel itself looked like one.

After a couple of days I felt some built-up angst. Surely someone was looking for me. I was missing swim practice and that concerned me more than running away and staying in a hotel for a couple of nights. *How was I going to integrate back into the swim team? What was I going to say? What tale was I going to tell?* I didn't have any answers. So I decided to check out of the hotel and get on a train and go somewhere. I started the ball rolling; my decisions were now starting to snowball out of control, but I didn't know that. I was making one decision to make up for the previous lie I just told myself and believed. I did know that I was miserable and I needed to take matters into my own hands, so to speak. I needed to do something drastic to get out of the situation I hated. I hated being bullied for being an American. I hated training with Terry and wasn't sure if he was the masked tormentor in the paper, and I hated driving through the Devon moors with the heavy thick fog not knowing what creatures were on the other side of that fog. I hated it all. I especially hated the garden shed.

I didn't hate the swimming part because that was where my talents lay and it seemed like that part of me needed to be protected at all costs. That wasn't my thought; that was my parents always telling me that I have talent and that I couldn't waste it. I attributed running away to possibly falling in the wasted category.

I took the train to the home of a young swimmer I had met. I was hiding in their backyard and then I knocked on the door. They had been called by the police as a possible place where I might have gone. I'm not sure why they didn't call my mom who was actually in England at the time, but they didn't. When my mother got wind that I had run away and that the police and child protective services were going to look into what happened, my mother intervened and told them I got lost on the train because I was intending to visit her. That was never the case. But I was going with the lie because I wasn't willing to go to the police either.

The good news was that my disappearance got me out of there and back to America. I guess you could say "mission successful." After being pulled out of school early, I returned home to Madison which allowed me to enjoy that summer. Besides, my father wasn't going to let anything happen to me that would prevent my success with my swimming. Thus the end of my days in the garden shed.

CHAPTER 5

Turning Point

The running away adventure sent me back to America sooner for the summer and back to training in the comforts of my own home. I knew this wasn't going to last for long, as returning to England was still in the plans. My parents searched the country to find a school and training facility that matched with the education and swimming expertise they wanted for me. I didn't exactly get a say at this point and went along with the plan. My parents landed me in Coventry at the King Henry VIII School to train in a 50-meter pool with past Olympians and current swimmers in pursuit of their own Olympic dreams.

That summer at home, I tore up the pool breaking every record and finding my way back to my stellar star self. At the end of the summer, Senior Nationals were in Milwaukee, a short drive away, so I went to watch the event. On the last day, Mary T. Meagher swam the 200 Fly and broke the world record. I remember watching her glide across the water and swim with such grace that I wanted to be in that pool right alongside her. She was a person of spectacular power and elegance. I wanted to bring that grace into my races. I was captivated by that swim as I witnessed history. I felt what it meant to have a dream. It wasn't just the winning and the record that I witnessed but also a renewal of my desire to pursue my dreams. That made my transition back to England easier and purposeful again. I could let go of the shame that I had experienced after I ran away. I had found me again.

The only difference in my return to England was that my mother was going to come with me. My parents decided that they would live apart so I could be settled in Coventry at school and at training. I wasn't a fan of the plan because I didn't want to be the sole attention of my mother. I had pretty much shut my heart to her long ago and her joining me was only going to close me off even more. The idea of being with her without my dad was sad to me. I wanted to be able to come home and share my stories with him. I wanted to please him. I also knew he would think I was selfish if I didn't do what they had planned for me. Last thing I wanted was for my dad to be disappointed in me. I was going to do whatever I needed to make sure that didn't happen.

In Coventry, there was a Rolls-Royce plant; I soon internalized the symbol of what Rolls-Royce meant. After watching the world record of Mary T. and then taking in what it means to be a Rolls-Royce engine, I started to feel the strength of the brand within me, if you will. Now there was an ever-present reminder of my engine inside of me. The flame that drove me was the idea of this shiny engine of perfection. I was going to be that and become that. I could breathe in the greatness that Rolls-Royce exhibited and represented to me and the rest of the world.

While my insides were acclimating to our surroundings, my mother was finding us a place to live in order to adapt to my new external world of Coventry. At first we stayed in a bed and breakfast until my mother found a house that was near my new school. I was a little concerned about joining a new club with no one that I knew, along with getting a new coach who was not the intended coach my parents had planned for me to swim with. It didn't really matter to me that I had a new coach, Paul Hickson, since I didn't know the other coach that I was supposed to swim with anyway. It was all about the swimmers on the team and apparently this new coach had brought the top swimmers from his previous club with him, so I thought he must be good if they had come along with him.

I needed some time to get settled after leaving America. I felt a little distracted, excited, scared, and homesick taking in the new world all around me. I missed my dad, I missed him driving me to swim practice, and of course I missed the smell of bagels in the middle of practice. When it came time to meet Paul, my focus was on impressing him, and then there was my desire to gain the favorite swimmer spot; that was always the secret unspoken pursuit. I had a newfound coach to please and dreams to capture.

Coming off my spectacular summer of swimming in the US, I was a renewed person; my past had already been forgotten. I had a couple weeks off to just be me without the label or pressure of training for the Olympics. The downside of that is it takes a couple of weeks out to reconnect with yourself, or in swimming terms to find the feel of the water again. Combine that with meeting a new coach; your dreams are closer and seem bigger by the moment. All this led me to want to work extra hard to gain Paul's attention and regain the focus that I so desperately needed to find in England. I needed to make it work. Whatever it took I needed to make my time there work. I wasn't going to let my dad down again. I needed something to call my dad about, so having a spectacular workout was my new focus. All my attention went to performing in practice until the swim meets started later that fall.

I found a rhythm of life in my new school and in my training. My time with my mother was annoying, coupled with my newfound moodiness as I transitioned out of the little girl and into a young woman. The shyness that I experienced up to this point was starting to melt away from my body and psyche. I had developed into a lanky 5'11" stature with very broad shoulders that I wasn't a fan of, but they gave me the perfect swimmer body shape. My mind and body were rapidly changing in every direction while my chest started to develop as well, changing my perfect streamline in the water.

When I walked from school to practice I would pass by the famous statue of Lady Godiva riding her horse naked in the square. Every time I passed by the statue I would feel naked and wanted to cover up my ever-changing body. While my shyness was fading away, my feeling of nakedness was not. When I got to practice I would have this awkward feeling of being exposed and then I'd be met with Paul's eyes. When he looked at you it felt like he was undressing you as well. That feeling of him looking at my body made me feel awkward, but at the same time he invested his attention in me as a swimmer, and that felt good. The way it was presented by him was that he was perfecting me for greatness. He was training me to be an Olympian and that was the role of the coach: to perfect you as a person, all aspects of you from the inside out.

As time went on, Paul started to pay more attention to me. He would challenge me to a set with the boys, where I was never too shy to perform and rise to the occasion. I thrived on the challenge and yearned for him praising me for my success. There were only a few of the boys faster than me and none of the girls on the team were anywhere near me in practice. I had quickly earned the status of being gifted and special. I was the Sharon Davies of this team. Paul let me know how impressed he was with my training. He would tell me about upcoming teams that he wanted me to be on. We talked about the swim meets and what I needed to do in order to earn a spot. The first goal was to make the upcoming Junior National Team trip in Milan. It was just a swim meet against three other countries' teams: Italy, France, and Spain. Each country brought two swimmers per event. Paul and I had a goal with the real objective of making the Senior Team, okay let's be honest, the Olympic Team, but for right now it was this competition right in front of us.

The meet to qualify for the trip took place just before the holidays. It was perfect timing, right before my father arrived from the US to spend time with his whole family, so of course I wanted to make sure that I had something to share with my dad. It would be like a gift to him so he could be proud that I made my first international team. I would be just like him, able to share something with my father. Something I dreamed about since sitting on his lap as a little girl. I would be the countryperson that he would be cheering for.

The way the team was selected after the swim meet was by committee and coaches. I had won my races so it seemed like it was a no-brainer and, besides, Paul was the head coach and selector of the team. I knew there was nothing to worry about; I had won. Winning only brought me more attention from Paul and the swimmers around me. I started to become closer to Paul. I fell into a dependence on him. I started to shut down any personal awareness of those around me and I pursued this coach to have has his sole attention on me. I became his only female swimmer along with five guys. It was like having him to myself. I could always go over to him to get direction and he would drop everything to give it to me.

The selection of the national team is a big thing in Britain, success in sport is something that is rewarded with media attention and soaked up by the citizens. It would give me something special to share with my dad. I shunned my mother; I wanted this moment to be just between my dad and myself.

I really resented my mother at this point. I was struggling to become a woman in my body and didn't share this struggle with anyone. I had no direction or help on how to make this transition. My body was changing beyond my control and I wanted to ignore it in the hope that it would just go away or just happen. When I saw my dad over the holidays, I had fully grown into a young woman's body. It wasn't just that I grew into a woman's body; I had grown into a dynamic swimmer's body—I was strong and statuesque. I could see the Olympic dreams in the shape of me. I was getting that reflected back from my conversations with Paul and now with my father. He was impressed with the daughter I had become.

Over the holidays, I couldn't imagine what it might have been like for my siblings, coming to Coventry, a boring town where they had to listen to boring, self-centered conversation like their sister's success plans and ambitions without having anything as grand to report in exchange. We talked over and over again about going to the Olympics, which we knew would be held in Los Angeles in 1984. I had my exact target identified: the '84 Olympic Summer Games where I would be 16.

Making the Junior National Team gave my dad everything he needed to know about his investment in me. We didn't talk about school, detentions, my issues with the school uniform, mostly because he or my brothers had the same issues and it was just life in boarding school or school in England—you are uncomfortable and deal with it. There was a protocol to being British, and one of those unwritten rules was not to complain. Well, you could complain, but don't expect anyone to do anything about it. The focus remained on my swimming and success and that was it.

The holiday break with Dad had to end at some point since he had to return to work. My siblings had to go back to school, albeit I believe they were really going on a skiing holiday, a sport that I was not allowed to do because I was well into the protected asset class of human activities at this point which meant skiing was out. I was clearly handled like a prized possession. My short-lived moment of family was fleeting and soon it was back to the way it was.

After my dad returned to the US, I felt empty. I almost would have preferred not to have spent any time with him at all, as the pain of the goodbye was too much for me.

By New Year's Eve I was filled with excitement, anxiety, and budding sexuality as I stepped into my girly-athletic self. My swim team was hosting a party at a pub and I came with my mother who enjoyed being social with the adults. When we got to the party I needed to drink—the pain of missing my dad and not being able to train seemed best served with a drink. It helped that adults, including my dad if he had been there, would have been feeding me alcohol to ease the pain. It was how I was taught to manage my emotions, well, that and food. Alcohol seemed to be the first choice.

After a few drinks, I had enough courage to connect with one of the boys on the swim team, a teammate's brother. Besides, the adults were getting drunk themselves and who was watching anyway? We got a few drinks in us and decided to leave the party and do what teenagers do when there are drunk adults around; we went outside and found some privacy.

This would be my first interaction where Paul had actually followed us outside and was watching over me. He just stood there and stared. As I was making out with this boy I could see him out of the corner of my eye. I had a few drinks so I didn't say anything or do anything; it appeared like it was a figment of my imagination, or at least that is what I wanted it to be at the time. Even though I had a creepy feeling.

A few days later we were back in training. When I arrived on the pool deck Paul walked up to me and placed his hands on my hips giving me the directions to some warm-up that I had done for the past several months. He looked at me with those creepy eyes, and as I looked away he asked what happened with me and David, the boy that I had made out with. I wiggled out of his hold on me and jumped in the pool, knowing that David was training a few lanes down in another group. I was totally embarrassed by all of this and laughed it off because that is what you do.

That would be the beginning of Paul asking me about boyfriends at practice. Since I swam with five other boys, it became especially awkward to have this topic come up. It also didn't help that my body was also developing into a young women's body. I wanted to cover my chest and my heart at the same time, I felt so exposed. It wasn't just being in a swimsuit where I felt exposed; my person and my soul felt naked that day. It was how I felt when I walked by the Lady Godiva statue every day on the way to practice. It was like a gust of wind blowing past you for your soul to bare for others.

A few weeks later I had my first Junior National trip to Milan, Italy, with Paul as one of the coaches. This was the part of the swimming that fed my soul the most. The travel, more opportunity for praise, and the socialization where I would know every swimmer at the end of the swim meet. A cocktail of delight.

At the airport, Paul was there standing with the rest of the coaches, some I knew and some I didn't. Paul seemed especially friendly to me when I arrived. He was proud of me and bragged about my recent training set to other coaches as he introduced me to them. Of course I was coy and looked away not being able to accept the praise. I wanted the praise but knew better than to take the offering directly. Last thing I wanted was to be considered arrogant or cocky. I leaned into the British mannerisms to the best of my ability while also being clumsy and unaware of the space taking up this fully grown body.

Before the trip there was a write-up in the paper that featured not just me but my new coach Paul who said he seemed happy about my success just like my dad was happy for me. Now at the airport it seemed like Paul wanted to be praised in the same way that I did by the way he was bragging about me to the other coaches.

While this was my first Junior National Team, my presence also came with awe and respect based on my quick rise to joining the team where I was a couple of years younger than my teammates. When you're talking about minor years that is a lot of time; it seemed like we counted in months until we were eighteen and then moved on to years. Due to Paul's praise I felt like I fit right in with the team. I also felt British now that my American accent had gone and I was blending right in with my fellow Brits.

We arrived in Milan for this swim meet without a hitch. We stayed at a nice enough hotel and had roommates assigned to us which was always fun for me. All that wasn't new; I was used to travel for meets, but not so much in Europe with the language difference. That aspect was fun and exciting. There were also a few nuances in how they did things that were different than how it was in England and America. Adjusting to your surroundings became part of the challenge and what was expected of you to compete at this next level. I thought of myself as adaptable up to this point, so this meet was no different.

The meet was spread out over a few of days, Friday to Sunday. I was swimming on Saturday and Sunday with only finals on Sunday: the 800 freestyle. On the bus ride over to the pool, Paul sat next to me and wanted to discuss my races with me. He seemed to have started to focus his attention on me, since the rest of my club teammates, for various reasons had not made thee trip. It was just the two of us.

When we got to the pool, it was an older facility with high decks, big gutters, and the depth of the pool didn't have much of a curve for the deep end. For my first swim the pool wasn't feeling especially fast, but I seemed to have found my glide and rhythm. I especially liked that the walls weren't slippery, making it easier to do flip turns without being concerned about losing your footing. After a practice session with Paul I felt comfortable to perform. Paul reviewed the competition and felt like I could win the 800 free by the way that I was training. I believed him. He believed in me. That is what I needed: someone to believe in me.

The longer distance events are often left for the start of the evening session on the final day, in order to give the other swimmers some rest between warm-ups and competition. That seemed universal no matter what country you were in. I warmed up early with Paul to get ready for the first race at the start of the competition. I didn't like to go first; I needed mental time to get ready. I was more at ease when there was a race or two before mine. There was going to be emotion; that was guaranteed, and it set the tone for the races to come. It also gave more time to be distracted, but I wasn't afforded that luxury.

Before my race, Paul sat with me and discussed my race strategy. When we had that conversation, I was like a computer that would calculate a feeling in my body and then replicate that euphoric feeling when I swam. This is where honing my skills and the perfecting of my craft became an art form that I thrived on. It was also where I wanted to be recognized for my ability to take direction and respond with precision. This idea of you telling me what to do and then I do it perfectly is what defined me as an athlete, and in this case a gifted athlete.

I felt ready to swim my race after Paul and I spoke. I had my strategy of how to control the race to reach my max output. I trusted the plan. The race started with a bang. For swimming in general it's important to swim your own race and not be concerned with the competition. There is a tendency to go out fast and lose your sense of self. I wasn't that swimmer at all. I was a builder of speed; if I moved too quickly, it would throw off the whole system, especially my heart and breathing. I needed to gradually increase the intensity to excel. And that is what I did. I stayed focused on my race. I was connected to myself in my own world, or the zone as some call it.

What made this race different from the US was the counter to tell me what lap I was on in the water before each one of my turns. In Europe they have the counter on the pool deck which requires you to look back and break the rhythm of your stroke slightly, so it wasn't something that I did every lap. Here I needed to think about it. I was so focused on my swim and in the zone that I lost track of where I was. At some point in the race, I knew I was so far gone in my mind and soul without a swimmer in sight.

When I touched the wall I could hear this intense cheer that didn't quite sound like I had won and I couldn't figure it out. As I watched the next swimmer come into the wall, she did a turn while I was sitting on the wall thinking I was done. I realized what had happened. My first thought was to fake something to squash the embarrassment, but I didn't see that playing out well so I quickly put on my goggles and sprinted the last lap hoping to catch up and take my rightful place of first but didn't quite make it happen and touched within a tenth of a second of the winner of the race. I was so devastated by what had just happened. All I could think about was what a failure I was. I could hear my dad's voice calling me a fool and stupid. My eyes started to well up with tears. I put my goggles back on to exit the pool on the side trying to hide the fact that I was crying and made a mistake that was not allowed at this level. It was not acceptable to me.

When I got out of the pool Paul was there to comfort me. He sat me down on the bench right next to him and put his arm around me as I was still crying into my goggles—I didn't want to take them off. I didn't know how to comfort myself through this. Paul started to give me the excuses for the mess up and justified the error. As he started to do so, I started to ease up on myself when I heard that it might not actually be my fault and that Paul wasn't mad at me. He shared with me that this was my first international competition and we all make mistakes, it was okay. I swam a brilliant race exactly as directed and planned. Paul reaffirmed my talent and told me we would work on this for our next race. Paul assured me that everything was going to be all right. I trusted him.

When it came time to talk to my dad about it, I had all the reasons that Paul had shared with me and we had made our plan to address this error. My dad became impressed with Paul and entrusted him to coach his daughter. I had gained my dad's confidence in this process and that was something I feared I was about lose. It felt safe with both Paul and my dad that I was going to be okay. My dreams weren't over. In fact, they were now both invested in my success. That was what I needed and wanted in that moment. The pain of failure was too much for me to take. That physically hurt more than any practice or race ever did.

When I arrived back in England with Paul, I had a deeper, more meaningful relationship with him; it had matured into a coach-athlete relationship. I also felt like I had moved my need for my dad's praise over to a need for that same praise from Paul. Even more, I wanted to perform for him, and become the swimmer that he believed I could be.

CHAPTER 6

Lights, Camera Action

Returning home from Milan was bittersweet. On the one hand I swam fast if you didn't factor in the mishap, but on the other hand I was disappointed with my failure and that was hard to recover from mentally. It wasn't like it was a regular pattern; it was the fact that it happened at all. There was no room for errors.

The dynamic changed between Paul, my mother, and I. I felt like Paul was there for me and was going to support me as a swimmer and that was comforting. I redirected my attention to training and more or less laughed off the Milan incident like it was nothing. The only thing that was really missing was the glory from my success. The level of my swimming was rising fast and that was all that mattered.

I needed to have some bargaining power between Paul and my parents, and I felt like I accomplished that after the trip. I promised my dad I would swim fast at the next meet and make the Senior National Team. My mother was just there to ensure I got where I needed to be to continue to excel.

My mother and Paul's relationship started to develop as they discussed all the opportunities I had to shine that year. It became especially important for my mother to make sure I was on the right track for success.

Everyone at this point seemed happy with Paul and how he was bringing me along. I was in his top swimming group, the only girl with five guys. I was on the path to stardom and that path was starting to be clearer by the swim meet. Paul was the head coach and had influence with making sure that I was on the team. The next event coming up was Winter Nationals and that created an opportunity for me to make my first Senior Team. I knew I needed to please Paul and train hard while doing whatever it took to make that team which was selected based on the coaches' discretion after the upcoming Nationals.

The competition in England was starting to get harder as I was no longer competing as an age grouper; I was now competing with the top talent of Britain and the world. It was always what I wanted to be: the youngest and the best in the world. I was doing it. The British team was already filled with world record holders and champions, just not as many as in the States. The competition wasn't anything to balk at. There was a level of excitement to join those ranks—I felt what my dad had felt the day we watched the Olympics together. The British pride was starting to grow inside of me.

While practice progressed, so did my conversations with Paul. He began talking to me about my training and what I needed to do to make the National Team. We discussed my future and the path towards greatness. We had a plan. Paul began to have the same dreams and vision as my father had for me. My feelings for Paul started to grow; I wanted to excel and shine in practice as well as in competition, with the praise from a great set being just as satisfying as winning a race. I thrived on what my workouts would bring. As I built a stable of excellent workouts, my confidence to perform grew exponentially.

When Nationals rolled around I was ready, and Paul was ready for me to shine as well. I had become his new rising swimmer. When we arrived on the pool deck I had confidence in myself and the confidence that Paul had in me. My focus was to make this upcoming team because

Paul had committed to me that if I swam in the top three at Nationals he would make sure I was on the team.

Meanwhile, my mother's connection with Paul and his wife grew close. My success proved that the sacrifice my parents made was worth it. After a great practice Paul would reaffirm that my mother would have something to report back to my dad, although I would rather be the one to tell my dad the wonderful news and have him all to myself. I really just wanted my dad to be happy with something that I had accomplished despite the fact that the bar would continue to move. I wasn't ever quite sure if he was pleased with me as it was a moving target. But that didn't stop me from chasing it.

When it came time to swim my race, Paul pulled me aside to go over my strategy and how I was going to swim the race. What splits I was going to hold, the almost always request of swimming faster on the back half while pacing myself at the start. This all translated to "swim my own race." Paul was starting to consistently feel too comfortable around me as he would casually place his hands on my hips. I was uncomfortable about it, but more uncomfortable to do something about it. It was the look in his eye filled with the confidence that I was going to do just great that kept me locked into his gaze. I felt assured about the upcoming race. I knew I was going to execute as directed; I didn't have any doubt in my mind. Besides, Paul kept alluding to the fact I would easily make the team with him being on the selection committee. Going into the race all parts of me were a go. Paul wasn't the same with the boys, well, they were boys and older, and I supposed they didn't need the nurturing and care that I did.

The race was a blur, but the accomplishment was not. I don't remember my race at all. I only remember the feeling of getting out of the water with Paul greeting me in the warm down pool with a smile and his piercing eyes that looked right through me. I felt like I wanted to keep only my head above the water as he kneeled down to discuss the success of my race. I did everything that was asked of me. I was second to one other swimmer who happened to be one of top ten swimmers in the world for our event, the 800 Freestyle. As my dad would say, "It wasn't bad." Paul thought I should make the team with that swim, although I would need to wait and see what the coaches said.

At the end of the swim meet the coaches got together and decided on who was going to be on the National Team for a dual meet against Russia. After the team was selected, Paul called my mother over to let her know that he selected me for the team. It seemed like it was a sense of relief for my mother; her sacrifice from Dad was becoming worth it. I had just made the Senior National Team. The path to making the World Championship in Guayaquil, Ecuador, was made much clearer as well as me making the Commonwealth Games Team at the end of the summer. It was like the yellow brick road had lit up just for me.

When I woke up the next morning the team was announced in the national newspaper. Since I was the youngest person on the team the renewed media attention continued. One of the first R-rated movies I saw was *The Jerk* and one of my favorite lines in that movie is when Steve Martin gets a phone book and points to his name and says, "My name in print!" I had a similar feeling. This time I felt pride, unlike during my first big interview where I felt I had to swallow my pride and my love for America. Back then I didn't feel a love for Great Britain; I only knew my dad's love for his country. Now I had my own pride and love for my dad's country as well.

After walking through town there was a little skip in my step with my newfound pride. But that didn't change me feeling exposed from the inside out as I passed the Lady Godiva statue. That part of me didn't change that sense of my soul feeling naked before I even got to the pool. I had become someone and it wasn't a mature woman; it was just a kid with a dream that was starting to show up in color.

When I arrived at practice that afternoon, I was greeted by the Sky TV national news crew that wanted to do an interview with me. I learned of this when I walked onto the pool deck with my swimsuit on and had leftover feelings of being very self-conscious, mostly because I wanted to be in the water. I wanted to be shy and have the attention all at the same time. Then there was the idea of getting out of practice or at least the warm-up. I liked getting out of something, especially for the attention and praise that was right in front of me.

Paul was unaware of my previous media experience when I was at Kelly College, so this wasn't my first rodeo. He pulled me aside and wanted me to feel comfortable with doing the interview and being on TV. He was treating me like a kid. I was, but it felt protective and possessive. It wasn't a reaction that I had experienced with him before.

The rest of my teammates arrived as the crew was setting up. Paul didn't leave my side but stayed with me and gave the rest of the swimmers the usual warm-up. I wanted him to go back to being a coach and let me have my time. It wasn't looking like that was going to be an option.

Shortly thereafter, a woman in her late thirties or early forties, attractive and well-put together, explained how the interview was going to go. She pulled me aside, out of Paul's earshot, to share the questions that she wanted to ask, mainly around being the youngest person on the British team and how I felt about that, and of course she had to ask me about my American roots.

When it came time to start filming I sat on the bench, they adjusted the lights, moved the boom mic in place, and then Paul interjected himself to sit down next to me. There was a pause in the moment and it was completely unexpected. I looked at the interviewer questioning this arrangement and then looked at Paul. He turned to me and said he wanted me to feel comfortable. Then he started talking about my talent as a swimmer and the records that were in my reach; he talked me up beyond where I had expected the interview to go. He said all the right things that made it okay for me to have him there.

The interview proceeded with Paul sitting right by my side. After the first question was asked, Paul placed his hand on my thigh and started rubbing it in a sexual and comforting way at the same time. I remember looking at the interviewer—she glanced at that and didn't skip a beat. She went right into the next question. I was lost in the moment. I didn't know what moment to be in: the one with the feelings about Paul and what he was doing to me, or the feelings of doing a TV interview and the idea of being praised. I was lost in a swirl of emotion that held no clarity for me. I also knew that I had no defense against Paul. I didn't have a "no" or a "stop" in me. There wasn't one in the tank, if you will.

At school the next day after the piece aired, classmates whom I didn't know started saying "hi" to me in the halls. The teachers that I tried to manipulate paused from giving me a bad grade or forgot what they wanted to scold me about for my behavior. I earned something from the people around me. I earned their respect, their admiration, their awe. It was a mysterious feeling I attributed to Paul for coaching me to this place. I wasn't just getting the attention that I desperately craved from my dad, I was now getting it from my coach, friends, parents, and strangers. I was recognized as something special.

A few weeks later would be the swim meet against Russia held in Blackpool, England. I was not a fan of the city, a tourist trap with a saltwater pool that was often used for competition. It was also the venue for the upcoming World Championship trials so it was essential to be able to race in it prior to the trials to get a feel for the pool.

I was the youngest swimmer on the team accompanied by three of the five guys that I trained with. Paul had four swimmers on the team. I was a little shy and nervous to be part of the senior team. Only a few years ago I had admired and wanted to be like these swimmers and now I was part of the team, one of them. It was weird for me to make that adjustment from being a fan to being on the other side of having fans.

All this attention triggered my shyness and need to be feel connected to Paul more. I became needy and sought out his protection and comfort. The competition itself was uneventful in the sense that I swam my race, and swam fast enough to become world ranked in the 800 Free. That in itself was good enough to set me up for being on the World Championship Team. It was a solid second place behind Britain's fastest swimmer in the 800 Free at the time.

My relationship with Paul was becoming more chummy, where we could joke around with each other. As our relationship got more chummy, Paul wasn't shy about how he expressed that on the pool deck and at team events. I became a possession of his. I was a product of his coaching and expertise. I was something that he was enamored with. This was the perception that I had from outside looking in. His open admiration for me was feeding a part of my soul that I needed fed.

At the same time that Paul was expressing his admiration to me, I was seeking that same feeling from the boys on the team. I wanted one of them to like me the same way. After the meet was over there was a party and it turned out to involve drinking. I found that I liked to drink and hang out with the older swimmers. It was considered acceptable; after all, we were British and that is what British people do, drink. I ended up getting too drunk and getting together with one of the older boys on the team.

What I learned at practice when I returned home was that there were no secrets on the team; coaches knew everything and swimmers knew everything, and this incident was no different. Paul wasn't going to let it go and let up on commenting on it when I returned to practice. I was stuck in an embarrassment loop with him.

Shortly after that swim meet I was off to Sweden to swim in another meet; my schedule had gotten full now because I was swimming in all the junior competitions for the National Team and now for the Senior Team as well. I was traveling most weekends to trips around Europe and Paul accompanied me on all of those.

The more we traveled together the more friendly Paul became with me. He became especially interested in the boys that I was interested in. When we were in Sweden I befriended an Italian boy that was so sweet and nice. We got together on the last night and did what teenagers aren't supposed to do. Paul learned of this, not sure how, but really everyone knew everything, let's be honest.

The touching and the intrusive conversations with Paul gradually got more involved. Paul wasn't just interested in the boys that I was engaged with, he wanted to know more. He wanted to know what I was doing with them. His questions only embarrassed me. I answered them not because I wanted to, but because I felt like I had to. I felt like he was entitled to the information. My mother was also intrusive with questions, but this was just her style of communicating. She harbored a lack of trust that you are going to be forthright based on the assumption that you are lying and therefore she needed to interrogate you to figure out the truth.

I had a secret and my secrets were started to compound. Paul knew it. I was at his mercy with the guilt of my actions. I had this notion that I only told my parents the good stuff and left the rest of my dark actions to figure out for myself. Why would I tell them anything that they disapproved of? It was how I thought about things as a teenager. It wasn't like they were really attuned with my life to have a conversation about anything other than swimming. All necessary talk was about how I was performing. My existence was based in time and performance and nothing else. School had very little weight. Flunking out was perfectly fine, despite the fact that I was extremely intelligent and gifted and never had to apply myself. I was also protected from accusation because it was always someone's else fault and certainly not mine.

Paul never let up on talking about boys and sex with me. He seemed to find moments where I was alone and no one could hear our conversations. He made it look like it was about coaching and my success as a swimmer. It wasn't long after that Paul asked if I was on the Pill. I literally had just started my period for the first time the month before. He knew that as well because it happened when I was on a trip with him. He said, "You'll get pregnant and that will ruin your life." I didn't want to ruin my life and swimming career either. Getting on the Pill seemed like an easy solution so I could continue to have fun and be a teenager. Paul had an ulterior motive that I would learn about later.

Paul wanted to talk to my dad about putting me on the Pill. I really didn't know how that was going to go over until Paul said he would tell my father that it would help with my swimming and I would swim faster if I was on it. I was concerned at first that he was going to say something about me being sexually active, but it seemed Paul would keep that between us.

Paul called my father up to talk to him about my training and about me going on the Pill. The way the story was told to me was that in the '76 Olympics, the East German women took the Pill to increase their hormones, essentially creating an advantage, now a debunked story. Nonetheless at the time it was a story that was going around. Since the Pill wasn't on the banned substance list it was okay to take. Shortly after that conversation, my dad had the Pill prescribed for me.

Around this time, one of my older teammates whom I was friends with and who was from Paul's previous team, shared with me that she was having sex with Paul. Paul was married and his wife was a Jehovah's Witness and my friend was seventeen. She said that Paul could never get divorced because of his wife's religion; therefore, he was free to have sex with anyone. When I learned of this I didn't know what to do with the information.

Due to Paul's increased interest in me and speaking to my dad about the Pill, the World Championship trials, and all the other upcoming swim meets, my parents were taken by what Paul was going to do for my swimming career. After that conversation, my dad was convinced that Paul was going to be the coach who was going to get me to the Olympics. They were going to do anything he suggested.

At the same time my father's career was becoming bigger and more important since he invented the SPF (Sun Protection Factor) for sunscreen. As a result he traveled the world to give talks on that and on many subjects within his expertise. My father had an upcoming trip around the world and my mother was going to accompany him. After all, she had been with me for the most of the year. Paul was clearly developing me and bringing me on as a swimmer. My mother asked Paul if I could stay at their apartment while she traveled with my dad. He was very open and accepting of this idea.

My parents had what they wanted: a coach who would take their daughter to the Olympics. I was happy I didn't have to live with my mother for a while and at the time thought that anything else would be better. I wanted the space and freedom to be me. I was happy my father knew that my coach was going to take me to the next level of my career. Everybody was seemingly happy with this scenario.

CHAPTER 7

The Black Line

I was like an orphan dropped off at the doorstep of another person's home. Although I was happy with the departure of my mother, I didn't really want to be living at my coach's house. I know my mother felt I'd be safe and taken care of after she had a long conversation with his wife who presented herself as kind and nice. They lived in a two-bedroom high-rise apartment—a short, easy walk to the pool; actually a much closer and shorter walk to my school and the pool than my parents' house, which played right into the lazy, be-efficient athlete that I was. The only awkward part of this whole thing was letting go of my personal space. I knew how to connect to Paul and manage my space on the pool deck, and I also knew the drill of living with people, but this was going to be different; I'd be in his house and not out in the garden shed. This living arrangement seemed a little too close and uncomfortable for my teenage self.

I settled into my own room, and noticed there was only one TV in the apartment which was in the living room. If I wanted to be entertained I would have to sit in the living room and socialize with Paul and his wife, never mind eating meals with them and having actual conversations. I wasn't shy about directing the conversation as a way to get what I wanted and in this case it was to watch TV, especially American TV shows. *Fame* was a hit show at the time, but back then we couldn't record our shows to watch later, so the only time to watch the show was when it was actually on. On Wednesday nights after dinner I would get to watch the show and stay up a little longer because we didn't have morning practice; and I could sleep a bit later in the morning, before I had to go to school.

The dynamic between me and Paul was very much a servant-master relationship. He would give me a set and I'd perform that set. In return I'd get praise for how well I accomplished the task. Rinse and repeat. At this point in my swimming career I knew how to speak up when it came to something wrong with me or the set. Let me tell you it wasn't with grace, poise, or any other positive description. You could even make a case to call me a prima donna at times, although that mode was generally reserved for practices and maybe around meal times since I was always starving from swimming.

Paul and I were buffered by his wife the first night and by the fact that I was able to watch my favorite TV show, *Fame.* I closely identified with these characters, who were young teenagers like me trying to make it in the world with their gifts, while being challenged with outside issues at home. I connected with their passion, their pursuit of their talent, and who they were as people. I was in awe. That Rolls-Royce engine inside of me was getting revved up with the excitement. The show took place in New York City, a city that I craved to be part of the culture and grandness that it exuded. New York was a clear example of America's sparkle that I dreamed about. The show touched on every part of my desire for my own pursuit of fame.

The next morning, Paul entered my room and placed his hand on my back, rubbing it until I awoke. I was super tired in the mornings and never wanted to go to practice. It was always a struggle. I wanted to give every excuse as to why I didn't have to go. I wanted something to be wrong with me like being sick or something. For the barrage of excuses that went off in my head, I never had any that were convincing enough. When Paul started touching me that morning there were other voices that went off, but I shoved them aside not even sure what they were saying because my focus was to get up and out from his creepy touch. I took this as my coach being friendly. At least that was what I told myself at the time.

When we left the apartment together to go to practice, I didn't have the mental prep time that I was used to. I had to walk and actually converse with him. I was never a morning converser. I just wanted to get to practice and jump in, listen to the set, and be underwater in the silence of the nothing that floated through my mind. This is what I had come to love about swimming; it wasn't just my passion and love for the sport but how I could cancel out the world the moment I entered the water. I would stare at the black line at the bottom of the pool where there was no space or time. It was just me gliding along in the water. I had this long power glide that was my signature stroke. It was effortless to watch and I was in no hurry to perform it. I was so connected to me and all of me. Having to speak to Paul before I started swimming disrupted my rhythm and how I connected to the water and to practice.

One morning on the way to practice Paul asked me how long I had been on the Pill. It had only been a week at the time. It was an odd question and embarrassing for me. I knew when he asked that question there was danger coming my way. I also didn't know what to say or do about that. I ignored it and went about swimming like I normally did.

My spirit opened up in May as school was coming to a close for the year, albeit final exams were around the corner and then it was a summer of World Championships, Junior Europeans and then finally the Commonwealth Games. At this point I had a lot to look forward to, but first I needed to qualify for the World Championship Team at trials at the end of the month. That was also the other reason that I went on the Pill so I could manage my periods and not have my period during a major competition. When Paul asked me how long I'd been on the Pill that was the way I took his question.

The swimming season is generally from the fall until March for Winter Nationals. In April some international competition takes place and then you start training hard again for late July trials for the final competitions in August. This year was different in that I needed to be rested, or more accurately tapered, for the World Championship Trials at the end of the month. When a swimmer like myself started to taper there was much restlessness going on because I had nowhere to put all that pent-up energy. I couldn't just put it back in the pool to keep me docile, or tame if you will. During this time I was starting to lighten up on the training in order to be sharp for trials.

I had my school exams and could have put my attention in that direction, but I wasn't focused on school at that time. I had too much excitement for how close I was to having a breakthrough in my swimming career.

I had an opportunity to hide in my room until my show came on. This night was the final episode of *Fame* and I wasn't going to miss it no matter what. I was addicted and hooked.

The night of the final episode I was little more friendly with Paul because I didn't want to miss my show. I knew I needed to be nice and accommodating with him, like talking to him when I didn't want to. When I came out of my room for dinner his wife wasn't there, so I asked Paul where she was. He told me she was at her meeting of the Jehovah's Witnesses, and then afterwards she was headed to the pub with her friends. It was just going to be the two of us. We had pigs in a blanket that night. I had an appetite that was difficult to tame and would eat whatever I could. Mind you, I had a 5'11", 126 lb. lanky frame that didn't have an ounce of fat on it. I served myself and then went to sit down in front of the TV. At first Paul wanted me to sit with him at the table, but I sat in a single chair with a direct view to the TV, watching the show right before *Fame*, which didn't start until like 7:10, as they never started on the hour; it was always weird like that with their limited programming. I wanted to be fed and ready to watch without distraction.

Paul catered to me, asking if I wanted anything else to eat. I told him I was good, then he took my plate and cleared up after me. Paul now sat on a couch lined up against the wall at an angle to the TV. While I was sitting in my chair Paul asked me again how long it had been since I was on the Pill. "A couple of weeks," I said. It was then he got up and went to the fridge and brought me a beer. It was a big can, not the small American-sized beers, but at least twice that size. This was followed with a comment about the strength of the British beers compared to the weak American ones. I laughed because I felt it made me strong to be able to down a British beer without a problem. I also figured it was okay since my coach had just given me a beer. I could drink and not get into trouble was the frame of mind I was coming from. I wasn't a sipper at the time; I slammed the beer pretty much and started to watch the show.

As the alcohol took effect, I was getting sucked into *Fame* as the voice of Debbie Allen started to blare out in the opening, "You got big dreams, you want fame, well fame costs, and right here is where you start paying."

I felt like I was Alice in *Alice in Wonderland* as my mind started to spin from having downed the beer. I was trying to focus my attention on the show. Then Paul started asking me questions about boyfriends. I was starting to get embarrassed or awkward to say the least. I could feel myself falling down the rabbit hole as the beer took over my body and mind like Paul was doing with me.

Debbie Allen then started singing, "Oh, this is a special place, the magic is here to see, and when it works the universe is dancing in time with me."

Just when I thought I had settled down my mind, Paul came back with another beer. I couldn't say no. I didn't have that ability in any other circumstance so this was no different. Besides, I had just slammed alcohol into my body and my coach was letting me feel I could get away with anything. I had no restrictions, no rules. Isn't this what every teenager thinks that they want? I was experiencing that in this moment.

On the show there is a character, Paul, who is there to assess what teachers he can layoff to meet forthcoming budget cuts. He introduces himself as Paul to Ms. Sherwood.

Paul passes me another beer, my eyes began to blur, as does my ability to make sound decisions.

I sit there trying to focus on the show while Paul pats the couch for me to move to sit next to him. I get up without thought or hesitation. I am at his command. It is me responding to a set or a race strategy; I do as I am being directed to do. I am so well trained to respond to the call and know the repercussions if I don't: this time is no different. I sit right next to him without a moment of uncertainty. He puts his hands on my leg and starts to stroke the inside of my thigh. I take my concentration away from watching Fame. I am feeling a rush of adrenaline while feeling annoyed at the same time. I am living in two different moments of time. If not experiencing a multi-dimensional time world.

While Paul is rubbing my thigh, Paul the Fame character says, "Don't you feel the need to let go a little bit, you know, let off a little steam?"

As I sit there not responding to anything, I have flashes of the time he was watching me make out with my teammate, to how he would place his hands on my body, to how he would look at me. As the alcohol continues its effects on me, I lose all sense of me. It is pushing down my spirit to a place where I can't reach it. Like a snail retreating into its shell. I can feel myself go in that direction as Paul leans into me and starts kissing me.

With the show still going on in the background, I am walking down the hall with Paul's hand on my back leading me towards the bedroom. He says to me, "You are on the Pill two weeks now, right?" My innocence and unknowing, while my knowing at the same time, understands what he is asking me. The naive and young part of me isn't foreseeing my future moments ahead of me.

At this point, my mind is good and spinning while he is in full control of me. I am going to do whatever he asks of me. That is how well I am programmed to respond to a command.

When we get to the bedroom Paul knocks my teddy bear off the bed to the floor. He starts to kiss me and undress me, I do not respond to him. After I'm completely undressed he tells me to stand in the corner, as the sun is setting through the blinds. It projects a silhouette of my naked body on the wall. I can hear the blare of the TV outside the doors of the room, as the Fame theme song starts up. My bear is just face down on the floor. Paul starts to play with himself as says to me, "Your father thinks you're good enough to be a world champion."

I freeze in time, my head is spinning from the alcohol. I have little balance and am getting cold from my naked body being exposed to the air. I can feel my shoulders want to hunch forward and my body wants to torque itself to avoid being on full display. As I stand there, Paul stares at my body with those now-so-ever creepy eyes as he criticizes the shape and definition of it. The tone and the language he uses makes me feel like a thousand knives flying my way. The intensity that he plays with himself starts to swirl my thoughts as I am down the rabbit hole of no return. All I want is to be out of the world in which I have found myself as everything starts to blur from the alcohol.

Paul pats the bed, and I respond without hesitation. He might as well have given me a set of 10 x 200 on the 2:20 and that I am to start on the top, the next time the clock ticks to 00 on the minute hand. I am ready to go. I have no defense other than to respond to his command. Being that the alcohol has consumed my body, I am even further defenseless to his commands.

As the TV blares on the outside, my heart blares on the inside, now I have this man on top of me. I look the other way as he kisses me all over my body. I have turned off. That Rolls-Royce engine is starting to putter out inside of me. It feels like all the lights are shut down on the inside. There is no God in this moment. It is only me and the darkness of my actions. This goes on for a while as I am told that he needs to come inside of me because I am on the Pill. I stare at the wall as all the light from the day gradually disappears as I lie there in total darkness with my coach taking my spirit. It wasn't my virginity that he took; it was my spirit of self.

When Paul left I lay there for the rest of the night not moving an inch. Bear laid face-down in the same place, as both of us suffered our fate together. I was completely paralyzed from the inside, frozen in time and space. I wanted something, even if it was beer—I needed something to comfort me in that moment. I had nothing, not even a thin sheet to cover me. I couldn't put anything on my body that was connected to this person. I had no mother, no friend, no coach, no one to comfort me and I couldn't exactly call my dad—what would I say? I was stuck in a world of thought. I had no practice in the morning to wash away my thoughts. I was stuck in the abyss. I had no idea how to get out of it. I had several more weeks to stay here. I couldn't run away, I would get into more trouble for that. What was I going to do? I had no options. All I wanted in that moment was for someone to tell me I was going to be okay.

When I showed up for practice after school, walking by the Lady Godiva statue was especially revealing more than it was the first time I walked by her. I could feel the cold brisk air brush past my heart. If you have ever stuck your finger in a starfish, it closes at the site of the finger and then it hardens to the point where no one is getting in. One could say that hell had frozen over on my heart as the shame of my actions were on full display, half naked in the center of town for all to see. Yet the only difference between me and Lady Godiva was that no one else saw it, no one experienced it but me.

I arrived to practice all tense and unwilling to engage in conversation with those around me. It was brushed off that I must be on my period or moody or something. No one even considered something else may be going on. As a high-performing athlete, the objective is to overcome whatever life events you have gone through in order to be the best athlete you can be. It seemed the more disadvantages you shoulder, you have more value by the time the win appears. I allowed the chatter to be whatever they said. It didn't stop Paul from embracing me with those eyes that undressed you in the moment and the liberty he took to caress my body. I was now trapped in this cage with him.

When I arrived home that evening after practice we had a trip planned to see Macbeth at the Royal Shakespeare Theater. I was going with Paul and his wife. I was reading the book in school and had the final exam in a couple of days. Of course I hadn't read the book so going to the play seemed like the easiest way to get the story and be able to write about it. I didn't want to go, but I also didn't want to read the book either. It was hard to concentrate after practice and now it was even harder. Going to the theater became the lesser of two evils and, besides, I had no reason why I couldn't go. It wasn't like I was going to be left alone in the house, and not going didn't get me away from Paul. I figured I would suck it up.

When we arrived at the theater, Paul sat in the middle of us with his wife on one side and me on the other. The moment the theater lights dimmed his hand flew between my legs. I sat through that play completely disconnected from myself and could not remember a moment of the play besides the monster sitting next to me with his wife oblivious to what was happening. Here was another adult who missed a moment that wasn't right, right in plain sight. I was being let down and taken advantage of by the adults around me. How was I going to trust an adult? How was I going to get out of this situation? I couldn't help blame myself for what was going on. I had found myself stuck in what was starting to be a relationship with my coach.

The next morning he came in my room waking me up with his touch that had become gradually more invasive since I was staying there, going beyond any fourteen-year-old girl's ability to say anything. One, it was shocking; two, it was early; and three, I was already completely shut down and had absolutely no defense at this early hour.

I got up after he left the room. I wanted to leave on my own or figure out a way to get rid of this person. I lived at my coach's house and was about to be coached by the very same person that I stayed with. Where was I to go? We exited the apartment and waited for the elevator to take us down 33 floors. I couldn't help but feel like time had slowed to halt. I was holding my breath, hoping for a relief from somewhere, anywhere. We got on the elevator, and I watched the doors close only to see Paul's hands move towards the stop button. He stopped the elevator and started to make out with me. I was completely trapped. It was first time that I wanted to get in the pool and be the first one in the water; usually I liked to linger around before jumping in. It took some convincing to get him to turn the elevator back on. It took me being as nice as I could muster to get myself out of that position.

When we arrived at the bottom, I couldn't get out of there quick enough. I allowed him to walk in front of me. I could hardly bear to have this person on the same plane as me, in my eye view, in my space. I started to protect myself by putting up a barrier to my spirit. So much so that I needed to walk on the other side of the street just to put some distance between the two of us.

I don't know how much longer after I had to stay at that apartment. It may have been a few days or a week, but regardless it wasn't over for us. I had the World Championship Trials in a couple of weeks and it was important I redirect my attention to training for that.

I went quietly back to my mother who had returned from Japan with a present. The best part of seeing my mother again, well my parents in general, was getting presents after they came home from their trips. My mother had brought me the latest gadget, a Sony Walkman. It was the perfect distraction and the perfect option to protect myself from Paul.

At the time the hit band was The Human League. I ran out and bought a few tapes and now was one of the few kids, if not the only kid, with a Walkman and a way to create distance between Paul and myself. It was the perfect hideout.

The Walkman distraction allowed me to ignore adults and focus on being prepared for my race at the World Championship Trials. My event was on the first day, or at least the event that I was most likely to make, the 800 Freestyle. My event was only swam once since I was in the top eight and was swimming only in the finals.

We were staying at a hotel down the street from the pool in Blackpool. The hotel was okay, not American nice, but clean and comfortable. Thankfully I had my own room across the hall from my mother. The rooms were small, with a bed, a chair and sink and toilet with a little space to move around, essentially a tiny room for a single person. I stayed in my room out of sight to prepare for my race. I was supposed to be napping, but I was filled with excitement, anxiety, and fear.

I also liked to be prepared and not rushed to race. It's my thing to not rush me. I will get there when I get there. It was how I swam, precise without being rushed, a very controlled powerful stroke. I never liked pain—I liked the stream of power through me. I put on my Walkman to get my mind centered for my race and as I exited my room, I saw Paul leaving my mother's tiny room. I had a rush of concerning thoughts flow through me. I saw those creepy eyes, those eyes that he gave me the night on that couch while watching Fame. It wasn't something I could totally ignore. In that moment I realized my mother was compromised and he turned her loyalty against me, not that it was hard to do. I was openly disappointed with her. There was no loyalty for her anymore, in fact, the complete opposite.

I carried on from that moment, not missing a beat, and, yes, I refused to walk anywhere with Paul. I walked on my own to the pool. Yet when I arrived at the pool I had no choice but to engage him. I could act like a bratty teenager, but when it came to my swimming it was all business. There was no room for messing that up, as I had to report the results back to my dad. It would kill me if my dad was unhappy with me. The Walkman allowed me to be a disconnected teenager allowing my behavior to fly under the radar and I could also blame it on my period for being moody. I had both of those issues going on when I was swimming those trials. I also got to buffer myself from Paul a little bit with my fellow teammates so I wasn't all alone with him. That eased the awkwardness and embarrassment that I was trying desperately to hide.

I went to speak to Paul to get my directions for warm-ups, though at this point Paul never changed the warm-up. I had my cap and goggles on my forehead. He took the liberty to put his hands on my body as I squirmed out of his grasp while putting on my goggles. I dove in the water trying my best to avoid his advances. At the end of warm-ups I would do sprints to rev up the engine. When I would get out Paul kept touching my shoulder or wherever he could get his hands. It wasn't a pat; it was more sexual in nature and I knew that. At one point, I turned and snapped at him about my swim, not about the touching. It was about how I just sprinted, how the time wasn't good enough. He knew I was rejecting him. He pulled me close in to him and told me that I needed to settle down or I wouldn't be on the team. I pulled myself together and at the same time gave him my best "fuck you" attitude. I had confidence in my swimming ability and wasn't going to let him bully me.

I swam my race later that night and came in second to Britain's fastest swimmer. They took the top two to the World Championship. I didn't think I needed to be nice to Paul for the rest of the swim meet. I swam other races but had only potentially qualified in the one race. After the meet ended the coaches got together and decided on who was going to be selected to be on the team. Paul was the head coach and on the selection committee. Since I was his swimmer, he was committed to me and my success, and it never occurred to me that I wasn't going to make the team.

When I woke up the next morning the team was announced in the paper and my name was not there. I was so upset, which was really an understatement. I was beyond upset. What was I going to tell my dad? How was I going to explain this? Paul had told my mother and subsequently my father that I was too immature to go. Unless I did what he wanted me to do he wouldn't be putting me on the team.

I was now forced to obey Paul, his direction, and his coaching. I wasn't allowed to get out of line and talk back or doing anything that was going to jeopardize my swimming career. I got the lecture that my parents weren't spending all this money on me to fuck this up. No, my parents didn't use that word—they were far more civilized than that. After all, their efforts weren't just to make me an Olympian; it was to dine with the Queen of England and partake in the highest of society.

That summer I returned to the States for a month or so reeling from the disappointment of not being on the World Championship Team. I also had to deal with the fact that I just flunked out of school at King Henry VIII. At least they wanted me to go to their private sister school, one that was a more sporty school and less academically focused. I was so not interested in doing that. I had the summer in America to figure it out, to feed my soul with everything that I loved about my birth country. Standing on US soil made me feel alive and whole. A feeling that I so needed after the last few months.

The summer was shortened due to the competition of the Commonwealth Games Trials and immediately after these trials I was swimming in European Juniors in Austria. While at home I could focus on my swimming, return to the smell of bagels and swimming in the fast lane. That summer I was also breaking all the state records in my age group. I was lighting up the pool and getting regular praise from my dad. I had missed it and now craved it. I was also getting praised by my teammates; they too were in awe of my abilities, both in practice and in competition. It was fun and exciting for me. I had no one to fight with. I could just be me, swim, and love it.

The disappointment of not going to Ecuador for World Championships was dissipating as I found a renewed love for myself. But the love was only temporary as I was set to return to England and get back under the coaching of Paul. I was swimming fast and was well rested for my upcoming swim meets. Nothing was going to stop me. My mind was focused and I was ready. I got the lecture from my dad to behave. I promised that I wouldn't rock the boat as they would say. Secretly, I dreaded what was ahead of me but I learned to ignore that and focus on swimming fast. That was all I needed to do—nothing would get in my way if I swam fast. That was the mindset I adopted when I returned to England.

By this time I had mastered how to make the traveling run smooth and had learned to become quite resourceful. I also felt like I had cleared my being of any shame and embarrassment with my time away. I had come to terms with not making the team. I had accepted that I was difficult at times and it was my fault that I wasn't on the team. My spirit was in a better place and my focus and drive were ready to take on new levels. I saw a hint of my dad's twinkle over the summer; I knew it was still there and I was going to earn that back.

When I arrived back to train with Paul, it didn't take long, like one practice for him to begin to take liberties with how he embraced me and touched my body on the pool deck. My heart and voice retreated back into me with the idea that I wasn't to rock the boat but I couldn't help myself but respond like a bull in a china shop. I started to yell back at him and tell him to get his hands off me. I told him, "Don't touch me!" His response was always that I was immature and uncontrollable and if I didn't conform, I wasn't going to be on the international teams. I knew he was my gatekeeper. I was torn: Do I let him do what he wanted and sexually touch me with the intention of him wanting to have sex with me? It was hard for me to let that happen without causing a scene. My intensity was passed off that I wasn't swimming fast enough or just having a disagreement with my coach. Others saw me through the lens of how I responded to Paul touching me.

When trials started I knew I was swimming fast and nothing was going to stop my success. I could feel the anger that I internalized from Paul in my races. I wasn't going to let him stop me. I channeled all that frustration to determination.

My first event was the 400 Freestyle and I placed third in the race, behind two women who were already ranked in the top ten in the world. I wasn't far behind them, ranking in the top 20 in the world. For these trials they took three swimmers per event, as opposed to the World Championships with just two. I knew I had a good chance of making the team, with three more events to go. My best event, 200 Freestyle, was yet to come. That surely would seal my fate to make the team.

After my race, I went over to Paul to get my splits and wanted him to be proud of me and happy for my swim. He did what he had been doing, which was to touch me in a creepy and seductive way. I know it didn't look like that to the outside world, but to me I knew what he wanted and what he was doing with me. I sat there dripping wet next to him looking at my times as he placed his hand on my thigh. My focus was on where the hand was going, not on how I swam. I stated matter-of-factly that I would make the team. As he was stroking my body he provided me no reassurances and in fact said that I would need to be more mature and not have any outbursts with him if I was going to be on the team. I looked at him with compliance and submission. I said I would try and apologized. As soon as I committed to his request it seemed like he would make sure I was selected for the team.

When I called my dad after my swim to let him know how I did, he was happy for me. He also directed me to not screw it up. I know I needed to make sure that I wasn't causing a fuss and that I needed to not act out. I could hear my dad's fear of not being able to control me and that I would be messing up his dreams if I wasn't focusing my attention on my swimming. I promised my dad that I was going to stay focused. The next day was the 200 Freestyle. I could feel the rush of confidence that I had inside of me. I knew I was ready for that race.

The next day I swam in the morning and qualified easily for one of the center lanes, meaning I was one of the fastest morning swimmers. Lanes are assigned by fastest in the center to slowest on the outside. When it came time to swim that night, Paul was extra friendly with me and took his liberty with how he touched me. I could feel myself hold everything in, knowing I needed to do whatever he said so I wasn't going to let my dad down. I went with the gestures and advances as I was given pre-race instruction. When it came time for my race I was blessed enough to have this Walkman that no one had and barely knew anything about, so I was definitely giving off the rich American kid vibe and all the other derogatory anti-American stuff you could muster up to describe me. I was that, regardless if I acted that way or not, it was how I was labeled. I knew the Walkman was how I was surviving the moments with Paul; I could shut myself off with music. It wasn't that I didn't care about the label, but I had no defense to speak to it—it was bigger than me.

My focus and determination were in rare form that night during my 200 Freestyle race. I could feel the power of my determination drive me through the water. I wanted it. I wanted my dad to see me as being a star and worth loving. When I touched the wall and saw that I was second to Olympian June Croft, one of the fastest swimmers in the world. I knew I had made it. I knew there was no question about me being on the team and more importantly, my time also ranked me one of the fastest in the world. I was actually smiling after this race. I was proud of myself—all my summer training and finding that renewed love for myself was back. It felt like the passion that I had once felt was rising to the top. I could see myself being an Olympian, not that I ever had that doubt, but this race gave me the poise to know that I was special. I was the youngest person that would be on the team. I really was becoming the next Sharon Davies, who had since retired.

After the race, I went to speak with Paul, I was so happy with my swim. He did what he usually did and I accepted his advances as I was told to do. I didn't react, I didn't withdraw—I allowed him to embrace me the way he had in the past. I was more focused on calling my dad to let him know that I was pretty sure I would make the team having qualified in two events and being second in one of them, with the selection committee taking the top three. After all, Paul was selecting the team. I was behaving to the best of my ability.

That night I returned to our lodging at Crystal Palace where the Commonwealth Games Trials were taking place. It was a training center and lodging facility in London for athletes. All the rooms in the center didn't have locks on the doors and the center was mostly comprised of single rooms like the one I was in. After I went to my room, I put my headphones on and was falling asleep with the excitement of knowing I would soon speak with my dad, but it had to wait until the morning because of the time change. Just as I was starting to fall asleep Paul entered my room, whether he knocked or not is up to question because I couldn't hear much with the music blaring in my ears. He entered and sat down next to me on the bed and I felt that touch, a touch that I knew too well from staying at his apartment. As he began extending his hands under my pajamas, I jumped up and responded like I promised my dad I wouldn't. I couldn't take it. I didn't want him touching me. I turned very bitchy and grumpy rejecting him and his advances. Any happiness from my swim and excitement that I had to tell my dad was fast disappearing. I knew that I screwed up.

When I woke up in the morning, I had my head hanging between my tail having to face Paul. I knew I was in trouble. I still had two more days of competition and races to swim. That day was the 100 Freestyle. I actually needed to be in the top four as there are four swimmers in a relay. I managed to make it through the day without much interaction with Paul on the pool deck, mostly because my recent success also opened me up to new people, new friends, and many others who wanted to get to know me as the new swimmer. I also had many friends from being on the Junior Team and knew that we were going to Austria right after this swim meet so the pre-meet camaraderie was already starting to form. I was grateful for these many distractions.

When it came time for finals of the 100 Free, it didn't involve me having a race strategy; that was reserved really for long races, for the managing of your energy over a longer period of time. I had less time that I needed to spend with Paul. I swam the event with relative ease and was third in the 100 Free and earned another spot in the team. All together that was three races I swam and three potential positions earned.

I had one race left: the 800 Freestyle, the longest race but also one of my better races and the one to place me highest ranked in the world; well, the 200, 400, 800 had all earned me world rankings at this point in my career at fourteen, and subsequently I came in second in that race. I actually had beat the swimmer who had once beat me a few years ago when I first arrived in England. I had earned my spot back.

I was quietly happy knowing that I had a great swim meet and an excellent race. I tried really hard to not engage Paul after the race but I still had to go over and talk to him about my swim. That is what you do—you talk to your coach and take their direction. My good spirits seemed to mark a place on my body for his eyes, and it didn't stop him from placing his hands on my hips as he pulled me into his body. I couldn't understand how no one else was seeing what he was doing. When he did that I started to get mad at him. I didn't say anything about how he was engaged with me, it was something else, it was about my race. I needed to find a way to disagree with him about my performance. He replied with a calm demeanor to my reaction, but my real reaction was how he was touching me and controlling me.

I looked around as everyone moved along their own world that wasn't ever intertwined with my own. It was a bubble of existence and I was the only person experiencing it. That in itself was frustrating me with the lie that I found myself in and saw no way out of.

The trials ended, I had a really successful swim meet, qualifying in four events—more than just about everyone on the team had done except for a couple of other swimmers. All I wanted to do was let my dad know of the great swims that I had. I knew that my parents wanted to go Australia to watch me swim. My success was their travel plans.

The next morning, when I would normally have known about the team, I was heading to the airport with Paul to go to the European Junior Championships in Austria. He told me that they hadn't decided on the team yet and that it would announced later in the week. Now knowing what I subsequently came to know it was already decided, but he was withholding, albeit it wasn't in the paper the next morning like it normally was so maybe there was some truth to what he was saying. Either way, I had more time to try to not react to him and his advances towards me while preparing for my next competition at the same time.

I did get the chance to speak with my dad before we left for the trip to tell him about my great swims and how happy I was. I swore to my dad that there was no way that I wasn't on that team. I had qualified and was one of the top swimmers and surely the youngest swimmer on the team. I could hear in my dad's voice—how proud he was of me. All the summer training, the investment, the belief was all starting to have meaning for the both of us. He proudly referred to himself as Annabelle's father, not to mention the bragging rights that he would have with his patients, nurses, and staff who followed right along with my career as well.

This swim meet in Austria was a little more fun than London; I was with swimmers my own age, although I was still one of the youngest on the team as I had two years left of competition as a junior competitor. I loved to travel and meet new people; language was never a barrier to communication for me. I had learned at an early age I was gifted to be able to read people and their thoughts. I could respond in my language or a version of charades that reflected back that I understood what they were talking about. It made it more exciting. It was a good distraction, let's just say.

The facilities in Austria had an open locker room set-up, so we had to change in front of our coaches, meaning that Paul had direct and clear access to all the minor girls on the team. I, of course, could spot his creepy stare from anywhere on the pool deck and it always seemed to home in on me. I believe this was where I started and perfected the art of the sly deck change to have some sort of privacy from his invasive vision that would almost certainly lead to his invasive hands on my body.

My interactions with Paul were met with me basically holding my breath and trying really hard to not react to his advances. It was the stroking of my back or my thigh that would make me withdraw inside. I wanted so badly to say "stop," but I didn't have a kind way to do it—that was what I was trying to figure out. Paul was starting to call out my reactions as being unruly by either speaking to me in a harsh tone or grabbing my arm to settle me down. At this point, Paul was telling me that I wouldn't be going to the Commonwealth Games if I was going to let him have sex with me. I was in the trapped.

After practice and before the competition I wanted to go shopping or do something to get away from the hotel and Paul to clear my head. I started walking aimlessly around Innsbruck with tears in my eyes, not knowing what to do. I wanted someone to comfort me who wasn't going to harm me. I had nowhere to go and no one to turn to. I also needed to focus on my swimming and prepare for my race.

After I returned to the hotel I was summoned into Paul's room to explain where I was and why I didn't tell anyone where I went. He could see that I had been crying. I dropped my head in shame just wanting to get out of there. Paul came over to comfort me, his version of sexually touching me and putting his hands up my shirt; he needed to have his hands on my skin. I tried so hard but just couldn't take another moment of this and said, "Just fucking leave me alone!" I turned and left.

At breakfast the next morning I was sitting with my teammates getting ready for the competition and Paul told me he needed to speak to me. I got up from the table and with a stern voice he announced that I was not going to the Commonwealth Games in Australia as he felt that

I was too immature, and unless I could control my temper and myself, I would not be on any international teams. It felt like I had a knife thrust through my heart. I could barely breathe and sure as hell was going to cry.

They ended up taking a younger slower swimmer who only qualified in one event. I was experiencing the most painful moment of my life in that moment and I had no one to comfort me. I had no one to tell me I was going to be okay—I had no one.

I was more concerned with what I was going to tell my dad. I knew that I needed to swim fast here so he wasn't mad at me for not making the Commonwealth Games Team. My parents would have been so upset if I screwed up again. They trained me to have better manners than that and to be polite and kind. I was everything but polite and kind, at least that was what the word on the street was about me. I was getting a bad rap for being an unruly American.

The fuel of my anger and disappointment was channeled into my swimming at that swim meet. I ended up placing second in the 200 Freestyle and broke the British Junior record. With that came the media interest and accolades that I so desperately needed to get over the pain of my disappointment of not going to Commonwealth Games. It would ease the conversation with my dad when I talked to him about not making the team. I needed something to give him.

CHAPTER 8

Airmail

After not making the team I was so devastated and broken-hearted. I was more upset with disappointing my dad and fearing him not loving me. He wasn't ever going to physically harm me—that wasn't his temperament. My father wanted his daughter to be the best in the world and a member of the highest social class. After all, that was the kind of family from which he came. My father grew up in a very upper-class family. While he left that world to make it on his own in America, it was still something he valued more for me than the American dream. It was his British dream if you will.

My parents brought me home after my disappointment to recharge and return to the fighting shape that I needed to be in to find my way back. They weren't going to let me be without making sure that I got the lecture of how to behave and what I needed to do to become a world-class athlete. The first thing they needed to address was my talking back. I grew up with the code "children should be seen and not heard" and that a child must respect adults. I felt like I was back to being lectured when I was eight and got busted for shoplifting a Bonne Bell lipstick. My parents told me I had to turn over a new leaf. This leaf seemed to be more serious than the last one.

The whole time I was at home before returning to school, all I expressed to my dad was how I wanted to quit swimming. I didn't want to do it anymore. I whined and complained just about every night I was there. I never gave a reason other than I didn't like it anymore and I didn't want to do it. I said, "I hate the training, I hate getting up in the mornings, I hate swimming. You don't understand, I hate it." My dad would try and console me with, "You just need a break." Sometimes during the consoling there would be a drink involved, and that seemed to take the edge off and bury some of that pain.

Since I was having these issues with my coach my parents decided that my mother wasn't going to return with me and maybe that was the problem. On the one hand I was happy that my mother was no longer going to overshadow me and on the other hand I was still going back to the coach who'd just broken my heart.

My mother made plans for me to return to England to live at one of my friend's houses. The only problem with this arrangement was that I was secretly dating, or more accurately having sex with, my friend's brother, David. My mother worked out an exchange where their daughter would stay at their house in America while I would move in with her family. I was good with that arrangement, sort of. I felt like I could have a normal childhood experience and have some separation from Paul 24/7, but this wasn't going to be a long-term solution for me especially based on my very open dislike for him.

Why anybody even sent me back was another story, at least find me another coach. No one thought about that; all they thought about was me needing to be more mature and not talk back.

When I returned to England I was going to go to the public school that was close to the family that I was staying with. Since the Commonwealth Games that year were held well into the fall Paul wasn't back and coaching yet. I had some time to be depressed with my teammates being gone and not swimming with my coach—he was still "my" coach regardless of my hate and dislike for him. There was an unwritten rule; it's a marriage of sorts. I hadn't broken up with him so he was still "my" coach. I was just now in what I later termed an athlete domestic violence relationship with Paul. I was married to him even in his absence.

This time was quite lonely for me; it compounded to pain that I only learned to stuff further inside of me, and I didn't have the level of training intensity to allow me to release it. I had to resort to other things like having sex with a fellow teenager and drinking. It wasn't that difficult because there wasn't anyone really supervising us.

After a while I was no longer calling home as my parents were often traveling due to my dad's career. He was thriving and striving to be the best doctor in the world who treated the most complex cases. I'm pretty sure he felt like I too should have the same focus and initiative as him. My dad wanted to restore that back in me. He started to write me letters. I always cherished a letter dropping through the mailbox for me since it was like the only human love I knew I could carry with me.

I had another bad confrontation with Paul, with me acting out from his continued repeated advances. They were getting bad where he would follow me into the bathroom. I only got out of the water to get away from him; I could have easily and more likely have peed in the pool. The bathroom was where I went to collect myself, many times not returning for one excuse or another.

This led to Paul needing to call my parents and tell them I had to either take his direction or I wasn't ever going to be able to swim for Great Britain and my Olympic dreams would be squashed. My father was not happy with this at all—what parent would be? There was never a consideration that I was actually not the problem in any of this. It was always my fault. I had no defense against the accusations. I was labeled as immature, unruly, an out-of-control American. Whatever derogatory name you had for me, I was it. The character assassination that I was enduring was bigger than me. All these attacks led to me saying I wanted to quit, as there was no other pathway forward.

Not long after the phone call, I received a letter from my dad. I only ever got letters from my dad. I don't recall my mother sending me a letter or a card for my birthday; a letter that meant something to me had to come from my dad. When I received those letters I was always over the moon. He would be encouraging, and I could hold onto his words and the praise went beyond just a memory; it was in print, the handwritten love of my father. I could prove to myself that he loved me. I would read them over and over again. The touch of the paper and the connection to his handwriting that I could barely read was as close to my father's or anyone's love that I had in my life at this point.

When I opened the letter from my father, my tough-self became unglued for a moment. It pretty much wasn't safe to show my emotion, not as an athlete and not as a stranger in someone's house. It just wasn't safe. I was touched deeply by my father on the inside. I could feel myself well up. I wanted the inside world just for me. I didn't need to read the words: I could feel the love of my father just by holding this flimsy paper-thin letter with my dad's doctor's prescription handwriting I needed to decode before I could read it properly.

As the tears started to roll down my cheek, I read what my father wrote:

Dearest Little Annabelle...

I know you are upset but I do believe that it's better to stay with Paul and have better swimming facilities in Coventry, then coming home.

Jack isn't available to coach you here in Madison right now. If you leave England now then your international debut will have to be delayed, so stick it out for 18 months....

Now about your sadness and not earning a spot on the World Championship Team or the Commonwealth Games Team, that you rightfully earned, we think it will cheer you up, and give you something to look forward to, if come to Hawaii and train with Jack and his boys over the winter break...

We want you to go, under one condition... if you listen to Paul and do everything he asks of you... he says you aren't following his direction... You need to do what he says, you need to learn to get along. You need to stop being so stubborn, if you are going to be a world champion.

I love you, little Annabelle, I believe in you. Go out there and make me proud.

My tears were a mix of joy, sadness, and defeat. I was backed into a corner that I had no idea how to escape. I was living with a family that was despising me more and more every day, a boyfriend that I had broken up with who lived in the next door bedroom, and a coach that was bullying me and harassing me. I didn't know what those terms meant or understand what was going on, other than experiencing a feeling of being alone and being frustrated with the world I found myself in.

My dad offered me freedom with a trip to Hawaii, but it came with having to submit to the very person I wanted to get away from. The only saving grace was that I wasn't living in his home. But that didn't stop him from finding places to pressure me into compromising situations whether it was the weight room, a team bus, or in plain sight on the pool deck. I was restrained from overreacting. I had this internal stopper that allowed it up until I just could hardly bear the pressure. Hawaii: I could see this place of paradise in my future vision. Having grown up going to Greece just about every summer, the idea of drifting off in the ocean was so peaceful to me in my mind. I could just see myself laying there in the ocean away from everyone and everything.

It got bad when I was traveling with Paul to international competitions. I had to really behave and follow all the team rules. Mostly because we also traveled with two journalists, Pat Bedsford and Anita Lonsbrough. Anita worked for *The Daily Telegraph*, a conservative paper, and she brought that personality with her. Pat worked for the *Daily Mail*, mostly, and she seemed to always have a fifth of alcohol going. I seemed to have more of a connection with Pat for obvious reasons. I loved her paying attention to me and that she was fun and always curious in her questions with me. Sometimes a little too curious like she knew what was going on.

Little did they know that I was broken on the inside not saying what was really happening, a teenager who was lying to everyone about what was going on. The way I saw it was that I needed to overcome the idea of what the other coaches and staff thought about me. To them I was this uncontrollable, unruly American who had no restraint when it came to my coach. The funny thing was I was nice to every other adult, staff person, and coach, and only got the reporters' attention because of my interactions with Paul. That was what told the whole story about me to them. Anita seemed to have one opinion and Pat had another.

Our next scheduled trip was to Gothenburg, Sweden, in December for the European Cup. If you haven't been to Sweden in the winter it is dark for most of the day, with maybe four hours of daylight. We stayed at this hotel that was right in the city on what I initially thought was a quiet street as there was no one out. I attributed it to it being too cold. Who could withstand that kind of cold? I grew up in the cold of the Midwest, but this was a new level of cold. Little did I know that the whole city came alive at night. A very festive bunch, that's for sure. All their noise woke me up. Now I had a mix of pre-race anxiety and a need for something to put me back to sleep.

I got up in the middle of night looking for something to eat or drink. I ran into Paul drinking in the bar with the other coaches. It wasn't something that I expected or was ready to address. He got up and wanted to know what I needed. There was a moment of care for me around the other coaches. It was an odd kind of embrace, or maybe it was me being too tired to have my guard up. I asked for a Coke, or something like that. He got it for me and started walking me back to my room. The first moment of Paul's creepy stare came in the elevator. I looked away and took a sip of my drink. As I approached my door I put the key in assuming that he was going to his room and I was going to mine. It was that touch again on my back, that gesture of him wanting to enter my room. I couldn't help but respond with, "Get your hands off of me!" and slammed the door.

I was sitting on the other side of that door in fear and dread for what I had just said and done. I had managed myself mostly well up to this point. I knew that I had pissed Paul off to a point of no return. I could see that rejection. All this new fear and dread wasn't going to help me fall asleep especially since Sweden's drunken stupor was getting louder by the minute.

I also knew that I needed to get through this swim meet since I was flying right out to Hawaii after it concluded. It was like holding my breath up until this moment. I couldn't contain myself any longer. I needed to redirect my attention to performing. At this point, it was another opportunity for me to break more British records. Every swim meet had meaning when it came to my accomplishments, praise, and public recognition. I craved that attention and I sure wasn't going to let this moment take that away.

The next day at the pool, I walked in with my friends. I often surrounded myself with friends in order to avoid any extra time spent with Paul. Some of my teammates preferred to spend more time with their coach and less time with their teammates; I needed to find the swimmers without their coach on the trip or ones who didn't want to be around their coach. However, I had this pseudo obligation to Paul. I had a commitment like I belonged to him and my harem consisted of mostly men with me as the single female swimmer. There was only so much avoiding I could do; after that it would appear that I was the terrible and immature troublemaker, and all the other words used to describe my behavior.

It became a known conflict when my performances were improving in leaps and bounds, mostly because I was getting physically stronger just about every time I raced. I knew that I was compromised on the inside. I knew about my inner struggle that no one could see. I knew I had more talent to display. I knew that it came through when I was free from harm. I had so much talent that my potential wasn't understood. How could it be compromised in the situation that I had found myself? I was still great to the outside world, but to me I wasn't doing what I knew I could do. It was swimming with this internal burden while beating everyone and then hearing that was great because you won. What I wanted was for someone to see this burden that I was carrying that was plain as day to me on the inside.

During warm-ups I went through the usual routine, the warm-up, and then ended with 12 meter sprints, mostly to practice my dives and garner my speed. The first day was 200 Freestyle, my favorite and best event. It was also the most painful event if you didn't swim it right. When one does those sprints you get out of the side of the pool, back where it was easy to pop right out of the pool with extreme ease. It seemed like those were the most vulnerable moments with Paul who was giving me feedback and I was clenching up from his hand creep. What would set me off would be how slow my sprint would be. If I was off, it changed my tolerance of Paul and his advances. That morning I was swimming faster than I had in the past which gave Paul more liberty to express that on my body. I was less apt to say anything or do anything when I swam fast or at least not make as many sudden movements and complaints openly.

When it came to my race, I remember swimming that race with determination and focus. I had the energy of getting away from Paul, the idea of breaking the British Junior record and all the benefits including being interviewed for my success. With all that came the praise I desperately sought. I wondered if more people saw me swim, would that better my chances of someone protecting me. When I touched the wall and looked up at my time, I had broken the Junior record. You'd be hard pressed to get me to smile in that instant but I did. When I got out of the pool, Paul put his hands around my waist as I was dripping wet from my swim. He walked away with me to the swim down pool. All this was fine and acceptable. I swam fast and therefore all the liberties were allowed and accepted in the open public. I knew from the last rejection I still needed to behave. I was going to Hawaii—that wasn't the issue now. It was the recognition, the report back to my dad. I still had more races to go. It didn't stop me from diving right in the water and speaking to him from the pool. I found ways to escape but it was getting exhausting. The hate that I had for him was growing by the second.

When it came to my final race, there was still a record to break. I had had enough of being nice or withholding my emotions and expressions. After I swam and broke another record the tension between us grew to a point of aggressive communication, okay yelling, and me talking back. I wasn't happy with the time, albeit I broke the record. I wasn't happy with how Paul was imposing his will on me. He kept wanting me to be kind to him, and when I was he took liberties and when I wasn't he threatened me with removing me from the team for misbehaving.

After my swims it was Pat who wanted to interview me. I was sure Anita did as well, but her interviews were more formal and posh. When Pat interviewed me this time she seemed curious about my relationship with Paul. I don't recall the exact questions but she wanted to know why we argued all the time. She even referred to us like an old married couple the way that we talked to each other. I made up some lie about being strong-willed because of my American upbringing thinking that was what she wanted me to talk about the situation. None of that conversation made it into the article; it was mainly about this young rising star that I was becoming.

When the swim meet ended, Paul was quick to inform me of his abilities to have me on a team or not. He reminded me that breaking records and swimming fast were not the only requirements for making the team: it was how well I responded to his coaching. That coaching included all of his touching and advancements with his intention of having sex with me. I could feel the doom and gloom inside of me. Yet the well of my "fuck you, leave me alone" attitude was full and ever-present. My charismatic personality to the outside world was what hid all of this so well. Meanwhile I was dying inside every swim; I thought the only way to save that part of my soul was to swim fast, get praise, and then my father would love me. I was stuck on the wheel and had no way of knowing how to get off. All the wins, records, and praise weren't taking away the thoughts that all I really wanted to do was die. I saw that as the only way out.

CHAPTER 9

The End of the Beginning

After breaking records and the curious attention from Pat, I left Sweden on a high note and caught a helicopter from London Gatwick Airport to Heathrow to catch my flight to Hawaii. I was happy to be on this journey, to putting some distance between me and Paul. However, my internal anxiety and fears still needed to be pushed further inside of me.

I arrived in Hawaii at night to that warm evening air. I was no longer in dreary Coventry. I wasn't going to find myself face to face with Lady Godiva feeling naked and exposed. The engine inside of me needed something to get it going again. The smell of the ocean permeated throughout the airport.

It felt like I was home and an American again. I had dropped the accent and was back in the local dialect since I had perfected this skill over many years in order to protect myself. It felt good to speak with my American accent and be an American.

There was some excitement and nervousness with a mix of *I'm free from Paul. I'm free from looking over my shoulder. I'm free from those creepy eyes.*

I'm free from it all. My insides were in pain. I can't say that I understood the pain, the pressure cooker that was in me.

It was late when I arrived at the dorms at the University of Hawaii campus where I was staying with the boys' team. I had my own room and never saw my coach, Jack, that night. I was taken care of by the team manager. It was weird to be treated with respect by someone. I was having to always fight for something I wanted or needed, but now there was care and consideration for my well-being.

That morning I got up early for practice; it wasn't too much trouble with the time change, the thrill of a new place, and the sound of nature coming through the room. I had a sense of peace for a moment. I got to the pool without that morning dread that I had been feeling for months. When I arrived on the pool deck Jack was sitting in the bleachers reading a paper. He barely looked up as I walked up to him. There was an air about Jack that was like my dad, a little aloof with a stroke of military order. I knew to stay in line with Jack mostly because the set he would give might get a little more challenging. He was quiet until he yelled at you, usually deserved I might add.

I started to get in a rhythm with training with Jack and the boys. One, it was nice to be the only girl in practice with the boys, and be able to keep up and at times actually lead the lane. The college boys started to respect me in a kind way. They became very attentive to me and treated me like I was part of their team. It might have been because I swam in the mornings with them back in Madison, plus my dad was the team doctor for the team. My dad was a character to them the way he swam. He would get in the water and just start swimming butterfly. Butterfly is a stroke for anyone to do regardless of talent; you dread having to do it, knowing how much it will hurt, but not my dad who got right in and just swam it like it was the easiest stroke to do. So to the boys I was little like my dad that way, just without the butterfly.

After morning practice it was the fun part: stuff your face in the cafeteria with okay food, but a lot of it for a starving swimmer. Breakfast was the best. Afterwards we found a different beach each day. We explored the island.

Training was hard, well more accurately, it was very hard. I was always exhausted after practice and needed a nap to prepare for my afternoon workout. It served a couple of things that nap: it turned my mind off from the anxiety of performing and I was able to restore myself back to high performance mode. Having to do a hard workout when you're tired is doubly painful. I was training every day, twice a day for more miles than most people drive in a day, and adding tired on top of it was just a whole new level of pain.

The beach trips often came with being taken from the fresh smell of the ocean that swirled around you to one of those sleep-woke states where you wished you were on one side or the other.

I could feel the disconnect from the life at home and the life that I was having in Hawaii. The joy of the saltwater on my skin, the fish, the fear of a shark, you name it—it was all a great distraction coupled with not having to be on guard when I was swimming. I could feel at ease or at least I could feel myself distancing from the memory of Paul. All the boys cherished me and took care of me like a little sister.

Despite the proud little sister label that I acquired, I wanted to feel like I was part of the team, not necessarily one of the boys, but I wanted to do what they did to become a peer of sorts. As you can imagine a bunch of college boys found their way into drinking. Since that was quickly becoming my favorite pastime, I started to add drinking to my daily training routine right along with them. The boys liked it because it meant that I might be slower in practice or at least suffering the same hangover as they were. A competitive advantage, if you will, for them.

At the same time that mostly daily drinking started, the despair over Paul would fill my night. I saw flashes of Paul being on top of me. As the memories appeared, another drink seemed to be the way to acclimate or at least redirect those thoughts so they didn't exist. I didn't want them to exist. I wanted to be training and in Hawaii, in paradise and not mired in the misery of my time in England.

Here was the cycle of my training life: I started drinking at night till I passed out, then morning practice, followed by eating copious amounts of food, swimming at the beach, a nap, and then afternoon training. It was a cycle of busy, of being tired and it shut off the thoughts. It also came with a competition at the end of the trip. So there was some excitement and dread of the ending. It was hard to think of the future while also fearing going back to Paul at some point. I knew in Sweden that I had taken it too far in pushing back and arguing with him. I also knew that I was now a British Junior record holder and second fastest in Britain in three events behind one of the fastest swimmers in the world.

The combination of good and bad in my mind was a constant battle. I was also concerned that Paul reached out to my parents to complain about me not behaving the way I should. When those thoughts came up, it was often when I was at the beach or pushing down a drink where I could go back to pretending that everything in my life was great.

I was also very social which was a good mask for the pain. Especially for my age. I started to hang out with some swimmers from the Northwestern University when we went to the same beach or if they were in the cafeteria at the same time. Thankfully some of the other college teams had female swimmers with whom I became friends. One of those swimmers was Ginny.

Ginny started to talk to me about how she drank as a young person and that she cleaned up her life. She also started to share with me how she accepted Christ into her life. It wasn't something that I wanted to hear. I had a godmother who took her job a little too seriously when I was a child with all the Bibles and Bible verses. It was never something I knew what to do with. I had this disconnect between me and anything spiritual. I always believed in God; that wasn't the problem. It was that I never believed that God believed in me. If that was the case then I would not be stuck with the situation that I was in back home. What I liked about Ginny was her kindness and her friendship. It felt good to have someone listen to you.

I shared a little bit about some of the things I had done in England. She was kind and compassionate taking it all in. There was always a Bible verse or something to console me. I never heard it or took it in. I wanted to be drinking. I wanted to disconnect—it felt like a better option to me.

For the first time in a long time I felt like I was part of something, part of a team. I was liked so much that the coach at Northwestern started to recruit me and wanted me to start college there the following fall. I would have been 15 and back in America. The only problem with this offer was that I was better than anyone on that team; there would be no competition, just a group of gals who would have taken care of me. That was all I wanted: for someone to see me and take care me. I wasn't going to show that card, but inside that felt good to me.

The Northwestern team thought there was a possibility of me joining their team that fall, never mind the fact that I wasn't really going to school anymore. I was gradually not showing up for anything academic, but no one really knew about it because there was no one to tell and no one paid attention to that part of my life. I did read the *Financial Times* and *The Daily Telegraph* as well as the other papers because I needed to consume information. I was a well-informed kid on just about any subject. It wasn't like it was evident to the outside world what I was doing. I wanted these people to be my friend so I was willing to listen to the teachings of Christ, Bible verses or just about anything else to not feel alone in the world.

The time in Hawaii was nearing an end. We had New Year's Eve and New Year's Day, and then on January 2 a swim meet for three days. A day after that it was back to England. That meant that our beach days were limited for the rest of my stay. This also meant that the hard training was going to ease up for a few days. We would only have one practice on New Year's Day in the afternoon and then three days of competition which was much easier and more fun than training, not to mention the social sitting around part that I loved the most. Of course, this was an opportunity to be praised by many and I also got to watch other people race.

As New Year's Eve came around, the festivities and the drinking didn't disappoint. The boys made sure we had enough alcohol in the dorms for a week of partying. We all were pretty heavy drinkers, at least from my drunk perspective. I carried on right along with the boys, no problem; puking and passing out became part of my drinking habit.

New Year's Day was a big beach day at Pipeline Beach on the North Shore. The visit was saved for New Year's Day when we had more time and could enjoy the beach properly. Getting out of bed was easy, or least falling out of bed seemed more like it.

We got to the beach, and it was so beautiful, the water was spectacular. I walked on the sand and it held that morning quiet like nature wasn't up or tucked away from the night before. There weren't any lifeguards or other beachgoers that I recall. It was just me and the boys. They of course brought the cooler to carry on from the night before. It wasn't long after we settled down that the Northwestern gals arrived at the beach. I was very happy to have my friends there.

I moved over to join my friends as we sat and watched these perfect curl waves. It was very mesmerizing to watch. I started to hear the call of the ocean, that or it was starting to get hot and I needed to cool off. I was also lazy and slow to get in the water. I wanted to watch the waves; I wanted to be one with the ocean. It just seemed so peaceful. There was nothing like the silence of your mind under the water. When I swam I got a break from me trying to destroy myself with my thoughts. As the hangover wore off these thoughts were starting to intrude.

One of the girls on the team asked if I wanted to get in the ocean. I never said no to a request to do something. I grabbed my goggles and stood at the base of the waves as they came crashing up to my feet, sometimes getting my legs wet. The water felt so warm and nice against my skin.

The waves themselves were bigger than any of the other beaches. Pipeline in the past had been known for its big swells, although it had been tame for some time now, but that didn't take away from the fact that its waves were still bigger than any of the other beaches we had been to so far on the island. I wanted to do something with a friend so getting in the ocean seemed like a great idea at the time. When the next opportunity came, or when it felt right, I put on my goggles and walked towards the waves waiting for that right moment to dive through the base of the wave. When it came my friend and I looked at each other, we walked towards the wave and dove right in.

As I was under the water I could feel the force of the ocean pushing against me; I was so lightweight that I was easily tossed around in the undertow. I had a moment of disorientation not sure which direction was up but quickly recovered and pulled myself to the surface. As my head popped up I looked for my friend, but she was nowhere to be found. At the same time, I was faced with a massive wave with only moments to dive under before I was completely crushed by it. I swam quickly to the base of the wave, and then paused for a quick second to gather my air to go through the wave.

As I swam through the wave, a parade of thoughts from my life entered my consciousness. I could see myself in the baby pool desperately wanting to be in the big pool. I could feel the determination of my spirit as the strength of the wave was stronger than the one before. I could feel that little girl's energy swimming alongside of me like an angel helping me navigate the underworld. I watched the air bubbles indicate the direction of the surface. My hair was mostly short except for the top of my head where my hair flowed behind me like a mermaid's. I rose up from the long breath once again unable to see my friend in the ocean.

I looked around for my friend and in that split second there was another wave right behind it. I took a huge gasp of air knowing that my last breath was barely enough for the size of these waves. As I dove into the base of the wave, I reached with my right arm, giving myself a surge forward hoping that I could make it far enough under the wave that I wouldn't be tossed around. My attention and focus were becoming one in the moment. The wave's force was something I had never felt or experienced before. The little girl all excited to swim her first race was suddenly nervous on the blocks about what was to come. I knew I could do it, I knew I had the passion in me, well, that was what I knew. It was now the "what do I do?" "how do I perform?" part. I just knew what I loved to do and everything else was "figure it out along the way." I was doing that in the ocean. Each time I went under the wave I was having to stretch my air out longer and longer not knowing when I was going to be able to get back up to the surface. This time I started to get a few convulsions when my air was about to run out. I could see the sun breaking through the clouds as I approached the surface again. That moment when you can fill your lungs back with air was something that I had to do, not because I wanted to but because my body needed to.

In my next gasp of air when I came up I was no longer looking for my friend. I was now focused on the task at hand of getting myself out of this situation, with only a few seconds to gather more air and go under the next wave. There was no time for anything else besides doing what was the next thing right in front of me. The waves were getting progressively bigger, at least it seemed that way when you are lying in the water looking up at this giant wall of water in front of you.

There was something that I didn't lack: my confidence in my ability to swim. I believed that I was one of the best in the world, which I was. I also believed that I was going to be the best in the world one day. The idea of that deep inside of me usually led me to doing the next right thing. However, at some point that idea started to form into something else. The ocean started to wear me down and exhaustion was blocking the positive thoughts of how much I loved swimming and being in the water.

I was getting to that point where I wanted to swim to the side of the pool and get out. I was done. I wanted to pop out of the ocean and throw my goggles down in the sand because I had had enough. I wanted to tell my coach that I wasn't going to swim in the dark. I wanted to have been able to just get out of the ocean and be on the beach. All those wants and desires weren't available in that moment. It was only me and the swell I had found myself in. There was no one to call and talk about my frustration. I wanted to tell the ocean to stop for a second like I wanted Paul to stop when he raped me. I wanted to tell Paul to leave me alone and just let me swim. I wanted him to support me and not throw me around. I wanted my dad to say, "I love you" and tell me that it was all going to be okay. I wanted to be loved and seen in that moment. There was no one coming for me—not now, not ever. I was going to have to do it all by myself. It was going to be me against the wall of water.

There was no looking back for help, as lifeguards were not on duty; it was New Year's Day. I doubt anyone really knew where I was or was looking for me. I was also pretty sure that no one would be thinking that of all people Annabelle was struggling or in trouble. I was lost in the trauma of the ocean. No one was coming for me.

I had a moment of rest, like maybe an extra few seconds, just enough to settle down my heart, get some air, and readjust my attitude and confidence as the next set of waves were coming in. I had found a rhythm. As the waves got bigger, so did the darkness of the water I was diving into. I wondered if there were any creatures like sharks lurking around, I wouldn't know. I couldn't see them but could only sense their presence. Kind of like I could sense Paul's presence in my life. I wasn't thinking about how I let him into my world—I was trying to figure out how I could make it work with him. My dad told me I needed to make it work. What would I need to do differently so he would just coach me and otherwise leave me alone? All these thoughts were wearing me down emotionally and mentally. I didn't have an out of the situation. My temper wasn't going to work. My determination was keeping me alive, but my passion to be present in this moment was drowning out.

I was getting thrown around in the ocean in 16- and 20-foot waves, being pushed in directions that I had no idea where I was. I had lost my sense of time and space. I would come up for a breath and soon go back down. My spirit wasn't getting what it wanted. I started to turn my thoughts towards just being part of the ocean. Would anyone really care if I was lost at sea? That didn't matter. What mattered was that when I got stuck I wanted to quit and now I was so far stuck without any help that all I wanted to do now was die. At the same time I didn't want to quit whatever struggle I was in. I needed something to give because I wasn't able to keep up this struggle. I wanted something to give with Paul but that wasn't happening. The dread of returning to him started to creep into my mind. I loved Hawaii but not the struggle. I loved swimming but not the struggle. I loved my dad but not the struggle. I hated everyone and everything in that moment. I was tired and exhausted. I had been in those waves and the ocean for well over an hour trying to save myself. My mind needed a break. I needed a break.

While I was connected to God in a knowing way, I wasn't connected in an active believing way. I wanted to believe in something that could help me in this moment. The long walks home after spending the bus money seemed like a walk in the park compared the torture I was experiencing here in the ocean. The way my eyes and mind saw the ocean was no longer that crystal blue Hawaii paradise water shown on magazine covers. It was now dark and solid as far as the eye could see. The sun was now hiding behind the clouds. The reflection back onto the water wasn't giving me the shiny diamond reflection of comfort. The only thing reflecting back to me were the dark thoughts within the depth of my soul. I saw no way out.

In that moment the ocean stopped in front of me. I had made it past the surf line to the other side of the wall of water. I was rolling with the punches. I took a moment to just lay on my back and go up and down with the rolling of waves as I stared up at the clouds wondering if the sun would ever appear in my life.

I sat up to see where I was. In one direction there was nothing but ocean, not a stretch of land in sight. I spun myself around in the water and could see a sliver of something off into the distance. I knew my eyesight wasn't failing me with my more than 20/20 vision and farsighted vision beyond the average person's. I could barely see land at all. All I could see was a wall of waves rolling towards the shore. I was basically locked out of life with nowhere to go or turn.

I found myself all alone with just me and the unknown predators of the ocean. There was nobody coming to rescue me. It was just me. The moments in the dark dreary shed seemed almost comforting. I was tired of swimming, and I was tired of fighting; I was just tired of life. I couldn't fight it anymore. I laid back and looked up at the sky and closed my eyes. I decided in that moment that I was done with life. I was done with being tossed around. I wanted to drift off to wherever this world was going to take me. I sure as hell didn't want to go back to the life that I was living. I just wanted to be that little girl who wanted to swim. That was it. The innocence of that little girl was all that I wanted to protect. The only way I knew how to do that was to give up. I started pleading to God asking Him to just take me. I could believe in that moment that was the best option for me. I repeated this over in my mind as I was carried by the movement of the water.

As I was letting that mantra spin through my mind it was interrupted with someone saying, "Do you need some help?" I sat up wondering where that voice had come from. Where was I? Where did I go? I sat up and the land was still barely in sight as my ears drained the water. I put my finger in them and shook my head to clear out any water thinking I must be hearing things. Then I heard it again. "I'm a lifeguard, do you need some help getting in?" I spun in the water again and there was a guy in the water a few feet away from me. I look at him dumfounded. "How did you know I was here? Who are you?" I also wasn't trusting this person. It wasn't the distrust so much as the idea that someone helping me was not allowed in my world. I had to do it all myself. Then he asked me a third time, "Can I help you swim to shore?" I answered this time, "I know how to swim." I didn't want someone's help. I was trained to not accept it and most likely that training came from me. I was also prideful. *I'm one of the best swimmers in the world and someone is asking me if I need help swimming?* That wasn't going to happen. But there was a persistence in his voice, "Let me help you swim in. I can show you how to swim to shore."

It seemed like my plan to float away was being interrupted. The nonbeliever in me was wondering maybe there was a God. There was clearly a lifeguard who showed up to help me. I might as well take his help. Where was I going to hide or avoid this situation? Nowhere. I had no choice really but take this person's help. Setting my pride aside, I said, "Okay, how do I swim in?" The lifeguard explained by pointing at an angle towards the shore. He told me where I needed to track on land, pointing at a collection of palm trees. Then he said, "I'm going to swim right next to you." I was good with that. At this point I had rested and restored my energy; it doesn't take long when you're young and highly trained. All I could think about was that I needed to swim faster than the lifeguard.

We set off swimming towards shore. For the first several minutes I was looking back at his splash out of the corner of my eye. I was comforted by this person swimming alongside of me, and then eventually I lost all sense of time and space, and was focused on the landmark that he directed me to swim towards. At some point I became conscious of the fact that I had outswam the lifeguard. The idea of my talents and being the swimmer that I was meant to be started to fill my psyche again. I could feel the passion of swimming again. The dark thoughts of torture were drifting away as I made it closer to shore. My focus now had become accomplishing the swim. There was a charge inside of me being able to say that I outswam the lifeguard at the North Shore.

As land started to get closer, all of my struggles were left in the ocean. I wasn't going to give up and felt myself push into a higher gear of trying to ride the current of the wave in unison. As I approached the last wave that would bring me to shore, I looked up to some of the gals from Northwestern awaiting my arrival.

When I could stand in the ocean, I pushed through the pressure of the water pushing me back into the ocean with all my force. I fought my way towards land and knew I had won when I broke free of the water and started to high step towards the fresh, dry hot sand. Someone handed me a towel as I fell to the sand utterly exhausted from the inside out. All the while I maintained a presence of "that wasn't that hard."

I had drifted way down the beach from where we started. After a few moments I got up to walk back when I had a thought that I needed to stay for the lifeguard to come in and thank him for swimming with me to shore. The ladies who met me were confused as they asked, "What lifeguard? We have watched you swim for a ways and never saw anyone out there with you." "I was faster than him," I shared with a confident chuckle. Someone else said, "No lifeguards are on duty today—must be a surfer or something, they can't swim fast," and we all chuckled at our superior swimming abilities compared to our other water friends.

I walked down the beach wondering about my experience at the same time not thinking anything more about it. I was more concerned with the fact that I had an extra workout and we had a swim meet tomorrow. That was the End of the Beginning.

CHAPTER 10

Road Less Traveled

My adventure in the ocean gave me a confidence about myself I hadn't experienced before. I survived something only I knew the struggle involved. It wasn't something that was relatable by anyone else; very much like the night I was raped by Paul. These would be feelings only reserved for me. I know others have felt trapped or have been raped and sadly too many people have. I'm talking about that alone feeling that made it unique to me. And I mean alone in the spiritual sense, not in the physical sense.

The idea of conquering those killer waves and making it back to shore gave me a sense of my talent and ability to survive the un-survivable. I was riding on those thoughts and my path for life when I showed up the next day at the swim meet.

I remember swimming the 500 Freestyle at that swim meet, lapping some of the competitors without another swimmer in sight. I was so strong, and it was so easy. I wasn't rested at all for the race, meaning I wasn't peaking for the performance; it was like a workout race, an extension of training, if you will. When I touched the wall, I looked up at the clock and it was a good 10 seconds faster than the pool record. I had just broken the pool record, the age group record for Hawaii and Wisconsin, (because my swim club was from there) and all the other possible records in that swim. It had to have been one of the easiest swims I had ever done. All the training with Jack, surviving the ocean, and feeling like I was back to myself again contributed to my success in that race.

It was definitely something to write home about, or in this case, call home and tell my dad. It made his investment in me all worth it. So much so that these swims always came with a reward of sorts. I really wanted to get a nice bikini before I left. I wanted to be a girl and feel like a girl with my broad shoulders and tiny hips while being so tall. It meant the world to me to fit in with my peers, not that I had any. If I did, I wanted to be like them. Years before, that was the sole reason for stealing the Bonne Bell lipstick. I had just evolved to wanting newer and shinier things.

After my successful swim meet and trip, I had one more big day on the beach before my return to England. My spirit was ready to return and I felt like I was well rested, at least in my attitude and preparedness for training with Paul again. I was going to be well trained and much faster, so it was bound to be easier when I got back to Coventry—at least that was the story I was telling myself.

We found a nice fun beach for our last day, and at this point in the trip I was emotionally and physically exhausted. We set up shop as I unveiled my new bikini. A little embarrassed with the boys to show off my body, but at the same time I was a little bit of an exhibitionist. I wasn't much into using sunscreen despite my Dad's creation of the SPF standards. I had the bright white British stomach that had never seen the sun and it was very evident. I could have been mistaken for a lighthouse on the beach it was so white. Without a thought, I laid with my back on the towel and tuned into the sound of the ocean that sent me into one of those zones where I heard everything around me while not totally drifting off.

I had crashed so hard that I woke up to drool and the groggy-from-too-much-sun-exposure feeling. My first thought was that I didn't get a tan as I glanced at my stomach. I proceeded to get dressed and could feel the heat of my stomach like the oven warming up to its desired temperature.

When I got in the water for my last practice, I started having a hard time doing flip turns. The heat from my stomach was intense. I had to get out of the pool early, which is something you just don't do. Especially on my last day. I liked getting out of things, but I didn't want to get out for this, yet the pain was already unbearable. I went to the dressing room and when I took my swimsuit off, my stomach was the brightest red I had ever seen in my life. I can't begin to tell you how painful it was. At least I knew who to call. My dad prescribed me this heavy-duty cream to put on my stomach that at least took the sting out.

The next day I flew back to England with this bittersweet experience. On the one hand my swimming was restored to the level of success where I knew I could be, and on the other hand I was in so much pain I could barely move. I could barely have anything come anywhere near my stomach it was so sensitive. The next 24 hours was the most miserable traveling experience that I would ever have. Even the first trip to England with all the luggage without wheels was better than this. A slight bump and I was over the edge—that is how bad it was.

When I finally arrived in Coventry all I wanted to do was to crawl in bed and have a little comforting from the family that I was staying with but, when I got to the train station in Coventry, no one was there to pick me up. I found a payphone and called the family, no answer. After waiting a bit longer with a few more phone attempts, I hailed a taxi and went to the residence of the family where I had been staying. There was no answer and there was no one home. I was standing outside on the streets in January. It was cold, dark, and little windy. Even the pressure of the wind on my stomach made me wince intensely.

After a little bit, I found a payphone and called my parents. I was so tired and exhausted and in so much pain. My mother said she would sort it out as I waited in the phone booth, my only form of protection from the outside elements.

My mother managed to find me a place to stay a few days with the family that managed the local swim shop. My mother was a shopper who befriended the owner and they were happy to have me as their customer. I doubt they were happy to have me live in their home, but they did come and pick me up.

When I arrived at their house, they showed me to a spare room and fed me like an orphan from the streets. The only difference was that my face and body were not covered in street soot, but they should have been.

After a day or so of sleeping 20 hours straight I came to learn that I had sunstroke. It was amazing that I had even made it to safety at all. All the sleeping and the layers and layers of skin that peeled off my body didn't allow me to make it to practice for a while. The idea of wanting to go to practice, but having to swim with Paul, was too much for me. Every day the family I was staying with would come in the room in the afternoon only to find me sleeping. They needed me out of their home desperately. I'm not sure how long this went on, but probably for at least a week. To be out of swimming for a week was unheard of. The pressure of not being there was starting to weigh on my mind. It was building this fear about having to face Paul any day now. I wasn't entirely delaying the inevitable, but the sunstroke was doing it for me.

Then one day the family came to my room when I was awake; they had been leaving food for me for when I woke. This routine had continued for many days without any conversation about me staying there. But this time when they woke me up they told me that I would need to stay somewhere else because they were not allowed to house me. I had to pack up my stuff and the family took me to my parents' empty house.

When I moved into my parents' empty house I also returned to training. That coy, shy version of me needed to carry on with practice like I was fine. I was for the most part, well, except when it came to be in Paul's presence. There was definitely a tension between us that was still there from me being "rude" to him. That was the way he described me to others. So much so that he made sure that no parent on the swim team was allowed to house me, not even the family that owned the swim shop. He threatened to stop doing business with them if they let me to stay at their house.

After a few days of staying in my parents' house, they found a place for me not too far away in a poor family's home that could use the money to put food on their table. I had a room in this house without any heat and barely any food to eat. I would say that the garden shed seemed slightly better, in that I at least could come and go. Here, there were some rules that I wasn't a fan of, and let's be honest, I wasn't a fan of any rules.

My time was now spent going to practice which seemed to have been cut down some as Paul had changed his training style or I wasn't training like I used to. It was changed to more of a heart rate training with a lot of sprints and less distance, which was really what I should have been doing. My interactions with Paul were starting to become more distant. I was moving out of his focus to some degree. However, if I would let my guard down for a moment and laughed with my teammates it seemed to invite his unwanted advances.

While all of this was going on I had officially stopped going to school and would go hang out at my parents' house during the day where there was heat and no supervision. It quickly became known as the place to go and do drugs. Random strangers would show up there during the day wanting a place to sniff glue or whatever they were doing. I would need to go to practice while I had these thugs in my parents' house that I needed to get rid of. My fear of missing practice was greater than the idea that these people would destroy the place.

This became a cycle until it was time to go back home for summer break. Since school continued well into July in England, my parents pulled me out in early June to come back. The whole year was a crazy blur from the time I returned from Hawaii until I returned to the States. My parents needed me to get back in shape for both Junior Europeans and Senior Europeans Championships that summer. I had already qualified for the Junior competition and then I returned to Trials after that competition with the intention of qualifying for Senior Europeans in Rome.

When I got back to America it was always a place where I could breathe freely and feel like I was in pursuit of the American dream. I felt safe there. I felt out of harm's way there. I felt connected to myself there. But I didn't have much time to get back in shape and start performing again since there were only a few meets to get myself back in competition shape. I was training hard and after a week or so of being home I could see my sets start to build on each other and I would outperform myself one day after the next. I had about six weeks to correct the ship.

I was used to coming and going at this point with my family. A few weeks with everyone was a long time to maintain any type of equanimity. It was also all the time that I had for my dad and I to reconnect. I got to drive with him to practice in the mornings. I got to feel that competitive spirit of his. I knew he wanted that for me. There was something pure and innocent in his desire for me to be the greatest swimmer in the world. There was never any ill intent. I saw that my dad wanted the best for me. I wanted my dad to love me. It was a simple exchange, or so I thought at the time.

After my fill of Dad time, America time, and praise time, it was time to be sent off back to the world that I was trying to navigate through without telling anyone what was going on. I was talking to my parents in plain English by saying Paul was doing this to me and how he was treating me. I just didn't have the language for the right communication to happen. The only world that was being monitored were times, records, and wins. So all the other behavior that would have been a dead giveaway to the layperson that this minor might be harmed was being overlooked because I kept bouncing back and swimming better than before. When my parents sent me back to England I was in fighting shape again.

Thankfully, when I arrived back in England I was not only swimming well again, I was also confident in myself again. I knew that I had on my armor to protect me from Paul. My trip was planned so I would only be in England a few days before heading out to France to swim at the European Junior Championship. Before all our trips there was a training camp. This trip was no different. Most of our training camps were held at Crystal Palace where the doors didn't lock, but I would at least be with some friends to drown out the interactions with Paul.

If I wasn't concerned with the way Paul touched me all the time, I was always concerned with how he trained me. When he gave me a set or something that I didn't feel was right for what I was doing I would say something, and when I did, it still never came out kind or nice. Paul wasn't one to respond to me in the moment; he would always wait to say something later that would be conniving and hurtful. I couldn't predict what he'd say, but I knew it would be something.

On all our trips we always had a chaperone. On the Senior trips it was an older woman named Joyce who was clueless about what was really going on. She was more like a wannabe headmistress wanting to control us but never figured it out; we were always one step ahead of her. On the Junior teams so far the chaperone and the trainer were the same person, and this was again the case for this trip to France. On the first night of training camp, Paul hooked up with the trainer. He made sure that I was aware of this and closed another door or pathway for me to say anything about him.

Paul was also very good about making the officials at the swimming association aware of my "argumentative" interactions. These were all old men who wore this massive display of medals around their necks and displayed them around the pool deck as they passed out medals to the winners. I never understood what the medals were for and quite frankly they looked arduous to even wear around the pool. It was like a scene right out of *Gladiator* wearing those things. These men would turn their nose up at me for my lack of sophistication that I brought to the sport with my loose mouth and unwavering ability to challenge something that wasn't right to me. It wasn't getting me any closer to the Queen, that was for sure. I was still too American in their eyes.

Of all the people who traveled with us on the trip, the only person who seemed to take a liking to me was Pat Besford, the journalist. Anita didn't usually attend the Junior trips because that might have been beneath her, but not Pat. I would sit next to her and we'd have long conversations on the buses in between destinations. I don't recall much of those conversations in regards to their substance, but she seemed to be protective of me in her own way. Every story she wrote about me was always kind. Still, all that kindness didn't take away from the torture and the anguish that was inside of me from my interactions with Paul.

To no one's surprise, I continued to be Paul's only female swimmer on that trip as well as back in Coventry. My ability to connect with another coach was the equivalent of cheating on your boyfriend. He was still my coach and there is an ownership and belonging structure that comes with that dynamic. It was part of the unwritten rules of sport. Something that we all had to abide by. The moral code of going outside that dynamic had repercussions to the athlete that would have been even further aggravated beyond the constant need to protect myself from Paul's advances towards me. It wasn't always his hands; it was what he would say to me in the moment and how he would try and break down my defenses and my guard.

Here I was in a quandary of growing into the swimmer I was destined to be, while at the same time dying inside from the pain that I was enduring in order to try and fulfill that destiny. As the training camp ended and we moved to France. I was living in two worlds: the one Paul had described to the outside world and the one I knew for myself. I also couldn't stop my drive for the praise and recognition. The cocktail of sabotage and the pursuit of praise was quickly informing my choices.

When we arrived in France I was already emotionally drained from being around Paul and doing the dance of death with him. It was so troubling that it was affecting my sleep, my mind, and my being. There was something in his voice that I responded to without putting up a defense to it and being tired weakened me. It made me angry and mad and all that did was give Paul the leverage to shift accountability to me. I had no solution for that and felt alone in my experience.

When I was at swim meets there was a lot of down time to play cards or something to keep busy. When not racing, I started playing cribbage and spades which were the games of choice amongst my teammates. This was another area of my life where I also liked to win. As we sat around playing, it was an opportunity to share about Paul a little. One of my teammates started talking about how creepy he was. They shared about how he would try to put his hands on their legs and rub them, all gross behavior. I could feel my insides churning as the other kids spoke about him. We all knew that he was disgusting.

Then that conversation turned to talking about what would happen if you drank Coke and aspirin. Could you die from this deadly combination? The idea of that sounded good to me. It sounded like a peaceful way to exit the life that I had found myself in. It seemed like an accessible and easily executed plan. I liked all the options of this exit plan and I felt like I needed one. The time from when I left Hawaii to now had been nothing but a shit show for me. Of all the people with whom I had interacted with, the only person who maybe had been anything but curious and kind in my life was Pat, the drunk journalist. Well, maybe we had that in common.

I had knowledge and some camaraderie with my teammates, and they knew who Paul was as a coach, but they weren't experiencing the anguish and pain that I was going through. It was something that I needed to keep to myself. I knew that the chaperone/trainer was now fucking him and was open with the team about her relationship, so that wasn't something that was hidden. All that did was cut off an angle for me to bring up something about him. The longer this went on the more I was seen as the problem.

We had a few days to get used to the pool before the competition, so I went to the store to grab supplies for the room, okay food for the room, to eat outside of mealtimes. This time I decided to add some Coke and aspirin, not that anyone noticed anything since the rest of my purchases were junk food and the Coke fit right in. As a young swimmer, sitting around and eating was always my favorite pastime.

On the night before my first event, Paul came to my room to talk about my race. I had mostly spent my time up to this point avoiding him. I found others to spend time with or sat with Pat on the bus going places, doing anything to not put myself in direct contact with him. It wasn't obvious to the outside world other than I was this sassy American. I carried on with that label.

Paul freely entered my room, then put his hands on my shoulders and started to rub them as I stared at the bottle of Coke and the aspirin sitting out on the desk. I wondered how this was going to affect me, and would it even work? It helped me pass the time as his hands reached towards my breasts and down my shirt. I grabbed his hand and held it place on my chest to not move it any further. He leaned into me and told me that "If I'm not coachable with him I would not be traveling to any more international trips with him." I lightened my grip slightly as I got up to go to the bathroom that was actually down the hall and not in the room, thankfully.

I left my room with Paul right behind me as I headed to the bathroom. I stayed in there for an extended period of time waiting for him to leave the room and the dorm room floor. These constant interactions that I was having with Paul were making me feel crazy. I was spinning down the rabbit hole with him. I saw no way out of it. I really just wanted to swim, and deep down at the same time, I was so prideful that I wasn't going to give into him either. That fighting spirit that I swam with, that determination was also driving me in this internal and external conflict I was going through.

I stayed up most of the night dealing with the conflicting thoughts about what to do with my life. I was tired and wanted to just give it all up. It sounded like the best path. However, I also had this drive and passion to swim that I didn't want to let go of either. I was battling this internal dialogue of death and victory all at the same time; it was a duel of life versus death. My body was absorbing all these thoughts and experiences.

When morning came I was happy to embrace the daylight despite the fact that I was tired from the torment of that night. It seemed like a good thing to start drinking coffee, and right then would be the launch of my coffee drinking days. When I got to the pool, Paul was in tow with the trainer, not leaving each other's side, and they had an air of "we fucked all night." We might have been teenagers, but we weren't stupid.

When it came time for my race I was barely awake and barely ready to compete. As a result, I just barely made it into finals, qualifying in lane one, seventh. Eighth place was one of the East German swimmers, and you know that they were getting it a lot worse than me. It was good that I qualified, but they were about to be punished in one form or another. That was the thing—there was always some situation that you knew about that was worse than yours which gave you that needed pause to not speak up or say anything.

Between prelims and finals, I actually got some rest and was able to shut off from the world around me. My only obstacle was playing nice with Paul and sleep seemed to make those moments more manageable and go a little smoother with him. When it came time for my race I had no pressure on me as I wasn't even considered one of the best in the race, despite the fact that I was second in this Junior Championship the year before and was poised to win it this year without much challenge.

When I dove in for my race I could feel the rush of the water rolling off my back. I had that euphoria of racing that I knew so well. I had found what I was searching for. I might as well have been flying as the water separated in front of me with every stroke I took. I could feel the power of my glide and strength of being both inside and out. It was like all my troubles, all my sadness, everything was being washed and cleansed from my soul. I was free to be the person that I was, a swimmer in a complete state of joy. I saw no one around me¬—it was me and the open lane. All the competitors in the middle, faster lanes were not even in my sight. I touched the wall to look back at the clock totally expecting to see my name and place in first, but saw to my shock I had been touched out by an East German swimmer, Astrid Strauss. I never saw it coming.

That swim was exciting enough for Pat to write something up about it. I broke another British Junior record and was the only other swimmer from the British team that placed in the top three, of their event. The other swimmer was my teammate who was also coached by Paul. The downside of all this was that the story made it appear like Paul was this great coach because the only two British swimmers to show promise were both his swimmers.

I left France on a high with my accomplishment and suspected that I really should have won that race due to the rumors of the widespread doping of the East Germans. I didn't really have time to waste on solving that problem when I needed to focus on making the European Championship Team with Trials starting the following week.

When we returned back to England Paul had taken a new job in Swansea, so I picked up and moved right along with him. This time I was back to staying in a hotel until things got settled later in the summer.

The first order of business was to train for a few weeks and get ready for the European Championship.

I figured that my latest accomplishments were enough to carry me through to the next competition. It wasn't about coasting; it was about being established as a contender and as a rising star. The media attention certainly saw me as that. It gave me some liberty to not feel restrained when Paul continued with his harassment and his advances toward me.

At the new pool in Swansea, I was around new team members that I wasn't particularly interested in getting to know. I was only into getting to my training and leaving. But it didn't quite work like that. Paul wanted me to come to his office under the guise of discussing the practice in advance. Most of Paul's efforts were with him getting me to lighten up. What he meant by that was that he wanted free access to me, my body, and everything about me. Most interactions started off with non-verbal communication that I tried to grin and bear to the best of my ability. This time was no different. When it came to me getting in an argument with him was the moment of my demise. There wasn't anybody around to see or pay attention to his advances with me.

After every argument with Paul led to either a great practice or a terrible practice. There was never an in-between, and on that particular day it was so bad to the point that it appeared that I had just given up. Paul would reference my workout as the reason for him to not take me on the next trip. My choices were either to grin and bear it or mouth off and swim faster to the point that he had no reason to not take me on the next trip. I also knew that my nine lives were coming to end with Paul.

We got to the Trials and I would be swimming in the 100, 200, and 400. Over the course of the year I had lost my stamina in the 800 Free despite it really being one of my better events. Well, 200 Free on up were my better events. There were 400 Free and 800 relays that required four swimmers, so my chances of making the team were increased significantly, especially since I was second fastest in Britain in the 200 Free. I also knew that my poor training at the beginning of the year was going to compromise my strength combined with the uptick in extra competitions. However, I also had the will and the confidence despite my challenges with Paul.

It wasn't just having the will; I was a year out from the Olympics and that was now becoming my primary focus. My father also felt like I needed more international competition before I went to the Olympics to give me the greatest chance of not just making the team but winning the gold medal. At this point it was looking like the 200 Free was my event and the one that was going to give me the greatest chance of winning a medal. But before I got to that part of my career I just needed to make the upcoming team.

At this point Paul and I were barely speaking. I would ignore him with my Walkman or not give him my full attention when I needed to get a set from him. I made every choice in the world to not have clear and direct contact with him. I can tell you that he still didn't take those signals. I could feel his pants and crotch as he pulled me towards him while he gave me a race prep conversation. It was the eyes, the creepy eyes that just went right through me and made me feel like I was naked and completely exposed to the world.

During the meet, I wasn't swimming my best. I was very lethargic but still placed third in the 100 and 200, earning at least a spot on both relays. My ability to swim distance was completely compromised. When I spoke to my dad about it, I had one excuse after another. They all made sense at the time and not one was about how Paul was talking to me, touching me, or threatening me that I wouldn't be on the next team because I continued to act like a spoiled brat. So I talked up my race and shared about someone else's great swim to lessen the blow. I knew that I would be reassured by my dad that I was fine with Paul and all was going to be okay.

When the team was announced the next morning, my name was not included. They actually took two slower swimmers, the fourth and fifth place finishes. How was I going to explain this to my dad? How was I going to convince him that it wasn't me? I was devastated beyond belief. I wanted to quit. I wanted out from swimming with Paul. I wanted out from life.

As I sat there completely broken hearted, the phone rang and the person who answered said it was for me. I was confused not really knowing who would know where I was. The British Swimming Association knew where I was because I had to leave my contact information of wherever I was staying so they could contact me at any moment, for the media or for a team request of sorts. I walked towards the phone trying to find some composure to pretend I was happy. My whole insides were broken and devastated and here I was needing to put on my party face, but it was too much. I couldn't handle the pressure much longer.

I answered the phone, with a "hello" in my questioning voice. There was a pause and then I heard the person on the other end say, "This is Pat, Pat Besford from the *Daily Mail.* I'd like to talk to you about European Trials and not making the team. Are you willing to sit down and do an interview with me?" I was so shocked and happy that Pat had called me. I went into my polite British version of myself. The sophisticated one.

Then she asked me if I had an opinion on why I didn't make the team? I paused and thought about it. I wanted to tell her everything, but we were on the phone and I didn't trust saying anything, despite the close relationship that I had formed with Pat on our previous trips. I just said, "I have no idea, maybe because they still think I'm an American." By this point every paper that covered me knew that my father was from a prominent British family and I was loosely related to Sir Stafford Cripps, a famous politician and Winston Churchill's right-hand man during World War II.

We ended the conversation with her saying that she would make a few other calls and then she would call me back to schedule a sit-down interview. When I hung up the phone with Pat, drunk Pat who had taken a liking to me and saw me unlike anyone else, I felt like I was being seen for the first time for the swimmer that I was.

It couldn't have been but five minutes after that call with Pat that I got another call and this time it was from the British Swimming Association informing me that there was an oversight and that I was meant to have been selected for the team. How long would it take me to get to London to start training camp? I got on the next train and was in London later that day.

The only saving grace at the time was that I didn't have to call my dad and explain how I messed up and didn't make the team. I got to call him with joy and say that I made the team. I made my first major competition and was heading to Rome for three weeks to train and compete. First stop London for a couple of weeks of training and then on to Rome.

When I arrived in London for training camp, I was under the assumption that I would get to race in the events that I had rightfully earned which turned out not to be the case. No one was willing to say what events I was going to be swimming; I was just added to the team at this point. I was happy to be on the team with my friends and on the National Team for a major competition.

The best news was that I wasn't assigned to swim with Paul; I was assigned to swim with the sprint coach because that was all that I was potentially going to swim at the Europeans. One could say that there were some benefits like I wasn't getting into constant arguments with him. I did, however, have to prove myself to the other coaches that I was coachable as Paul had created a reputation for me as being unruly.

The group to which I was assigned was mostly older swimmers and one of those swimmers was the best in the country and all of Europe, June Croft. I was a fan. I placed second behind June at the Commonwealth Games Trials, so she wasn't new to me. We had been on the swim meet circuit all year with her beating me just about every time. I was super excited to be on the team with her and train with her. We quickly became friends despite our almost five-year age gap. That was a lot for a young person in pursuit of an Olympic career.

The only reason that I got to swim and train with June was because her coach, Keith, was banned from coaching at the international level by the British Swimming Association because he hitchhiked to a competition and expensed for a train ticket, which gave him a lifetime ban from being able to coach his swimmers, even though he had several on the National Team.

After practice, I found myself going with my new friends and teammates to the pub at the Crystal Palace training facility. I found a routine that was working for me: I was staying out of trouble per se, since I wasn't having to fight off Paul at every turn. I felt part of the team and wanted to blend in with my fellow Brits. I could be British this way.

After a couple of weeks, it was time to move the whole team to Rome for the competition where we were staying at the competition hotel with the rest of the other countries. Our hotel had a 50 meter pool where we trained. We were in this contained environment, eating three meals in the restaurant, with bread and pasta being my starter at every meal including breakfast, and then at the pool training twice a day.

There are some stereotypes about being British and one of those is being uptight, or some might say having a stiff upper lip. Since Paul had for the past couple of years broken down my defenses to do whatever he asked of me, it was taken to a new level when we got to Rome. I now wasn't the only person susceptible to his sexually alarming requests. In one of our practices, one of my teammates took her top off and trained topless, I don't know if this was in the hopes of getting a tan or if it was an underhanded request from Paul. Either way, my teammates started to take their tops off to train.

I remember standing over my lane as he seemed to make it a requirement that I take my top off and do 10 x 50 fly. I did it without thought, without fight, without resistance. It didn't stop Paul from commenting on the size of my breasts and nipples. Then the other coaches also chimed in. All I could think about was that I was on the team and. I didn't want to create waves so to speak. What else was I going to do but comply? All I can say was that set was painful; the water was cold on my breasts, and they were sore from hitting the water when I came out of the pool. It was a distraction from my real feelings and thoughts of embarrassment and shame.

While I had time apart from Paul coaching me, he was still my coach of record as my club coach, and we weren't disconnected from each other. I still had accountability to him. He was training the distance swimmers and since I wasn't swimming any distance races it made sense for me to be in the sprint group. While I managed to blend in with my teammates and stay out of harm's way with Paul for the most part until we arrived in Rome, my interactions with him began to shift again towards him taking liberties to feel like he owned my body when we were alone. He would hold over me the question of what I was swimming as that wasn't completely decided. I didn't really know what I was training for other than to please Paul. He needed to come to my room and talk to me and he summoned me to his room more frequently. Due to my undefined role on the team I knew the options to ignore him were limited.

At this point, I had decided in my mind that I couldn't train with Paul any longer. I wanted to train with June Croft who was one of the best in the world in 200 freestyle. I held that thought and the idea of leaving Paul. I wasn't set on Swansea; I had no school or home set up in my future, but it appeared I was going to have to return with Paul. I just couldn't take it any longer. I wanted to win and train for my event. I also knew that the struggle wasn't over with Paul because he was the head coach and all roads led through Paul whether or not I was swimming with him directly.

After about a week of training, Pat and Anita arrived to cover the event. They always traveled wherever we went, including all the times we were tourists. One day we all visited the Vatican and Pat was riding right along with us. I hadn't spoken to her since our call when she wanted to know why I wasn't on the team. I sat next to her on the bus on the way to the Vatican and she wanted to know what had happened with Paul and me. I didn't have an answer for that question other than I wasn't sure what event I was swimming. Then I really started talking about training with June and how happy I was to be swimming with such an amazing swimmer.

When we arrived at the Vatican I wasn't really a fan and didn't even want to get off the bus to go inside. I had this aversion to the institution; it might have been from my childhood teacher, Sister Mary Kate and the principal making me run around the school or my deep rooted dislike for the religion and not wanting to have any part of it. I didn't want to go in and stayed talking to Pat.

When the bus started to pull away, the team manager informed us that the Pope had offered to meet one person from every country in a private meeting. They decided that they would place everyone's name in a hat and draw a name. It turned out that my name was drawn to meet the Pope.

I returned later that evening to the Vatican for a private tour with swimmers, divers, and synchronized swimmers from the other countries.

We had a small tour of the Vatican leading us to the Sistine Chapel where the Pope would arrive to give us a blessing of sorts.

I wasn't that fascinated with the Vatican having been there several times in my extensive travels with my family. It was curious about the Pope. Here I was with the one person on earth who was meant to be the most holy of people. I had turned away from the idea of religion and really pursued the religion of being an Olympian. I never saw room for both, God and greatness of self—just the opposite. I left the Vatican that day with this feeling of there being even more distance between myself and God.

I look back at this interaction with the knowledge that the only reason that I was standing in front of the Pope was to cover up my sexual abuse by Paul as it was being ignored by every official throughout the swimming associations. Similarly, the Catholic Church was running a worldwide network of pedophilia without much awareness in the mainstream media. It was right under our noses just like my sexual abuse. I knew intuitively at that time, but not consciously what was happening in the church. The thoughts and feelings were so deep inside of me that they couldn't make their way out to be heard.

CHAPTER 11

Wonderland

I felt the excitement from the pre-competition events and knew it was all part of the pursuit of greatness, to rub elbows with the highest elites of society, something my father had said he wanted for me, something he groomed me for. The Olympic gold medal could open up access to this world. It was the premise and the guiding principle of my existence.

When the Europeans in Rome started, I only swam the relay on the first day. The lazy part of me was happy that I was done and could drink the rest of the time with my teammates, but the other part of me was really disappointed I wasn't going to be swimming in the other events for which I clearly qualified.

For most of the competition I was sleeping in and missing the morning session, drinking with the older guys, and crawling across balconies to carry on my drinking with them. Then a few days into that routine, I was told I needed to provide a blood test for the drug-testing protocol. I was good with that since I wasn't doing drugs.

After a few days, I got a knock on my door and was told I needed to give a blood and urine sample for testing. It didn't even occur to me that alcohol was in my system. I did what was asked of me, mostly annoyed, though, because it woke me up too early.

A day or so later, I found out that my alcohol level was .26. This became the ammunition for Paul for not selecting me on the team to begin with. I had now nailed my own coffin for competing internationally again if Paul had a say in the matter. Paul was very clear with me: if I wasn't going to respect his coaching, aka his sexual advances and submit to his sexual desires, then my chances of representing Great Britain again were fading. I couldn't explain this to anyone without implicating myself and my choices along the way.

I left Rome in complete defeat. How could I continue to train with Paul? My only out was that he had moved to Swansea and there wasn't really anything there for me to pursue. The result of the test wasn't official and therefore not actionable. All it did was weaponize Paul to continue his character assassination of me and hold this piece of evidence against me as this immature, un-coachable, and all-around bad person. I wasn't exhibiting the behavior of an elite athlete.

When I got home for a few weeks after Europeans, I was adamant about not returning to train with Paul. After the several missed times that I should have been on the National Team, my dad was mad at him enough to see that it was affecting the track of my career, so much so that he was willing to listen to me. My idea was to train with the fastest person in the country and one of the best in the world at the time: June Croft. It wasn't like I presented a bad option; it was well thought out and met the quality of training that my dad desired for me. A win-win for everyone.

Soon I was off to a new city and a new swim team in Wigan, located between Liverpool and Manchester in the northwest of England. There wasn't much there besides the usual city features of Britain: church, cobblestone, and of course a swim center with an awkward pool length of 55 yards, which was slightly longer than a 50 meter pool. It brought character to my training having to swim faster to be satisfied with times that I was doing in practice.

When I moved to Wigan, I was considered a grown adult in the eyes of the adults around me, self-sufficient in my ability to take care of myself. The days of living with a family was a thing of the past. I was moving into a bed and breakfast as a permanent guest. It was perfect in the sense that I had my own room and shared bathroom down the hall. This all came with no immediate oversight. I could come and go as I pleased, and I didn't have to be mindful of being in someone's home.

My sole focus now was to make the British Olympic Team. The opportunity only came around once every four years. And the move to Wigan was important to remove any distractions from my life. The main distraction was school. At this point, everyone had lost track of where I was with school anyway. I had stopped going in Coventry and was really bored with it. The general consensus was to focus on swimming. The life span of an elite athlete is finite.

I wasn't going to lose sight of my dream. I saw myself going to the Olympics as a young girl and nothing was going to stop me. I was happy to just be swimming. Well, for the most part I was happy. I had a lot time when I wasn't swimming and it was hard to sit with just my thoughts. But I had found something to shut off those thoughts when I wasn't swimming. I was curious about the horse races and learning how to bet on them. I found out I was quite talented at seeing talent not only in people but also in horses. I had sense of seeing things beyond the veil of illusion that we are all in. It was an interesting discovery about myself and my talents. I would go hang out with the old smoking men and tell them which horses I could see had "it." I loved sharing my intuitive connection with others and it gave me something to do in between practices.

As my time in Wigan progressed, I was starting to settle into being the swimmer I knew I was inside. It took a few months to let my guard down with my new coach, Keith, mostly because for the first time I wasn't the best female on the team or even the favorite. The praise dynamic that I'd had my whole swimming career changed while training with Keith. What I loved about his coaching was that the sets were hard and challenging, but he was not. He was nice and pleasant while asking you to rise up and outperform yourself. There was never a moment where I was threatened emotionally, physically, or sexually. To some degree it almost felt uncomfortable to settle into this relationship with Keith because it was something that I hadn't ever experienced.

I was training with June, swimming on her toes, well at least trying to. I hadn't ever trained with another female swimmer who was better than me. It was a new position and new challenge that I loved and welcomed. I could see in my swimming sets how much I was becoming the swimmer I had dreamed of being. That little girl was happy and in her element again.

Later that fall the swim meets would resume with the European Cup in December and another trip right after to Hawaii for some hardcore training over the holidays. There was no time to take any time off during an Olympic year. The only difference this year was that my whole family would join me in Hawaii.

The several months of training and developing into the next level athlete gave me my confidence back. I also felt that now that I had a new coach and was no longer under Paul's control, I could go in peace if you will. He was no longer "my coach"; we had officially broken up. I was also excited to be traveling with my new friends as there were five of us that made the team. Even though Keith wouldn't be with us because of his ban, I felt I was protected. I had a new set of teammates and we would surely be together with the same adopted coach.

When we got to the airport to go to Germany, I learned that I was going to be coached by Paul and under his control again. He had also taken "ownership" of a couple of my other teammates, so I wasn't entirely alone in that way. I wasn't happy about it. Yet I felt that I could deal with any interactions with him now. I felt like I was in a stronger place. I was training exceptionally well with a coach that I loved, so what could go wrong?

It didn't take long for Paul to resume bullying and harassing me. It always started out with an off-the-cuff comment to lighten me up that was sexual in nature about boyfriends, how much sex I was having, anything to pry whatever information he was trying to finagle out of me and point my thoughts in that direction. It was a set up for him to talk to me about sexual endeavors. My guard was disarmed. It was that first gesture of placing his hand on my back and rubbing it while thrusting his groin uncomfortably too close while I was standing on the pool deck at his mercy for swimming feedback. I was the only one who knew what was really going on. Everyone else was doing whatever they were focused on.

It didn't help that our language as teammates was not far from this line of talk from Paul. It was fine to sit around and laugh about this stuff, but when it came to your coach and one who is pressuring you to engage with them sexually, it felt wrong but there was no one and nowhere to go with it. I kept telling myself that I was uptight or an American prude. I felt all this shaming and needed to convince myself that it was okay and that I was the problem. It didn't take away from the fact that I absolutely hated this man and wanted him out of my life. No one would help me with that, at least that is what I thought at the time.

There was always something in the future that I wanted that would deter me from speaking up. It could be a record I wanted to break, or a trip or some material item I was promised by my parents I could have when I accomplished whatever it was that was in front of me. In this case, it was breaking as many Junior British records before I turned sixteen, in a few months. The need to perform always had a silencing mechanism attached to wherever I was at in my career combined with not having the language or the communication skills to speak about it. I was never able to see it other than it was my own fault.

Swimming in Germany with Paul as my coach brought up all that anger and the feelings that I had with him. I thought moving to another swim program would relieve me of those feelings and allow me to go about my swimming in peace. How I was training and performing in competition was also proving to my dad that I was not the problem. My parents could see that all I needed was a fresh start with a new coach so all my troubles would go away.

With another trip to Hawaii in my immediate future, I knew that my interactions with Paul, were going to be temporary. But it didn't change our dynamic when I trained for him on a daily basis. It seemed like he was wanting to silence my voice while also wanting me to swim fast. He was pulling me from two directions: one that felt unguarded with the idea that another person wanted for me what I wanted for me, which was to be a champion. Then there was the challenging engagement of the idea that if you are going to be the best in the world then you also need to be able to overcome any hurdle. There wasn't a description of what challenges marked you as a real champion if you could overcome this issue or if that issue crossed the line. There was no line. It all fell under the guise of becoming a champion and that was what I was going to be. All because I had a dream.

I left that swim meet having brought myself back up to fighting shape in a solid second in June's shadow and was without question the fastest Junior swimmer in Britain. I went to Hawaii not as broken as I was the year before. All this was called maturity, when in reality it was because I wasn't fighting Paul off on a daily basis. I was free from being tormented.

In Hawaii that winter, I spent a lot of time with my family in between training and wasn't as much of a partier as I was the year before. I was training and swimming as fast as I ever was. It was clear that I was happier in life and could manage life better. All this did was up the ante if you will. It added pressure as to the level of accomplishment that I was to obtain. My father saw what he would say was a true champion. My coach in Hawaii, Jack, the military gruff one who barely smiled or gave me a compliment, was impressed with my potential and the trajectory of my swimming. He witnessed me perform in practice like a world champion. I could swim at world record pace on a regular basis. I was becoming known as a fantastic workout swimmer. I knew that a lot of this was due in part to chasing June back in England. She too was a phenomenal workout swimmer. I wanted to return to England to be able to swim on par with her.

Returning to England still had its flaws since I wasn't happy with my living situation. I was bored and lonely outside of swimming and needed my own place. I spent most of my time in Hawaii complaining about this. Like all needs it was presented with a reward, a gift, a carrot or whatever you call it. All I wanted was to have my own place and with that came a renewed focus in practice and competition. I had new goals to accomplish, which of course were met without much challenge. I knew what I wanted and needed.

My focus upon my return was to break the British Junior records and have a new apartment. Shortly after I returned, a small team was taken to an annual swim meet in Paris. To be selected for Great Britain meant that you were one of the elite swimmers. I stepped right into that role. The great news for me was that Paul wasn't going to be on this trip, but neither was Keith. I had one more trip after Paris that was scheduled with Paul to take me and a few other swimmers with the intention it would be my last swim meet before I aged up.

What I loved about the Paris swim meet was that the American team also brought its elite group of swimmers. It was a very competitive meet and I was proud to be a part of it. Any time I got to swim with the USA team it brought me joy and pride that I knew so well. I was able to feel the patriotism within me that I had to hide from my British teammates and others. It reminded me that I hadn't lost my love for America or my desire to be as great as the American swimmers are known to be.

All my positive desires fed into my Olympic dream at this swim meet. I can't tell you if I won or not; I believe I was second. I also believed that the winner was an American which was more acceptable to me than losing to one of my teammates. The memorable part of the swim was breaking the Junior records or more like smashing them. So much so that I was very close to also breaking the British records as well. I swam fast and actually impressed myself which wasn't an easy feat. The standard that I set for myself was set at an early age to be the best and my swims brought me closer to that standard.

After my record-breaking swims Pat the journalist was right there to interview me. I was labeled as the star of the meet and got the most attention, not a small accomplishment against my teammates who were world record holders and among the best swimmers in the world. The praise competition was getting tougher and tougher as I moved through my career, but I had found my way back to it. Pat seemed curious why I swam so fast. I know she knew that an element of this was because Paul wasn't coaching this trip. It wasn't discussed but implied in our conversation. I mostly pointed to training in Hawaii and my new coach in Keith. There was always this unspoken conversation that the two of us tip toed around. I really just wanted her to read my mind as I wasn't going to say anything that might cause me further harm. I did not trust in people in general and the world told me to not trust a drunk, but she was the only person that I truly trusted at this point.

When I returned to England I was moving into my new place; my parents bought me a condo. I was coming off of this high of not only breaking records, but I was also ranked in the top ten in the world with my swim. There was so much to be excited about. Yet my success didn't offer me any comfort in the empty spaces when I wasn't swimming; it was too much for me. I was alone in the world without another person to process and share what was really going on with me. When I won and swam fast everyone assumed nothing was hurting me and if something was, I was a champion and had the inner strength to overcome all challenges. I was proving that in my swimming.

All these positive feelings were fading away fast as the next swim meet came along. The thought of traveling with Paul and a small group of swimmers was starting to become unbearable. It was draining every emotion and positive feeling that I just acquired from the swim in Paris. My parents just bought me this new place, I had new independence, but with that came obedience and compliance to whatever I just committed to. My mind started swirling in fear with how I could get out of going to this swim meet. What was I going to say? I had many people who needed answers—it wasn't just my parents. I had a swimming association, I had a journalist who was curious about me, and a coach who was living a multi-personality life the one that I had to deal with and speak to was different than the one that the swimming association would engage with. How could I bring all these different entities in alignment with my will?

This set off a pattern of needing to take the edge off. My new place was across the street from a liquor store. Every night after practice I would go and get a bottle of wine and a pack of cigarettes as I now sat in fear of having to be in the presence of Paul. I built up so much anger and angst with him that it was literally killing me inside. I had no coping mechanism. While the time in the pool and training cut off the negative and worried thoughts and I had relief in those moments, it didn't last long enough when I got home and my mind started to wake back up again to the dark chatter. I would drink the bottle of wine and then smoke a cigarette so I could puke and pass out on the bathroom floor. I would wake up in the middle of night and crawl into bed feeling like my own form of comfort or nurturing was the moment my body felt the comfort of the bed. That comfort wouldn't last long before I had to wake up for morning practice.

All this cycle did was tire me to the point where it was dragging down my practices and my spirit enough to imply to my coach that I was getting sick and couldn't travel. I desperately needed to forgo this last opportunity. Being rundown in an Olympic year was something that everyone could buy into as a valid concern. I believe I had found the right solution to not raise concerns with the people around me. I knew I could not take another moment with Paul. I didn't have the mental energy or capacity to be near him. There weren't enough destructive choices other than my death that would let me escape this torment with him.

Soon I was back to training and focusing on my next competition: the Short Course Nationals and a few other long course competitions before the Olympic Trials only four months away. All focus needed to be on swimming fast at those meets. I was no longer a child really; I was an adult now that I was sixteen. My nightly visits to the liquor store were curtailed as I got closer to the Short Course Nationals. I reserved those trips for weekends when the loneliness was too much. Drinking became my significant other, almost like I was in an on-again, off-again relationship with much of it on. I also had to feel fresh to swim. I hated to swim in complete pain; there was a zone that I always wanted to find. I was constantly trying to manage that and hide what I was doing outside of the pool and training.

When Short Course Nationals came around, I was restored to the high that I felt in Paris. I had established myself as a clear second to June with the desire to overtake her. I was getting closer to the dream of being an Olympian—that was only half of the dream—the gold medal was in there too. I saw a hint of the dream starting to fill in with color during my swim. When I lined up to swim 200 Freestyle with June, she and I were in the center lanes; we were friends and friendly competitors. The thing with June was that she was always nice to me and we got along great, but she had something that I didn't—this extra dig at the end. During that race I thought I was going to finally overtake her when I pushed off on the last lap of the swim. I was ahead and swimming close to world record pace. There was something that struck me in that moment, where I didn't feel worthy enough to win. I was hit with this negative self-talk that completely shut down my muscles, almost paralyzed me. To the outside world it looked like I had died, meaning that I couldn't sustain at the pace that I was going, or one could say I ran out of gas. I knew that wasn't the case based on the self-talk that I could hear. I knew when I could hear that talk I was no longer in the zone or connected to the source or the gift from within. I could feel myself block off from it. However, I still swam fast and clocked my best time, a 1:59. Swimming under two minutes at the time was still impressive even if it was short course meters.

After that swim it was looking like June and I were a good one-two duo for Britain in that race. I was labeled as the young swimmer in June's tracks as it was expected that she would retire after the Olympics. I was stepping into my own and working on taking over the British championships. I was doing all the right things in the pool so that everyone around me could see I was fine.

As Olympic Trials neared, my destructive behavior became less evident. I actually felt strong as a person on the inside. I had found myself training with Keith and the rest of the great team I was part of. I had the confidence that was unwavering about whether or not I was going to make the time and I knew exactly what time I needed in order to go to the Olympic Games. In swimming, and in other timed-based sports, there is a time established for one or two persons to go per country. The faster time of the two athletes goes to the Games in accordance with the established "A" time. The slower time, the "B" time, only one person can qualify for the Games; I had to swim faster than the established "A" time. The "A" was based on being in the top 16 in the world. I was already ranked higher than that from swims that year.

When it came to swimming at Olympic Trials, my parents of course watched me swim. They weren't going to miss that; they generally didn't miss the big competitions. I had been dreaming about this since that fateful day of watching the Olympics with my dad just eight years earlier. Here I was about to make my dad proud, where he was going to be able to cheer on his daughter and fellow countrywoman. It brought so much joy to him to have me swim for Great Britain and be able to go to the Olympics. It was something that he never accomplished, and he never let go of the pain of not being able to go. I was now at that moment where I was going to surpass my dad's accomplishments in one area of his life.

It was not just my parents who were advocating for me but Pat as well. She wanted to interview me after my race. The question that she later asked me was about not being overlooked and how did that feel. She wanted to know if being on the European Championship Team prepared me for this competition. I never thought anything of the questions. I was honored and proud that she wanted to continue to write about me. I was still young and interesting as far as a story went.

When I look back at my life, I believe that I was confident of making the team because I knew I could earn a spot based on my performance. I wouldn't have to deal with Paul. I was now one of Keith's swimmers. We were the powerhouse swimming club in Britain when it came to depth of talent. I was proud to be part of this special club. Keith didn't treat me any different than June. He trained us the same and connected with us together but separate. I never felt any jealousy, just camaraderie and teammates supporting each other.

On the first day of Trials was the 200 Freestyle. I swam in the morning and easily made finals in one of the center lanes. I swam as directed knowing that I needed to swim fast that night to make the team. The final result was all that mattered. When it came to standing behind that block there was nothing stopping me in my mind—no worry, no doubt, just an inner belief in me. Annabelle an Olympian. I knew what time I needed to do and knew how far June could swim in front of me from where she was going to be from training with her over the past year. I wasn't really a "swim someone else's race" person; it was always from within that I would drive myself. I remember touching that wall and seeing that I had swam faster than the "A" time, coming in second to June. There wasn't another swimmer that also qualified, so the waters weren't muddy for me, at least that is what I thought in the moment. The third place finish only had the "B" time and if that person was selected it also meant that June wouldn't be able to swim and I knew that was never going to happen. I knew in that moment that the two of us made the Olympic Team. I felt free with an ease within me of not having to wait for the coaches' meeting at the end of trials. I could go to my dad and feel his praise without an excuse or to explain a relationship or struggle that was ongoing with Paul at this point.

As the meet went on, I would limit my interactions with my parents, mostly to concentrate and not be annoyed by them, well mostly my mother. I was a teenager and was annoyed easily! I still needed my dad's approval, praise, and love. I felt like I had lost the little girl connection with my dad. I missed him calling me "Little Annabelle." After knowing in my heart that I had made the Olympic Team, I wanted to see my dad. I wanted him to be happy with all the efforts that they'd put into my life and into my career. I did it. I was going to be an Olympian. There was an excitement and awe from having a dream and starting to see your dream come true. I had this idea that you had dreams, but they didn't come true; maybe you'd come close to it if you worked hard, but the whole thing couldn't come true because it was a "dream." Not anymore, it was now reality.

After setting off on a strong note with Trials, I continued to have successful swims for the rest of my races. My only disappointment was not making the 400 Freestyle, my other event. I placed third behind Sarah Hardcastle, the younger swimmer who beat me in my first competition in England when I was eleven and she was only ten—remember, the one race that I lost. Here I was again losing to Sarah and June, two amazing swimmers and the second and third fastest in the world, not bad placing a close third to that.

As the meet came to a close, I was poised to swim the 200, 800 and 4x100 Freestyle relays in the Games. While I had to go through the same protocol of the public announcement the next day, I left the swim meet feeling like I was free from Paul and that I had now found my home and team. Keith's training got seven of us on that Olympic Team. The most swimmers by any coach.

I didn't think through what would happen after the Trials and what it would be like if Keith wasn't able to be a coach. I thought in my mind that if Keith had seven swimmers on the team then surely they would make him one of the National Team coaches. When they announced the team and I was on it, reality hit that I wasn't going to be coached by Keith. It was a detail that I didn't want to deal with. All my other teammates were in the same boat as me. I knew I wasn't alone with this issue. It was still devastating having to give up the coach whom you loved and who just brought you to the edge of your dream.

Once the team was announced, we spent a few days at home and then reported for training camp and other commitments with the team for the rest of the summer until the start of the Games, in about eight weeks. We would first train in Sweden for a couple of weeks. When I arrived, I was greeted by Paul who called me into his room. I was immediately on guard. I had been doing so well without him; I had been free from his daily sexual advances and everything else that I hated about him. I stood at his door not going all the way in as he informed me I was going to train with him leading up to the Games. I can't begin to tell you how disappointed I was. It wasn't even disappointment at this point—it was anger and frustration. Paul tried to come near me and I told him that I wasn't going to train with him. I didn't just tell him—I was adamant that I was not going to have anything to do with him.

Later that day we had practice and everyone went to their coaches while I stayed behind and said I was not training with him, meaning Paul. I wouldn't do it. It took some stubborn force and will to get someone to recognize that it wasn't going to happen. Yet all that did was validate everything that Paul had already described about me up to this point.

I was swimming some sprint races in the relay with the 200 being a sprint for some and an endurance race for others. In my case it was an endurance sprint as I leaned towards distance races. When they assigned me to swim with another coach I was relieved and free from interacting with Paul. It wasn't like I could say anything to the coach I was now training with about why I wanted out of swimming with Paul. I was mired in the shame of being in my teammate's room when I was twelve and had this idea that he had a judgment and feelings about what could have possibly happened behind those closed doors. I was carrying a secret and shame that closed another door, or avenue for me, to be able to speak up without fear.

While I got my way to be out of Paul's direct control, I did so at the sacrifice of the training that benefited me as a swimmer. While it was easier to train as a sprinter and proved less mentally taxing on me, it wasn't going to help me to perform at my highest level. But that was something that I was willing to give up in order to avoid being in a constant battle with Paul. I didn't have it in me to hold back my anger for him. It was the best I could do at the time to take care of me.

My time in Sweden was not abuse- and harassment-free by any means. Paul was sly and conniving when I was in his presence. My coping mechanism to deal with him was drinking when I could or thinking about committing internal harm to myself so I could quickly die. I also wanted to be an Olympian. I also wanted my dreams of life to come true. I was under constant attack from my internal voices.

After a few weeks of training in Sweden, we returned to London to get geared up for the Olympic Games. During this time there were also social events and media events to recognize the uniqueness of the individual athletes who were about to represent Great Britain. I was one of the youngest members of the British Olympic team, and had two younger teammates, Sarah and Zara. Several invitations and events came our way. The Cabbage Patch company, hugely popular at the time, made us a special doll for the Olympic Games. Then there was the invitation from the royal family to attend the opera at Royal Albert Hall as a guest of Anne, Princess Royal who was also the President of the British Olympic Association. As my dreams started to form, and the prizes of success started to show up in my life, where I was being recognized for the talent I was, it also closed the voice and the door to speaking up about my troubled interactions with Paul. My outside world looked great and exciting and all that I had ever dreamed of.

As our time wrapped up in London, it was off to California to begin our training camp in San Diego for a few weeks before finally making our way to the Olympic Village in Los Angeles. When we arrived at the Los Angeles Airport it was my first separation from the team as I had a different path to take from my fellow Brits; it was through the American citizen immigration line. My love for America when I stepped on American soil made me proud. I still felt my internal conflict of my pride for America and for wanting my American dream while also wanting inclusion in the high society which Britain had to offer.

I had already passed through customs ahead of the rest of the team and now had to wait to go through the Olympic credentialing with the rest of the team that took place at the airport. When Paul was reunited with me in the credentials area, he pulled me aside and launched into a tirade of backhanded insults about me being an American combined with his repeated requests for me to be more mature. Although that wasn't the language he used. He was asking me to be respectful of his wishes, which were about disarming me, and in that moment his hands and body leaned in my direction. It was another attempt to shame me into compliance that I wasn't buying.

After we left the airport, we all headed down to San Diego. We were staying at the UCSD campus that was situated on a hill from a beach called Black's Beach. The excitement of being in Southern California came with going to the beach. Some of us would head down to Black's Beach between practices. At first glance it was a beautiful beach and a great place to jump in the ocean, until that moment when you realize you are on a nude beach. When the coaches learned about this, a few of them decided to come down to the beach—one of them was Paul, of course. As the various nude beachgoers would walk by without a care in the world, Paul would lead the way in shaming the girls on the team to get naked. Paul wasn't the only coach to do so, but he was certainly instigating this behavior while also making sexual suggestive advances to other girls on the team. When he started doing that to the others it was easier for me to feel like, well, it wasn't just me. Some of the girls stripped down and took their tops off, while others pushed back and refused. Whatever choice you made it would be brought up later by Paul at the next practice or meal or something; you could not get away from whatever choice you made. It was in these moments that I wished Pat our journalist was traveling to these events so she could witness the sickness and behavior of our coaches so I didn't have to hold my secret any longer. Pat wasn't scheduled to meet up with us until we arrived at the Olympic Village.

As the time neared for our arrival at the Olympic Village, I was getting closer to being able to call myself an Olympian. It would become official when I actually competed. Up to this point I had just qualified for the Games. The dream was at my doorstep. My parents were making the trip to LA to watch and I made sure that they got tickets to all of the highly coveted events, which essentially were swimming, gymnastics, and track and field. I was also ignoring the fact that I had peaked in my swimming from a speed and endurance standpoint. While one part of the dream was coming into fruition, I was also preparing the story I was going to tell for my pending failure.

The British Team was housed on the UCLA campus and swimming took place at the USC campus. Part of our preparations were at the beautiful pools of UCLA and the other part of the time we had to trek across LA in traffic to get to the USC pool. The USA Team was also staying on the USC campus right there near the pool. That was all we heard in the lead-up to the Games.

The excitement of the Games really started at the opening ceremonies, also taking place the night before my first race which had its own set of nerves and excitement. Due to the ceremonies being the night before, I stayed behind and watched on TV with a few teammates of mine. After the opening ceremonies, I tried to rest but my head was spinning as I dreamed about winning while knowing that I wasn't swimming fast enough in practice to make that happen. I had to pretend that I had what it took to win while also preparing the excuse for failure. My mind was working overtime to figure all that out.

As morning came and it was time drag myself out of bed to go to the pool, I gathered up my stuff, put on my British Team gear and wore it proudly while admiring and being a fan of the American greatness that I was about to share a pool with. I had wanted to befriend and know the winners—I felt like them and would be like them one day. I was about to share a pool with Sippy Woodhead who was the greatest 200 freestyler in swimming history having broken the world record in 1978 when she was only fourteen years old; the other was American Mary Wayte, a relatively new name to me that summer but someone who I wanted to know and of course outswim. Those were the dreams that I couldn't feel but could imagine. I was stuck on accessing the hurt and pain of having to deal with my invisible enemy.

The day had come, or shall I say my dream had arrived, from the fateful moment of running across the pool deck at three years old. I was at the Olympic pool in LA. That moment of standing on the edge of the pool for warm-ups, my nerves were alive and well. I looked around the stands which were sprinkled with only a few early spectators. I was populating those stands like the subway filling up at rush hour. I needed to pull myself back into my body and the best way to reconnect from the illusion was jumping into a chilled pool, especially with a freshly shaved body. This was refreshing, but at the same time it reminded me where I was: about to compete in the Olympic Games.

After warm-ups, my focus was all over the place, wanting to know, and also at the same time, not know where my dad was in the stands. I also knew that my new coach Keith was in the stands to coach us from the sidelines. I had this sense of comfort knowing that he was there as well. I always felt he was June's coach first and then mine. Yet Keith didn't act that way. I put us in that position because June was the better swimmer than me and swam with him longer. It was me protecting myself from being hurt by another coach. My coach's son, who I was training with, was swimming this day as well so I felt I was out of a coach as the others were focused on their swimmers. This situation created a pathway for Paul to find his way back into my world. Out of convenience of giving up the fight on the outside, I held in my anger and my feelings towards him.

When it came time to compete, I could feel so many of my thoughts churning. I could barely focus on preparing for my race. The clear pathway was blocked and, in my mind, I was heading down the rabbit hole. With that came the fear of disappointment. I desperately wanted to start my race just to shut the voices off. Standing behind the blocks, waiting for the signal to get on the blocks couldn't come soon enough, but at the same time I wasn't ready. I was never going to be ready. When I dove in the water, I could feel the heaviness of my soul in the race. I wasn't smooth, the whole thing was a mental and physical struggle. I felt like I was out of shape and not able to perform. All my mojo to show up wasn't there. The well was empty. I felt my Rolls-Royce engine puttering and pushing me over to the shoulder to get out of the way. I might as well have been driving a Pinto at this time.

When I touched the wall, I was about fourth in my heat. I knew I didn't make finals; the dream of the gold medal was no longer a dream; it was a broken promise to myself. I could feel my heart start to turn to clay. I didn't want to see my dad; I didn't want to talk to any coach, especially not Paul. I didn't want to talk to anyone. When I learned that I had made consolation finals, my first thought was I would swim fast enough in consoles to make up for my bad swim in the morning by time.

I was never a morning performer and always shined at night. I convinced myself of this fate.

Due to the perceived traffic problem, Paul convinced me to stay behind so I could get enough rest before finals. It was still respectable to make consolation finals, but it just wasn't the dream that I had for myself nor was it truly representative of my talent nor of the training I was putting in either. I stayed behind at the USC campus and didn't got back to UCLA to get any rest there.

There was a tent for swimmers to hang out with several massage tents connected to the swimmers' tent along with various food tents around the complex. I was in the section where only athletes, coaches, and officials could be. Thankfully, I had my Walkman and I found a place to chill and listen to my music, most likely one song that I rewound and played over and over again. As I was lying around trying to find some rest, Paul made his way to where I was and started rubbing my shoulders. I was so focused on my race that I wasn't really connecting to what was going with me and him. There was nobody around except me and Paul. My broken heart from my morning swim was being consoled or at least he was trying to console me. I would like to say that I had a defense in the moment, but I did not. Even if I wanted to say something or do something there was nothing for me to do. I didn't have a fight in me. His movements and actions were also very sly, in plain sight, but often undetected. Sounds like a description from a predator on the Animal Channel.

When it came time to swim that night, it was part of the glory of the Games to swim in finals in the evening. While it was the 'B" final, I was still caught up in the excitement of it all. I was filled with shame from my morning performance yet felt that I could still redeem myself. I was already preparing my conversation with my dad for after my race before I even swam it. I was really bargaining for the praise that I was used to getting. It was plentiful when I was three; I had so much of it and it compounded in my youth, but as I moved closer to the top it became less and less. Without praise from somewhere I would fizzle away. I literally felt like a fish out of water without it. One could say that at the higher accomplishments, the praise was better quality or more meaningful, but the reality is that praise is praise. It's the same if you're three or sixteen and swimming in the Olympics. Ultimately, I knew this swim wasn't going to bring the praise that I desperately coveted.

When it came time to swim, my sense of self was right sized into 15th place in the 200 Freestyle at the Olympic Games. After my swim, I got out of the pool to make way for the final heat. I watched in awe, disappointed in myself. I also got to watch my friend and teammate compete for the gold and that was exciting to me. I finally understood what my dad felt when he watched David Wilke win the gold; I could feel the same for June. Yet I was really a patriot of America. I had this internal conflict of wanting Sippy Woodhead to win. She was the reigning world recorder holder who didn't get to compete in 1980 Olympic Games because of the boycott. I felt she deserved to be recognized with a gold for her exceptional talent. However, the Olympic Games is about that day, and in that moment and in that race and on that day it was Mary Wayte's moment.

Taking in the mixed emotions, feeling the loss for Sippy, made my disappointment more manageable for me; I didn't feel alone in my sadness. I could justify my race and terrible swim with the idea that swimmers don't win sometimes. The reality was I was hurting from dealing with Paul. I was living a secret life and all I really wanted was to be that little girl with the teddy bear. I wanted to be the little girl swimming on my dad's back. I wanted anything other than the failure that I was about to see from my dad. I also knew what made him proud was when I could brag about my accomplishments.

The saving grace of my swim was that I was young—I had youth on my side. The ideal of this Olympic pursuit was for one to match up their talent, their strength, and youth to the day of a competition that happens once every four years that also includes your preparation for even making the team. It really is quite a feat for anyone.

After my swim, Pat was right there to capture my moment as a secondary story to the many medals that the British Team took home that night. June wasn't the only winner; a couple of our great male swimmers won medals as well. While Pat was capturing my moment, she was strongly focused on finding out what my distractions were at the Games. I don't really know what she was asking me at the time. My line of thinking was around nerves, youth, and not being prepared. I didn't know if the question came with an opportunity to give another answer.

As the rest of the Games carried on, I had a few more events to swim. When I was in the Olympic Village there was a sense of what life would be like without the fiat money system because there was no exchange of money anywhere; all the services were free and provided for, right down to a haircut at the Vidal Sassoon salon with Vidal himself on location. I found my way there to get an official swimmer logo for the Games dyed into the back of my head.

I was living in a world that I could imagine as the structure for world peace while experiencing an internal world war. I would watch the actions of the coaches on the team, as one by one the coaches started to have sex with various swimmers on the team during the Olympics. When swimming came to end after the first seven days of the fifteen-day event, the coaches and swimmer hook-ups seemed to only get worse. As more and more coaches engaged in this behavior, I had no defense against Paul to be able to say anything or do anything about how he was treating me. What were they going to say? If I would stop fighting and have sex with him, then all my problems would go away—that was essentially the solution that was being presented to me.

What did I do with that? I found a way to survive because that is what I do. I joined my teammates and my many friends from around the world and we celebrated our success, but mostly we celebrated our sadness, because the only happy people at the Games were the gold medalists. The rest of us all had broken dreams in one way or another. At least we all had something to share.

After the Games closed with a fabulous closing ceremony, the sadness and grief hit me so hard. There was the grief of the end of the Games. The highs and lows that defined the moment. The meeting of new friends. Being one of only so few in the world that accomplished what I did. The specialness of now being able to call myself an Olympian. At sixteen I had reached a peak in my life and valley at the same time. The sadness of training for four more years to pursue a failed dream was too overwhelming to even process.

After I left the Games there were a few more social events, media events, and other gatherings to celebrate us Olympians. One of the first events that I attended when I returned to England was a visit to 10 Downing Street as a guest of the Prime Minister Margaret Thatcher. When I arrived at 10 Downing Street, we walked up this big staircase to a large foyer for a cocktail reception. I found myself at this reception in full conversation with Sir Denis Thatcher, Margaret's husband, where one was expected to speak only when spoken to at these events. I was trained with the right manners so I knew what I was supposed to do but nonetheless conversed because I could. After some time, Margaret came over and joined us in the conversation that turned to how I competed in the Olympics. I shared my results, which were 14th and 15th in my individual events and 6th place in a relay. I wanted to add an excuse and an explanation and point to Paul who was in the room as the culprit. But I pulled my excuse back and stood there waiting for her acceptance of my accomplishments. She thanked me for representing our country so well.

From being in the presence of the Pope to now Margaret Thatcher, I still held my silence. I don't know that I would have known what to say or how to ask for help, not to mention I simply did not trust people in positions of power.

CHAPTER 12

UnAmerican

After the Olympics I learned first-hand about the post-Olympic blues, depression or just plain old disappointment. Whatever it was I had a heavy case of it. The cash and prizes of the praise and validation cycle had come to an end and a new cycle needed to be created, but this time it wasn't from the innocence of a little girl. It was from a broken-hearted Olympian who was draped in disappointment and accomplishment at the same time. I carried the loneliness with me on my daily trip from my condo to the liquor store across the street.

When June retired it made room for me to step into her spot, yet at the same time I was left without my friend and training companion. There was an emptiness in practice, in competition, and in life. This was all part of that sadness after the Games, the loss of youth and friendship as the next season of athletes pushed their way towards their dreams. Since I was so young as an Olympian it was only expected that I would be training for the next one.

Over the next year, swim meets came and went with the focus on making the next big competition, and this time it was the European Championships in Bulgaria. The same issues that were in my past were also in my future—how was I going to get past Paul to make the team?

I was now back to being beholden to his final decision, challenged with having to push myself through the let down and perform at a high level.

After two successful trips to Hawaii, I had another in my future; however, this time the European Cup was in Ankara, Turkey, in December before my winter training camp. It was also the first time that I would be crossing paths again with Paul since the Olympics. The only saving grace on this trip was that there was no training camp. While that didn't change my interactions with Paul, it just meant I had less time for any involvement with him. Of course we also had Pat the journalist join us on that trip.

When the National Team travels and you are without one of your teammates you really feel the loss. It wasn't just your team—it included the other international teams as well. Among my competitors I'd see a swimmer that I had a crush on. The only way to stay engaged back then was to actually get someone's physical address and write a letter. While there was the phone, it was back in the days where you would start your conversation off with "This is a long distance call," informing your caller of the limited time and the speed as to which one must converse. The loss of your competitor just disappeared out of sight and kind of out of mind, but not really. Me being so social I felt the change on such a heartfelt level.

When we got to Ankara, I was confident that I was the fastest person in Britain now that June had retired, but I wasn't putting in the work to truly take that title. I was training hard and doing everything that I needed to in the pool, but then at night I was drinking to avoid the loss and pain that I was feeling inside. When it came to me interacting with Paul, I had mastered the general avoidance and silent treatment I would give him. I had no other defense or coping skills with how to deal with him. At the same time, this swim meet was an opportunity for me to be praised for my talents, where I was still young enough to be considered great and talented despite my disappointing results from the Games. That was only validated further when I won the 200 Freestyle. I had not expected that.

After my swim, there was the usual interview and Pat was right there to ask her questions. The line of questioning was in regard to recovering from my disappointment at the Games. I had learned by now how to answer these questions without tipping my hand or saying anything that might come back to harm me later. I always answered in a general way. This was really me having a general distrust for the system. I also knew that Pat had that as well. I realized she wanted to know what it was like to train with Keith and how I felt with him not being on the team. I know she didn't write about any of this, but it seemed the more interviews we did, she was getting closer to wanting to ask me this question. I never really gave her the space to ask anything about Paul even though I would see her watch us interact at the hotel or around mealtimes. She had one eye pointed towards us and the other towards the fifth of whiskey that she always had going.

On the final night of the meet there was a traditional dinner for all the national teams. These evenings almost always included alcohol, for the swimmers, and absolutely for the coaches, and on this night they were not shy about drinking. The evening came with unusual food that I would never eat, along with flowing alcohol and a Turkish belly dancer. During the entertainment, Paul got good and tipsy. He came over to me and grabbed my hips and tried to move them in sync with this belly dancer who was moving her hips in ways I never ever aspired to do. It took away any good feelings that I had about my swim. I also knew that I needed to let him do what he was going to do or I wasn't going to be considered for the European Championships that summer. I was stuck with his whims again.

At this point in my interactions with Paul I was starting to internalize all these thoughts and beliefs. I was starting to see how I was the problem. My inner life would reinforce the image of myself as the contrarian with coaches and officials. Yet around my friends I was well-liked, social, smart, and engaging. I could see these two different versions of me being spread among the ranks. My only saving grace was that I was not training with him on a day-to-day basis and could return to my home and training world with Keith.

The remainder of that year was filled with various international competitions mostly in Europe. In April of 1985 we had a swim meet in Montreal and a small select group of us was invited to go. This trip involved Paul as one of the coaches. At this point all I knew to do was to put up a wall of anger as my defense against this person.

Arriving in Montreal, I was excited by the idea that I was going to be swimming in the Olympic pool. The very pool where my Olympic dreams began. When I arrived at the pool, it was impressive in size, design, and vastness of space. When I walked into the swim center the first thing I noticed was the stillness of the water in the pool; it was so peaceful and calming. It's my favorite moment. I can always tell by the calmness of a pool and splash in the gutters of the water moving back and forth how fast a pool is to swim in. It was mesmerizing to watch the water move back and forth in perfect harmony. I wanted that from within me. I wanted to feel that in my races again. I wanted the innocence of that moment with my dad back again.

When it came time to race, I had hit my stride in this pool; it was exciting to feel that in me—I felt free when I was swimming in that pool. I was swimming without resistance from the inside and out. It wasn't like I was rested for the meet; it was merely an international competition to get ready for the Commonwealth Games the following year and a way for some of us to compete against our Canadian friends. At that swim meet I garnered the attention of some of the American coaches and recruiters in attendance after swimming very fast in the 200 and all the other events between the 200 and the mile. In the mile I clocked one of the fastest times so far that year.

My swimming caught the interest of one of the college coaches at Alabama. He wanted me to come down right away to their campus. The interesting part of all this was that I was being recruited as a foreign swimmer to join their team. At the time, the team was made up of many European swimmers, one of those was a boy I liked who was on the French Olympic team, and so I was motivated to go on this recruiting trip just to see him. Instead of flying back to England with the team, I flew down to Alabama to check out their program. I mostly did this because I was going to be free of Paul and my engagement with him, not to mention it felt good that someone actually pursued me and wanted me. It was a feeling that I wasn't currently getting. My father wasn't exactly freely praising me. It was on to the next Olympic Games cycle, so any praise had to be earned and not be freely given.

When I returned to England I called my parents and told them I was going to go to Alabama for college. There wasn't much they could do about it because I had a full scholarship; well, the reality was that I would get a full scholarship anywhere I wanted to go to college. My parents got right on the phone and told me that I was not going to be going to school there, despite the fact that I had already signed the contract. Well, lucky for everyone I was under eighteen and the contract became null and void. All I knew was that I wanted to get back to America and train in America. I was done. I was done with everyone and everything. I wanted to be training with people I cared about and respected.

After I was stopped in my tracks from going to Alabama to swim, I got a call from the coach at the University of Texas at Austin, Richard Quick. At this point Texas had just won its second national championship. The team was made up of world record holders, Olympian and National Team members, and was considered one of the best teams in the world. Richard had learned about me from one of the girls on the team as I was not on his radar during the '84 Olympic Games. This was the team that I wanted to be part of; on the other hand, I was also afraid to go somewhere with so many other great swimmers where success would be hard to come by and garnering any praise would be even more difficult. But being part of the best program in the country resonated with me, so I decided to welcome the challenge. Really I welcomed the identity of saying that I swim for Texas.

I returned to the States at the beginning of the summer to train and swim in various highly competitive meets around the country before I would return to England for European Trials. At this point, I was untethering from my connection to England as I saw a pathway back to America. When it came time to swimming at Trials, I was phoning it in. I didn't have anything in the well. I couldn't fake whatever I need to fake to swim or interact with Paul in any shape or form. With June retired, I had stepped into the winning position which was still not good enough. When it came time to be selected for the team I was overlooked. One could look at the situation in that it was a much smaller team that went that year, or one could look at the fact that Paul was back to selecting the National Team and I wasn't getting past that gate no matter what. I knew Pat couldn't come to my rescue on this one since the stated reason was they had to take a smaller team. There was no leeway to pursue any other explanation at that point.

My continued disappointment was wrapped in another colorful version of lies that everyone accepted as truth. This continued disappointment became even more motivation for me to return to America and get the training I needed with some of the best swimmers in the world. In order to make that happen I had to catch up with my schooling in a hurry. That fall I attended high school back in Madison. We worked out my schooling for me to graduate in December so I could start school at the University of Texas at Austin that January.

After the holidays, I headed down to Austin in my new car to start winter training with my new teammates. I'd gotten to know some of them on my recruiting trip the prior summer. I knew Richard's workouts were good, hard, and I could excel with them. Going to Texas was part of the American swimming dream. One being in America, and two training with gold medalists and world record holders. I was keeping the company that I wish to emulate and be.

The one thing that hadn't changed along the way was my desire to drink and arriving at college allowed me to blend in, kind of. I quickly found my way to the partiers on the team. They had what they referred to as the "freshman award," which was the first person in the freshman class to puke from drinking. Even though I was the only freshman to start in the second semester I still managed to win this award.

I had this idea that I could party hard and swim hard. It was what made me such a great swimmer. It was like part of my training and accomplishing my goals, my internal praise if you will, to mess up and yet still rise to the top in competition. It became what I lived for, how close to the edge I could go and still be great. It was my internal fuck-you to the world that wasn't telling me what it was doing and nobody around me would say anything. My measurement of success was to swim fast and stay in school. They, everyone around me, the athletic department, coach and parents, didn't really care what I did in school other than be eligible. I knew what the expectations were of me and thrived to barely meet them.

I found myself so happy to be back in the States, and with my new teammates I was swimming fast again. I had the freshness of a new coach and a new program. There were two foreign swimmers on the team: me and one other who wasn't eligible to swim internationally because of apartheid. At this point, my American accent returned. One could say that there was just one. I didn't feel like I was British at this point and had dreams and aspirations of representing the USA one day. I was back to leading a double life of embodying American patriotism and my loyalty to my father and our lineage.

That double life carried over into how I would develop my relationship with Richard. I had to learn how to deal with Richard because that was a whole other issue of concern for me. I was battling the image that I had for myself of what every coach thought of me while also wanting to please my new coach. What came with pleasing a coach was how I performed in practice. I knew I was an excellent workout swimmer and could rise to any challenge that was presented.

All that didn't prevent me from finding my way towards the partying crowd; it was how I managed to live with the torment that I was plagued with on a consistent basis. Despite those voices, there was always something so deep in my core that was driven by integrity and I demanded that of those around me, despite the fact that I wasn't in it for my own issues outside of the sexual abuse. I could see it clearly in others, hence my constant fighting with Paul and Richard was no different.

Early on in my training with Richard, he gave us a set of 4 x 50 on 32.5 seconds all-out sprint timed with a 200 easy in between. I was swimming with a teammate, and my teammate was being timed by the assistant coach while I was being timed by Richard. I would come into the wall a full body length ahead of my teammate and Richard would yell out a slower time than my teammate was getting from the coach timing her. I was particular about not leaving early off the wall and knew I left precisely on time. I was precise in my training as I perfected pushing off the wall for my intervals; it was extremely important to me to not leave early. I swam fast to get praise and my driving factor was being compromised in this scenario.

When Richard was yelling out my times wrong I started to yell back at him that he was wrong during my five seconds of rest I spent arguing with him. Every time I touched the wall my frustration grew as he continued to yell out the times wrong. After significant arguing and complaining, I pushed off late by 2.5 seconds and went on the 35 instead of the 32.5 on one of the 50's. As I came into the wall, sprinting, all out, Richard reached down and grabbed my arm as I stretched it out. As I was doing that he yanked me right out of the water across the pool deck several feet. I started to immediately hyperventilate while I was crying, barely able to speak fluidly. I explained to him, "I misread the clock." I was actually lying here, so don't feel so sorry for me. I didn't give up on speed, but pushed off late in a fuck-you way. I found myself having to cry my way out of this moment out of fear of whatever was next.

I found myself in this quandary with Richard where I was letting loose with talking back and advocating for myself and creating this version of myself that wasn't entirely representative of me. I was building a false personality of myself as a way to protect myself from my coach harming me. It was a knee-jerk reaction that had become a part of my swimmer's persona. It was also a reaction to a coach lacking integrity. This abusive event from Richard was no different than what I had experienced with Paul when it came to integrity.

Richard didn't want to be called out any more than I wanted to be called out. He was the coach and he won every time in that scenario like Paul had won every time in any scenario that was presented. All that event did was drive me to train harder and not speak up—it was a conforming moment.

Due to my late arrival in the middle of the season, NCAA came around quickly that year. Qualifying for NCAA didn't get you a spot on the Texas team even many top colleges would only have a few swimmers qualify. I was swimming on such a strong team we had to leave people behind. One of the blessings of my talent was that I could swim the full range of sprint to distance and was good enough for all the relays as well. My freshman year I qualified for all four events from 100 Freestyle to the mile and all the races in between.

Like back in England, I had that same fear about not being selected for the team despite my level of talent. I was concerned that Richard would leave me behind for someone who only qualified for one event. I always felt that I had to do more or whatever I was doing wasn't enough. Then there was the issue of being a foreigner and stepping aside for one of the Americans on the team.

When it came time for NCAA's that year, I placed in the top 8 of all my events and what was even more impressive was that I was sixth in 100 Free and sixth in the mile and finaled in all events in between. My contribution to the team score far exceeded the narrow gap that we won NCAA's by that year. I was part of my first championship team at Texas and the third one in a row for the team. A tradition at the University of Texas is to light the famous clock tower in the center of campus with the number one in burnt orange. The excitement of winning and being associated with greatness was exactly what I had wanted to be part of as a little girl. I was starting to feel a bond with the best college program in the country.

All this excitement and being part of something great had to come to an end for the summer as it was time to return to England for World Championships and the Commonwealth Games. Off I went back to my condo in Wigan and started to train for the rest of the summer with Keith. While I loved my British teammates and training with Keith, I also had to return to Paul selecting the team and coaching me again. Not to mention not being able to have my coach be at our international competitions. It was like I was without a coach and a country.

I had settled into being American and now I was going to have to don my British cap once more as well as my accent to blend in again. That in itself was a lot of work. My blood and lineage were all British, but in reality my family was living in America and referred to as the American cousins.

Since we had two major competitions that summer, we qualified for both competitions at one trial; however, to make the World Championship Team you had to be in the top two and the Commonwealth Games was top three. A much smaller team was going to World Championships in Madrid, Spain. The competitions were about three weeks apart from the end of the Games until we moved on to World Championships. All this meant was that I was going to be spending months around Paul.

I felt like the year in America and the recent success in college with the fastest swimmers in the world gave me enough distance to give me the strength and wisdom to manage it. It was clear that I wasn't going to be training with Paul at camp, and I was placed into the sprint group again with a different coach. I liked swimming there because it was easy, although too much sprinting would deteriorate all the endurance that I had built up training for Richard. I knew this was the sacrifice I needed to make to deal with the double life that I was living.

Despite the distance I put between myself and Paul, his presence and torment wasn't going away. We had a team-building event of sorts complete with self-inflicted humiliation and inappropriate skits influenced by the coaches. I was never one who wanted to participate in those. Early on in our time together as a team I learned that Paul had started to spread rumors about me that I was a pothead. The problem I had with this rumor was that I had smoked pot but it was just a couple of times and not a regular habit. My guilt over the couple of times of doing something illegal and against competition rules kept me silent. I wouldn't have tested positive and I hadn't tested positive for any illegal substance, either performance-enhancing or recreational. The sad part of this scenario was I knew actual teammates who were doing both of these things. I had a uncompromising standards when it came to clean performance having witnessed the East Germans' cheating regimen and I had to compete against them. I felt so defeated by the lie and having to face and overcome yet another rumor that Paul was pushing through the coaching circles and the selection committee.

The rebel in me was proud of my wrongdoing since it went with that fuck-you, I'm tough a person, while the integrity part of me knew that wasn't entirely true. I actually didn't like pot when I tried it; it wasn't my thing; drinking was my thing. At this point, I was over eighteen, and it was legal to drink in England at my age so that wasn't going to work like it could have when I was fifteen in Rome when I'd tested with a significant level for alcohol in my system. All I knew at this point was that it angered me that I was going to have act my way out of this situation and didn't have a plan for the lie that I was confronted with.

The first of the competitions was the Commonwealth Games in Scotland. The Games include all the countries under the Queen's rule. As a result, Great Britain is broken up into individual countries, meaning that I would be representing England for this competition, while the World Championships would be for Britain with a much smaller team with a combination of the best from all the countries. I had already won the 100, 200 and finished second in the 400 Freestyle to qualify for both teams.

When we arrived in Edinburgh for the Games it was a similar set up as the Olympic Games with the athlete village and all the countries housed in the same place. With these Games came many formal invites to meet with hosts, and in this case, there were many events planned with each member of the royal family. Here I was once again being invited as the representative for our team to meet with the Queen of England along with representatives from all the other countries.

The event was a cocktail party that took place in a private outdoor patio space in the village. The Queen walked around and had a social chat with everyone there. We were told that we couldn't take any pictures, not that I adhered to that. At that event, I had one eye on the Queen's interactions and one eye engaged with my new friends or friends from the other countries who I had gotten to know during our years of competition. Arguably one could say that I was standing in front of one of the most powerful people in the world and I was carrying a secret of pain from sexual abuse and torture that I had endured up to this point. Why couldn't I have said something? Not that it was the place to do that. Surely my connection to power was starting to become very clear in my life. What other eighteen-year-olds had engaged with the highest level of society? Albeit I had trained for this moment my whole life, to consort and be one with the highest level of society. I was mostly thinking my dad was surely going to be proud of me for having crossed paths and having interacted with the Queen. This was not merely a chance encounter; it was earned and chance at the same time. I realized there was something about me that was leading me down this path of influence.

These events didn't stop coming in my direction as next up was meeting Diana, Princess of Wales and Prince Phillip, Duke of Edinburgh at another engagement while at the Games. Meeting Princess Diana, who was considered terribly shy to the public, came across to me as dreadfully fearful. I saw something in her that I saw in me: a secret of sorts. It was something that I could detect in others who experienced some level of pain or wrongdoing. There was a bond in our souls of both holding back from the world. In the usual fashion of engagement there was the standard line of questioning of the "what are you competing in" variety and the basic pleasantries. Either way we had a moment of an unspoken bond. We knew each other's pain.

After the social events, the Games had yet to start, Paul was not letting up on the harassment whenever we interacted. This time he chose to hound me about my weight. He became obsessed with my body and my body fat. He would have the trainers constantly measure me. While I wasn't training with him he started to grab parts of my body and squeeze my hips, or my ass and thighs, commenting about their size. It was all embraced with those creepy eyes of his that would undress you. Paul was also threatening my participation on relays despite the fact that I was the fastest swimmer on the team. He always seemed to find something to hang over my head to maintain the control over me that he was looking for.

When it came time to swim my best event, the 200 Freestyle, Princess Diana was in attendance as the royal guest. I felt a kinship in our pain that came out in my swim when I was touched out for fourth place by a teammate of sorts from Britain, who on that day was representing the Scottish team. I would also swim later in one of the relays in that evening's competition. It would be here that I would have a shining performance by bringing us from behind to take the silver medal behind the Australian team.

Being the star of that relay race was another opportunity for me to talk to Pat the journalist after my race. This time she was curious about my training in the States and asked if I felt like I was American or British, or in this case English. She wanted to know if I ever wanted to represent the United States of America. I always answered that question the same: I express my loyalty to my father by following in his footsteps and exceed his accomplishments by being an Olympian. Pat wasn't letting up on this line of questioning around my nationality when, in that moment, I was going to be on the podium for England.

My father was also in the stands. I know he too was actually proud of my swim. There was always going to something wrong with it, but in reality I swam fast—it was my leg that pulled us into second. When I saw my father after my race there was an acceptance in my performance. Like it made sense for him to watch me swim that race and the money they invested in my career was validated in that moment. When that was validated I could get a moment of love and kindness, or really acceptance, of his approval. It wasn't like the little girl praise, but it met a level of satisfaction when I saw my dad. My dad was actually approving of me and this took me away from the struggles that I was having with Paul. It didn't mean that Paul wasn't harassing me like he did; it just meant that I had a little time where life was more manageable when my dad was on board with me.

I finished up those Games with two silver medals and did okay in my individual events. However, I mostly remember the amount of pain I was in swimming my individual events. At this point in my career and life I had only learned one coping skill to deal with pain and that was to drink—even my father recommended a drink to take the edge off of stress. I wasn't exactly hiding what I was doing, especially since I was drinking with my teammates. It wasn't just my teammates and fellow athletes who were drinking; the Games' events were also filled with alcohol.

On our final night of competition we went somewhere in Edinburgh where they had a massive tent set up for us with shots of whiskey covering the length of the table. You could slam as many as you wanted. There was a point where Paul was actually pushing me to drink more. I had already started and then here he was feeding me shots. Technically I was old enough to drink and it wasn't just Paul but the other coaches as well. As my eyes blurred and my senses started to waver, it was then that Paul started to take care of me, with his dogged hands all over my body. The amount of alcohol that I drank drove me to a blackout at some point. I was in the hands of the coaches who made sure that I got back via safe transportation to the athlete village. All I knew was that my guard was down, I wasn't functioning, and was open to whatever was going to come in the way of help and not getting in trouble. Essentially I was mostly concerned with not being kicked off the World Championship team as we were leaving the next morning to go to London and train before we went off to Madrid for the competition.

What was exciting about these World Championships was that my American coach Richard was going to be there with several of my Texas teammates. Everyone always admired the power of the Americans.

I was no different. I wanted to be that and be a part of that. It didn't take away from the fact that I loved everyone on the British team. But I wanted to associate myself with the power of the American dream and that was what those swimmers represented to me. They were many of the best in the world in their events. We had a couple of swimmers on our team who also held that title, but not in the depth of the American team. The idea of having "my coach" there who was one of the USA Team coaches gave me the pride and strength that I desperately wanted to have.

The importance of having "my coach" present was more for me to have another place to turn away from Paul and not feel like I had to engage with him as he desired. It wasn't like Richard gave me much attention at all; it was knowing that he was there. My teammates were the comfort and safety that I was gravitating towards.

In good Spanish fashion they had their daily siesta almost on par with a swimmer's regular life schedule of swimming twice a day with a nap after morning practice. The only problem with this siesta was that our hotel was in the middle of nowhere so I would leave the hotel to get away from Paul who had started to come by my room again after the drinking incident in Edinburgh. It was like it opened the door to have access to me again. I would try and walk around to find something to eat. I came back to the hotel one time and Pat was in the lobby, doing her usual story prep, going through her notes. I could see that she was concerned about me. It was her observations that I was watching. I knew she was watching the interactions between Paul and me. There were purposeful stares away from her notes. I remember getting into an argument with Paul there as he threatened to pull me off the relays again and he basically said that he would let me know if I was going to be swimming again during that meet. I didn't swim as I would have liked; I placed 9th in the 200 Free and missed finals which was another letdown—not as bad as the Olympics, but a letdown to say the least.

For the remainder of the meet over the next several days I took it that I wasn't going to be swimming for the rest of the meet based on my interactions with Paul. Then after several days of known drinking with my fellow teammates who were competing, I got called into Paul's room who told me that I was in fact swimming on the last day. I know he knew what I was doing. I know he wanted to watch me destroy myself in front of my American coach. I could see in his eyes that it brought him great joy to watch me fail and suffer. I couldn't get out of the trap that I had found myself in. I know it is no shock to anyone that I swam poorly. I was bad for business back in America with my coach.

It wasn't just me that was feeling the effects of Paul's ways and coaching tactics, not to mention how he was sexually pursuing every female on the team. After the summer of being around him far too long for everyone, a couple of teammates, including the team captain at the time, called the British Swimming Association to complain about his ways with the swimmers. Shortly after they called to complain, the Association made a public announcement that he was going to be the head coach for the 1988 Olympic Team. I knew that was the end of me. I now had nowhere to turn or go. It was going to be my fate to be at his mercy.

When I returned to the US after World Championships, there was a distrust that seemed to have seeped its way into my relationship with Richard. At least that was the story that I was telling myself. At the same time, I had academic issues because I wasn't going to class either. I knew what I needed to do to be eligible and still swim. I was trying to do exactly that and nothing more. This was proving to be a strain on my relationship with Richard both in and out of the pool. I could ride on the post big-competition blues for a few weeks into school, combined with the unknown/known partying that one does in college. I was riding all those excuses and when they started to run out, I started to complain about my shoulders hurting me when I needed to get out of practice. They were hurting me, but I wouldn't know what pain was at this point in my career. I was in so much internal torment that everything was pain. However, I felt the most acute pain in my shoulders as that was where the most pressure was on my body when I swam.

As result of my injury and excuses, my training started to falter so much so that when it came time for NCAA's that year I turned in an extremely poor showing by both my and Texas swimming standards. We still won and I was on a championship winning team again. With one less event to be able to compete in I shied away from swimming the mile because of my shoulder problems. I was given several shots and prescribed an anti-inflammatory to address the pain. The reality was it was all the internal pain that I wasn't talking about. My shoulders were bothering me, but I knew in my heart it was the anguish of the world I was in that was really causing the pain. I let up complaining about the pain when I was scheduled for surgery in May of the following year.

What I really wanted was to not represent Great Britain anymore and try and represent the USA. I couldn't take another moment with Paul. In order to pursue that I had to sit out of international competition for a year and my shoulder surgery would get me out of going back to England for the summer. So I opted for the surgery knowing that I wouldn't miss any competition. It was the perfect cover to make the switch.

I went back to my parents' home in Wisconsin to have the surgery performed by one of the most prominent orthopedic surgeons in the country. I had both shoulders operated on at the same time. I did this while my parents were out of the country. I had found myself all alone in the hospital, or really, in life again. I ended up checking myself out of the hospital and driving myself back to my parents' empty house a day after surgery. I was in this huge house all by myself with no arms to speak of as far as movement went. I had heavy duty pain medication they gave me after the surgery, but I never wanted to take that. I had become so used to the pain I was carrying that it truly became my friend of sorts.

I left my parents' home and drove back to Texas with the idea of doing recovery or something. When I returned there, I was just out of my slings for my shoulders, I had zero physical therapy lined up with the athletic trainer at Texas, as it was out of season and school was essentially closed. When I returned to practice and had to start training without full motion in either shoulder. It was one of the most painful experiences that I had ever been through in training. What made all of this worse was that I was swimming in a meet three weeks out from surgery without any recovery. Every single person around me thought this was okay. In fact, a new assistant coach complained to Richard when I pulled out of one of my races at that meet and that caused a rift between Richard and I going forward.

I had this conflicting drive inside of me to focus on going to the Olympics, along with the pressure of my father who wanted to see the greatness that he believed was in me, and finally me wanting to be able to just be in the grace in my swimming that I knew was the real me inside all of the pain. I couldn't access that part of me; it was so deeply buried that I had lost all sense of self. I wanted someone to magically see my pain and know what I needed to get out of the hell that I found my myself in.

As the summer progressed, I was determined I could do something about not wanting to return to England to swim for the British team. I finally got full recovery of my shoulders by sheer will and force. What was great during this time is that I loved my teammates; they were amazing. I couldn't have found a better group of women to train with and become friends with. I believe that is what helped me refocus my attention in the fall to take my training for the Olympics seriously again.

I didn't know how I was going to go about changing countries. The problem with wanting to switch to try and swim for the USA during this time was that it required effort, paperwork, and communication. That was something that I wasn't good at or able to do. Who was I going to talk to about this? What was I going to say as my reasons for doing so? It was a much harder team to make so why would I do that anyway? I carried this idea in my mind in hopes that someone would read a sign above my head that just said, "Help me." The invisible messages that I was putting out into the world should be intuitively known by those around me.

The notion of the country change allowed me to train hard again. Due to the fact that I just had shoulder surgery I was able to move my way into the sprint/middle distance lane. I was finally starting to train fast. My teammate and I were consistently ranked first and second in the 200 for most of the year. I felt like I was training for me and not having to train for the mile because we needed the points. The success that I was experiencing in my races was giving me the internal confidence that I could represent the USA in the next Games, especially since they took top six in the 200 Freestyle for the relay. As the year progressed so did my swimming. I was swimming as fast as I ever had. At the same time, I couldn't begin to describe the dark cloud that was looming within me.

I had developed this reputation with Richard of being a troublemaker. If something went wrong it was easy to just say it was me and move on. I took it all in and hardly said anything; the last thing I was going to do was rat someone out or redirect the allegations away from me. I figured I could handle the criticism better than someone else. Then the day came along when I was accused of not including one of the swimmers in my lane by not talking to her, despite the fact that I would lead the lane and only speak to the person that went behind me. It was not like you got a lot of rest on the walls, and one learned how to have conversations in five second intervals when you trained at this level and still wanted some kind of social experience. After that complaint I was moved out of that lane and into the middle distance lane, which to me was the distance lane. It broke my heart that I wasn't getting the training that I was thriving with. I let Richard know in my complaining and was not shy or holding back how I felt about it. That went nowhere except to close the door on ever moving back to that lane to train. And so began the next series of events of distrust for my coach.

The NCAA's moved closer, and being an Olympic year, it was especially important to get the training, the rest, and fitness timed just right for all the competitions that year. There was generally a three week tapering off leading up to a major event. During this time, our energy levels went crazy due to the light workouts and the increased sprinting and pacing that we were doing. It was also a time to get oneself into trouble, and that was certainly something that I found my way to. A few days before NCAA's and before we moved into the hotel as a team, a few friends came into town and we went to our favorite Mexican restaurant, where they made their margaritas with Everclear (180 proof), with a three drink maximum allowed. I took that as a place to start, or rather a dare if you will, five drinks later, I knew I had destroyed the zone that I had created within my body.

I soon found myself thinking destructive thoughts. The shame and the guilt was killing me inside. I wanted to drop out of school and hide. I was running out of desire to keep doing what I was doing. At the same time I needed to rise up to the challenge and perform for my school and be part of one of the greatest team programs of all time. I had qualified in all three events and was still swimming fast despite the wreckage that I was hiding from the team except the teammates who were there with me that Everclear night. At some level there was pride in performing with my demons at the same time and then there was this "why is this happening to me" question.

At that NCAA's I swam pretty well, placing fourth again behind three USA Olympians in 200 Freestyle, and in one of my other events, the 800 Freestyle relay, we broke the school record that subsequently stood for over 20 years. On the outside I swam good enough for my dad to praise me for my success. I swam good enough for Richard to not be as mad as he usually was with me. I got a marginal smile out of him, which spelled success to me.

The success of winning three championships and five in a row for the school meant that the last classes had won all four years and now I was part of winning three of those. I once again enjoyed the celebration with my teammates as they lit the tower up orange. Soon my torture of having to go back to England and be around Paul was causing me anxiety that I couldn't say anything about. So, instead I pretty much dropped out of school and stopped attending in what I would say was a cry for help. I had also missed any opportunity to switch over to being American for the 1988 Games. There was no discussion. I didn't say anything and nothing happened.

My demise in school was showing up in my training and in my attitude towards how I was speaking to Richard about my training and what I needed from him. He was strategizing how to remove me from the team for the summer. Richard called me into his office just as the semester was coming to a close to tell me that I wasn't going to be able to train with him that summer leading up to the Games because he was only going to train the Americans. It felt like someone had thrust a dagger in my heart when he said that. He did say that he called another coach, Mark Schubert, and asked if I could train with him in Florida. I knew it was an equally great option that Richard had found for me, but the idea of being rejected for not being an American just about killed me.

CHAPTER 13

Frozen

Arriving in Florida felt like a fresh start as well as an opportunity to swim with another great coach. At this point in his career, Mark had coached more gold medalists than any other coach, so showing up on his team was a much-welcomed opportunity for me. Plus he was accepting foreigners on his team, which I was at the time despite the comings and goings of my British accent.

Whenever I started swimming with a new coach there was that need to make a great first impression. It made it easier to settle into the coaching relationship, at least from my perspective. I had a value in the relationship which needed to be known from the get-go. They had this huge scoreboard at the pool in Florida and one of the first things Mark had me do was a timed 200 freestyle for the whole team to see. It was an effort in collective practice shaming if you will. However, that isn't what happened. I actually swam extremely fast and became an instant favorite of Mark's. It also confused him as to why Richard didn't want to train me after he witnessed that swim. My relationship with Mark started off on the right foot. His interest in me as mine in him immediately opened up that mutual trust I had been searching for in a coach.

Even with a new coach I was the same person who looked for fun, or who rather tried to keep the demons at bay. It didn't take long for me to find my way towards the drinkers on the team. At first I was hesitant to drink and wanted to behave and act as if I was doing all the right things to be the Olympian I was and would be again. That lasted until I learned that Mark had no sense of smell and wouldn't know if we were drinking the night before. The only requirement was to be at practice on time and swim fast in practice, which I could always do.

I stayed and trained with Mark all the way up to Olympic Trials that were held later in the summer due to the Olympic Games falling in late September that year. That summer was filled with many competitions around the US, and then altitude training in Flagstaff before I would head back to England for the Trials. It was agreed that I wasn't going to need to entirely rest for my Olympic Trials due to me most likely easily making the team based on being highly world ranked and one of the fastest in the world at the time, and easily the fastest British swimmer. I was also free and happy swimming with Mark. As I settled in with him, I was able to let go some of my sabotage behavior and focus on training more. The faster I got, the more willing I was to show up for myself. When we started on our travels and altitude training we had curfew and a stricter lifestyle to keep when it was with Mark and the team. I was good with that and didn't violate the rules when we were together.

When it came time to leave Mark it was hard for me because I had become attached to him, my teammates, and how he trained me. Mark knew how to get the best swimmer out of me, in ways that I had always desired to, but hadn't found it in other coaches quite like I found with Mark. I was finally training with a coach who had my best interests as a swimmer and athlete. Up to that point I had only felt that with Keith. I needed a coach who could coach me to the fulfillment of my dreams. I knew Mark would be able to do that for me. It was sad to leave Mark and return to England, but I knew we would be reconnected in Seoul soon.

I flew out of Flagstaff at the very last moment to return to England with only a few days to recover from jet lag before Olympic Trials would start. I was confident in me that I was the best swimmer and it was finally my time to shine.

I arrived at Trials out of sorts because I was having to adjust without my coach really being there, combined with seeing the new up and coming swimmers, and of course my old teammates that I loved. At this point, I was more comfortable training in the US with my American Olympians and my teammates.

The pool deck was busy with swimmers and coaches all over the place. It was overwhelming the level of chaos going on. The reality was that it was the same level of chaos going on within me. I presented myself as calm and confident when it came to swimming, but inside I was torn up with the anguish that I spent all day pushing down in practice. I had perfected the gift of avoidance from within me so well that I didn't even know I was doing it. I only become aware when my world was rocked.

Again Paul was persistent in his efforts to rock my confidence. It didn't take long from my arrival on the pool deck for Paul to be in my space threatening me with his control over me. He wanted to make sure I was aware that I would be suffering under his coaching. We silently agreed on our hatred for each other; the only problem was that he wasn't shy about moving in close with his gestures to see if I had changed my ways and if I was going to be friendly to him this time. My blatant rejection is what set off our struggle every time. He needed to know if I was willing to accept his sexual advances. My anger was very clear that was a no. My anger towards him was viewed as my immaturity by others.

I hadn't felt that level of anger for almost two years since the last time I saw him after the World Championships. Knowing he was the head coach I was at his mercy again. I knew making the team was based on time, so swimming fast was all I needed to do to make the Olympic Team. I also knew from swimming with Mark that I was on fire when it came to performing.

As the Trials started, I won the 400 Freestyle on the first day and qualified for that event; however, I was clearly a prima donna at this time and didn't want to swim that race at the Olympics. I really just wanted to swim the 200 Free, 100 Free, and 100 Fly, which was a new event—I had transformed myself into being an endurance sprinter. I didn't have the mental capacity to swim the 400 like I used to be able to. I knew I couldn't handle the level of pain it involved. My love has always been the 200 Free—it was my event; it was the one that I felt the most defined by since I was a young girl. I also knew swimming the 400 Free at the Olympics would force me to train with Paul again, and I just couldn't do it or even think about the idea of it, so I pulled out of the event. It made somebody else happy that they got to go the Olympics because of it.

When I got on my high horse there was no convincing or stopping me from going any other way than towards wherever I was headed, good or bad. As the meet carried on, I made the team in the 100 Free, winning the event as well as the 100 Fly. On the last day was the 200 Free; I was already on the Olympic team so this event was just for show, if you will.

The night before the event I was in the lobby restaurant eating dinner with my parents and in walked Paul. He came over to my table and placed his creepy hands on my body as he spoke to my family. My mother in her kind way interacted with him like he was her best friend. I was frozen in the moment watching this interaction only thinking to myself what a monster this person was and how much I couldn't stand him. Paul went on about training camp after Trials which was going to be in the South of France. I couldn't bear the idea of being in the South of France with him. I needed for my dad in that moment to see my pain but he had never seen my true pain; he had only seen my pain if I wasn't going to perform—that was all he seemed to care about. In my grumpy and irritated manner I asked to leave the conversation saying I needed to rest for my race tomorrow, the last one left and the most important one. I left that table with so much anger and hate while I was trying to figure out how I could get out of going to the South of France and how I could train with Mark in America.

When I started down this path of questions, I had a wild idea to help with my jet lag and sleeping issue, so I bought a fifth of whiskey and brought it back to my room. I was tossing and turning. I wanted to just sleep and wake up for my race the next day. I needed to shut everything off twirling inside of me. I ended up drinking the whole thing that night and woke up drained, exhausted and out of sorts. I had been here before and figured I could hide it and manage it like I always did.

I was so tired and exhausted that when I swam it felt like I was going in slow motion. I didn't have that fifth gear that I usually could turn on when it was needed. I was completely out of fuel. I ended up placing third in my event with a terrible time. I was so embarrassed. I had made the Olympic Team but was not going to be swimming one of the events in which I was highly ranked. I had qualified to swim three events, plus all the relays, but I had no emotional connection to any of them. They weren't the races that defined me as a swimmer, only the 200 Free could do that. How was I going to manage and get through this devastating realization of my fate?

At this point I wondered what I would say to get out of training with Paul. I was so adamant after my bad swim, regretting that I didn't taper for the meet and viewed that as the reason for my loss. I wanted to go back to America to right a wrong and get back to my form again. The only way I saw that as a possibility was if I returned to America to train with Mark. I sold my parents on this idea. I told them I was going to say that I needed to go back to Austin to finish school which was also where the USA Olympic Trials were being held at the University of Texas Swim Center. I could get away with the lie for who can deny someone their education? I had to tell Paul that I wasn't going to training camp in the South of France and that I would meet them at the airport to catch the flight to Seoul with the rest of the British Olympic Team. It was a contentious conversation and not one that I handled well at all. Success for me was getting a yes, at whatever personal cost.

While my parents had bought into this madness, they didn't exactly help with my plan. I had no idea how I was going to get to America, let alone Austin. I left Trials and headed to Heathrow Airport with the intention of buying a ticket to any city in America and then I would buy a ticket from that city to Austin. I just needed to get to the States. My inner self was running from a monster that I felt was sitting on my shoulders all the time, screaming in my head the same images and words from the night of the rape coupled with the Fame theme song playing in my mind. "Fame costs." That was all I could think about.

When I got to the airport I wasn't prepared to not be able to get a flight to the States. I didn't anticipate, that it was peak holiday season in the UK and everyone was going on holiday at that time. My determination was now driving me. I had committed to a path and was going to make it happen. I didn't even have a choice to go to the South of France at this point; I had already said I had to go back to school. This was a one-way ticket to destruction and I was the only one on the train.

After waiting around all day and not being able to book a flight, I didn't have a place to go and stay, so I walked around the airport trying to find somewhere to lay down and sleep or at least rest. I'm not sure why I didn't think to check into a hotel, but I didn't. I found a spot in the stairwell at the Hilton that was connected to the airport. I doubt I was completely sober as I'm sure I found my way to something to help me deal with the world that I had found myself in. I crashed there and then got up the next morning to see if there was a flight I could get on. I checked all the airlines, the best I could, not knowing who to start with first. I ended up doing this for three days, until I finally got a flight out to Philadelphia. It was like escaping from prison; the only problem was that I was still inside my own mental prison.

When I finally made it to Austin, I was happy to see my friends, some of whom made the Olympic Team while others were dealing with disappointment and sadness. A sadness that I knew only too well. I had just made the British Olympic Team again and here I was doing everything to destroy my childhood dream. I was carrying so much hurt and pain. I felt like I was a cartoon character with a sign above my head that showed all my pain. I thought by now someone could recognize what I was experiencing. I had convinced myself of how bad I was as a person inside. I had very few coping skills to deal with anything other than swimming with a coach who cared about me and who I could respond to. I had found that in Mark. When I left London I was chasing that moment.

My time was short in Austin since I only had a week before Mark would leave with the USA Team and I needed to find somewhere else to train. I was hell-bent on not returning to England which would lead me to the South of France and Paul. I couldn't do it.

My last night in Austin would be another defining moment on my path of destruction. Mark and the team all went out to dinner after Trials to celebrate those who made the team and really console those who had not. At that dinner I kept getting up from the table to head to the bar, slamming shots, and then returning to the table. Before I knew it, some of my friends and teammates were being taken back to their hotel while my other teammates and friends were all partying on Sixth Street, the famous Austin party street. I was proud of my school's partying of course because I was good at it and knew all the bartenders despite my underage drinking. I left that dinner with the alcohol not fully into my system and by the time I got downtown and parked my car at my friends hotel, I was unaware that I had started to blackout; I guess that is how a blackout works.

At the same time that I was in a blackout, I called my teammates who went back to the hotel and they wanted me to come pick them up so they could join the other swimmers that were partying on Sixth Street. The only problem with this plan was that I had lost my car in the parking lot, well my rental car, since they all looked the same, especially when you are drunk. A friend of mine stopped at every car asking me if it was the car. I have a spotty memory during this time that leads me to come to driving on the freeway. I knew at that moment how drunk I was and that I needed to get off the road. I had a thought that I needed to protect myself and others. I took the next exit and pulled over. I opened the door of the car and fell out of the car onto a red ant hill. If you have ever been bitten by one red ant you know how painful they are. I was bitten all over my body, just covered in bites.

When I was passed out, someone called me a cab to send me back to my apartment—all these events are now a general blur. I could finally disconnect from the torment inside of me. I was running out of ways to escape from the pain and be an Olympian at the same time. Right then I didn't care about that. I was so hurt and disappointed by my career and the struggles that I accepted that no one really cared. Yet I wanted someone to see me and see that I was destroying my life, yet no one saw it. What more could I do to make it clear and evident that there was something wrong going on with me? I just didn't have any skills to communicate anything other than I wasn't swimming well.

When I got up in the morning I had a flight to catch to Florida. Nothing was there, no coach, but only another friend and teammate that I was going to hang out with until I had to return to London to catch my flight to Seoul, South Korea. I would like to say in my story this is where

I was making good decisions, but the reality was me making even worse choices as the days got closer to returning to England.

My ideas were, "let's drink until the bar closes and then drive down to Key West at 2 a.m." not knowing it was an almost four-hour drive and dangerous. We drove there just to be holed up in a hotel with my friend with her eating disorder and my eating and drinking disorder that I referred to as having alcohol-induced bulimia. This lasted for a few weeks with limited training until the very last minute of needing to arrive back in London for the team flight to Seoul.

The flight to Seoul was long and it made it longer due to being confined on a plane with Paul. Pat was also on that flight, but she was off doing what she did, looking busy and hiding her drinking with an eye on what was going on around her. On that flight Paul made sure he asserted his authority as the head coach of the team. I would like to say word for word what the conversation was about, or any of these conversations, yet regardless of the different words, the tone, the touching, and the intended result was always the same. If I wasn't submitting to him, I was going to be swimming in an event that I did not want, and wrongfully removed from my earned spot. It was clear that no matter what I did, he was in charge and he was going to decide my fate. I constantly rebelled against that power and each time thinking I could win.

In Seoul, all the countries were housed together in one Olympic Village and the American team was housed near the British team. I was excited to see my teammates and coaches and was also excited to see many other friends from over the past four years. Since the last Olympics I had gotten to know many of the American swimmers, from either my team or swimming against them. There were so many special people on that team that year, one of those being my childhood friend, Jay, whom I knew when I was three years old. He and his family were at the country club pool on that fateful day when I swam a lap and my Olympic dream began. We trained together until I left home to train in England. Here were two of us from the Maple Bluff Country Club swim team that produced five Olympians and never won a meet. Now two of those Olympians, Jay and I, were about to compete together in the Olympic Games.

As my teammates arrived, so did my coaches, both Mark and Richard. I was still feeling the intensity of the rejection from Richard, who not only rejected me but had now rejected the whole Texas Women's Swim Team to take a job at Stanford. I was going to be returning after the Games to a program that at this point did not have a coach. With all this loss around me, the one constant was Mark. Mark had taken care of me all summer to prepare me for the Games. He was still vested in my success when he got to Seoul with Team USA and this made the interactions with Paul more bearable knowing that I had another coach to escape to who gave me direction that I wasn't filtering through my unspoken anger and resentment.

However, training with Mark had its challenges. There were times when our pool time overlapped with the US team and there were times when they weren't there. It was getting to be like taking your hand off the hot stove for a second to have some sense of relief and then I would have to engage with Paul. I would need to get a set from him and have him time me on my splits. I hated having any interaction with him as there was always a dominance and control dynamic.

When I would swim with Mark, I would have times that were amazing and fast. I wasn't killing myself for my poor training or lack thereof and started to tell myself it was my taper. I was swimming sprints and I needed this much taper to get my speed up. The only place where I had speed was in the first lap of my 100 butterfly, which was a relatively new event for me. At our Trials I had won both the 100 Free, 100 Butterfly, and 50 Freestyle and the 400 Freestyle that I turned down. I was swimming world record pace in training on the first 50 of fly. I felt alive and strong as a swimmer. But when practice came around with Paul, I felt like I struggled to just make it to the wall without dying. I found myself in this vicious cycle in the time leading up to the Games.

During our downtime, it was a standard affair for us to either nap or play cards. Since we were all tapered, napping was hard to do with all this extra energy we had to burn so we played spades. Mary Wayte, the USA Olympic Gold medalist in the 200 Free from the 1984 Games, was a fierce competitor. While I didn't have that fierce trait, I was a bit of a card shark. I had met my equal when it came to bringing those traits to a game of cards so we naturally formed a great card-playing partnership. We would play for like eight hours straight against anyone who wanted to lose to us. Over the course of that time we got to know each other really well and especially got to know each other's playing style. It gave me a break from the torment that would otherwise engulf me in anticipation of my performance. I was able to shut down all my thoughts of harm, disappointment, or anything else and just be at the Olympics with my peers and friends. I had this incredible joy and satisfaction of being at the Games as we won card game after game, that at some point a couple of our regular guys who played with us had to start cheating just to get close to a win. It was all in fun.

As the start of the Games neared, so did the arrival of my parents. My father had to cut short an event that was honoring him for his SPF invention in order to make my first swim on the opening day of the Olympics. He traveled with my childhood friend Jay's parents. Jay's mother was dying of Stage 4 cancer. My father took care of her medically, more or less, as her private doctor so she could watch her son compete at the Olympics.

As the Olympic Games kicked off with the opening ceremonies, I stayed behind to watch in the apartment to prepare for my race the next day while most of my teammates attended the ceremonies. As my teammates left, and the rest of the village emptied to a skeleton few, I was left behind to have to interact with Paul. He started to question if I was going to swim fast enough. No encouragement, only disparagement. He made sure that I was aware he was the head coach and that he could put someone else in any of my events. I ignored the comments in my typical fashion of walking away mid-sentence, knowing there was a tear that was starting to well up inside. The dam had so much pressure against it that the wall was starting to crumble.

I went to my room and didn't want the opening ceremonies to end; I didn't want my races to begin. I knew that this was probably my last Games. I knew how tired I was inside. I wanted time to stop in that moment.

That night I heard the excitement of the teams returning to the apartment while I tossed and turned in fear with nothing to quiet the voices of doubt in my head. I woke in the morning after not much sleep in fear and dread. But I knew how to turn that off and just compete. I had perfected ways to silence these voices, and today was no different.

I arrived at the pool for warm-ups. The thrill of the Games and being at that meet was met with the excitement and anticipation of complete joy or complete sadness and no in between. When I was sixteen I was still naive to some degree; I didn't know much about fear—that was something that grew as I became an adult. I now had a lot of it. It wasn't for my race; it was for the idea of the loss that was going to happen after this meet. When it came time to compete, I swam miserably. I knew that was going to set the tone for the rest of the Games.

In between sessions I would visit with my dad and have an explanation ready and prepared for my poor performance. I needed to think of something that would not make my dad irritated at me—it was getting easier and easier to do that. My mother would hear my excuses and actually side with me to shift my dad's disappointment away from me; she was right there carrying on with whatever excuse that she came up with for me. I wanted so desperately for my dad to be understanding and loving. I wanted to know that he could see my pain and help me like he was helping Jay's mom. I watched the joy in my father as he was so caring to Jay's mom, giving her the most loving gift of all—the gift to be able to see and watch her son win a gold medal before her death.

None of that changed how my dad was getting frustrated with me. At the same time, Paul was expressing his authority and power over me as he threatened to pull me out of events if I didn't swim faster. It wasn't like I was the only one swimming poorly; most of our team was. As were many of the Americans. It was especially hard to watch the 200 Freestyle and see that my friend Mary, the reigning gold medalist, place fourth. It was like disappointment on steroids, as I didn't have someone else's success that I could hide and escape behind. We were all swimming badly or at least not up to the expected level of excellence.

As the Games went on, I continued to deliver some of the worst performances of my career. I was known for rising up to the occasion at big meets. I was good at not disappointing others, but this time I had lost that ability. I was disappointing everyone around me. All that did was maintain Paul's harassment of me with snide remarks. He never asked what was wrong or what was going on—it was always a comment about my body, about something sexual in nature, being washed up or past my peak, and to him it was implied that I was too old to be sexually abused; he was into the young ones. He was making that clear every time I swam.

To be clear, I was swimming badly, but that was based on my standards; I was still faster than my peers on the team. As to my non-swimming bad, I wasn't doing anything to write home about. Journalists at the Games didn't have direct contact with the athletes like at our other competitions, so talking to Pat or her observing what was going on wasn't as obvious to pick up on. One of my teammates won the gold, so that was what she wrote home about. All the media attention went his way and rightfully so. I was no longer young and upcoming, as I was old in the athletic world and trying to hang on to my youth, passion, and drive that was about to completely stall out.

Towards the end of the meet as the disappointment racked up, race after race as I continued to swim subpar, after my last individual swim I went to the warm down pool. As I arrived at the pool so did Mark. I went to talk to Mark about my race. Mark was good at finding something positive about my race, or asking questions about it leading me to my own conclusions about my swim. I got to call it what it was for me. As Mark and I were talking, Paul abruptly interjected himself into our conversation to tell me that I was off the relay. He continued to tell me that he was going to put someone younger and more attractive to watch. He wasn't talking about performance; he was talking about his next pursuit. It was clearly evident to me. Paul walked away after dropping that bomb on me. I was fastest in the country in two of the legs of the medley relay and now I wasn't swimming either. I was left defeated and powerless. It was yet another thing that Paul would take away from me.

At that moment, in mid-conversation with Mark, I was so distraught by it all that the only thing I could think of doing was to put on my goggles to catch my tears so Mark or anyone else could not see me crying. I put on my goggles and stood there in front of Mark, which is something no swimmer would do—stand on the pool deck with your goggles on. Then Mark asked me, "Are you going to let him do that?" He was so disturbed by what had just happened and I had no words to explain what was happening. I was so tired and exhausted. I couldn't fight him anymore. I was done. I was done inside. I couldn't do it any longer. I dove in that warm down pool and just cried as I meandered through the water. I had lost the battle. He had sucked dry and drained every ounce of passion that I had for sport right out of me. He had won.

All I wanted was someone to console me and tell me that it was going to be okay. I wanted my bear to comfort me. I wanted someone to tell me that they loved me. All I was doing was filling myself up with shame as I cried my way through the pool.

After I pulled myself together, I went to see my dad to tell him I wasn't swimming in my other races. I desperately wanted the same love that he was giving Jay's mom. I wanted my dad to say, "It's okay my 'Little Annabelle.'" Instead, my dad's only response to me was, "Thanks for wasting my time" and he turned his back on me and walked away. There was nothing. I had lost everything in that moment. I lost the love of my father, my swimming career, and all the little girl's dreams that had now became a nightmare. When there was nothing left to praise, there wasn't any love for me either.

I was left frozen in my tracks as my father was done with me on every level. I was no longer "Little Annabelle" to him; I was no longer his favorite child. In fact I might as well no longer be his daughter. As we parted ways at the Games so did our hearts.

CHAPTER 14

Unwanted

Returning from my second Olympics Games was much harder than from my first and that was hard. I was tired and exhausted inside; I had lost the innocence of the pursuit of praise. My pursuit had turned to darkness while my youth was quickly fading away. As I was coming closer to the end of my swimming career, my heart was broken beyond repair. I didn't know anything besides swimming at this point in my life.

Every part of me wanted to quit swimming when I returned from the Games. I had not planned for that or figured out what I was going to do moving forward. Staying at home and giving up a scholarship was not going to happen. I needed something exciting to help me transition back to life and off the post-Olympic depression.

To my surprise and elation, it was announced that Mark was going to be the head coach at Texas. I felt like I had an ally in Mark who as a coach knew where my talents lay. He would train me for those talents and not just for the greater good for the team. There was a balance between the team contribution and my specialty that I never found with Richard who seemed to make me always sacrifice for the team because I was so versatile as a swimmer. The idea of Mark being my coach gave me the spark that I needed to keep going and shove the pain down as I knew how to do.

While I was happy with Mark being our coach, it changed our dynamic since he had not been responsible before for both my academics and my swimming. Mark was walking into my wreckage from school. I had flunked out of school or at least dropped below a 2.0, and needed to bring up my grades to be eligible to swim that year. Due to the Olympics being so late that fall, I was in extension self-paced classes that were of no interest to me. I was so tired from the world from which I came I knew I needed a break, an emotional break, I needed to step back from it all. I had no need for school. I never went growing up, but had managed to get by with the gift of persuasion when I needed it. If I wanted something, I turned it on. Now I was even getting too tired to even do that.

When Mark settled in as the coach I asked if I could take the year off of eligibility. It wasn't an unusual request as many Olympians are in the cycle of depression, sadness, and grief—that emotional hangover you get. I was no different and had a heavy dose of it. I wasn't emotionally equipped to handle school at the time and had zero communication skills to even talk about it or say what was going on. The skills I had were to drink, eat, and swim. When I asked to sit out the year, it was met with a resounding no. Mark had convinced me that he needed me to be part of the team because so many people had retired and he needed all the swimmers he had on the team as well as a friendly face. I knew I was in debt to Mark and wanted to do whatever he asked of me. I was so grateful for his coaching and how I was swimming when I wasn't sabotaging myself.

It wasn't long into school, a week or so, that I had a meeting with Mark, Donna Lopiano, the athletic director, and my academic advisor to really discuss me being a fuck up—that would be the simplest way to describe it. I was nothing but a pain in their ass; it was like herding a cat with me. My outward personality and what I showed you was a I-don't-care, whatever, nothing-can-hurt-me persona, but I was also well-trained to show up for commitments. I couldn't just blow them off. The day of that meeting, I had to run home and get my dryland training clothes, as my stuff wasn't already at the pool. In good entitled fashion, I was speeding home and got pulled over for speeding. Unfortunately for me, I had a warrant out for my arrest for a $25 unpaid ticket that was actually for someone else. I was driving my drunk friend home on her moped with expired tags, but the ticket was in my name as I was the driver. Since that ticket was unpaid and had gone into a warrant, the police officer decided to arrest and handcuff me and drive me to the city of Austin jail.

As I was carted off in the police car, I was begging to just pay the ticket. It wasn't paid because I didn't have the money but rather because I was lazy and everyone did everything for me. I knew that this was going to send me over the edge of no return. I never missed something. I always showed up no matter what. I begged and persuaded the police officer to stop by an ATM machine on the way to the police station. But the bank he stopped at would not take my card as the strip reader had melted in the Texas sun. I ended up going to jail that day and missed my appointment. While I had a good reason, I was in jail which wasn't exactly changing their thoughts about me but really only added to what they already believed about me. This was now the tone that I started off with Mark. It was a continuation of the world that I was creating for myself which wasn't a true representation of the person that I knew I was inside.

As I tormented myself about the continued misconceptions of me, I went the only way that I knew which was to live hard and swim hard, but this time it was more of a struggle than ever before to swim and get back into the cycle of training. I was doing it but I was also drinking almost every night. I would be the barfly in the bar until 2 a.m. and then roll out of bed to swim at 6 a.m., and then sleep all day for practice in the afternoon at 2 p.m. While I did this before, it seemed like it picked up even more during this time. So much so that at some point I did something, I can't even remember what I did, but it resulted in Mark kicking me off the team for a week. That to me meant more time to party and be irresponsible. The timing of this was right before the US Open and took place in December before the holidays.

The US Open was the big closing-of-the-year-meet and the last time to semi-taper before NCAA's in March. This was the first big meet since the Olympics. For me this was where I would really feel the post-Olympic blues; the old swimmers retired and the new ones were coming up. I ended up swimming much faster than I did at the Olympics and all last summer, as I won my new race that I was starting to love: the 100 Fly. I also qualified for NCAA's in all my events, an unusual and remarkable accomplishment. I was the only person on the team to even qualify early for NCAA's.

One would assume this accomplishment would have brought me back on track ready to commit to my love for swimming again. My relationship with Mark had started to wane before this meet as my aloof persona was not paying off. The outcome of my success resulted in Mark being even more pissed off at me. He sat me down to yell at me for showing him up after he kicked me off the team. I couldn't really win this battle. All I wanted were the accolades and praise for my success, but now it didn't matter what I did because it wasn't good enough or right. That took all the wind out of my sails—what was I doing this for?

When NCAA's came around, I had pulled everything I had in my being to make it to that swim meet; I wasn't going to let my teammates down. I may not have showed it at the time, but they meant the world to me; it was the only place where I was truly happy training and being in my element. It was all about to come to an end. The praise, the joy, everything was about to stop. While my parents were there to watch and enjoy the festive team environment, it wasn't quite the same for me since I had already cut my heart off to my dad and just about everything else around me. I was in full protection mode from disappointment of any kind.

I don't know if I swam NCAA's that year knowing that that was it for me. That was going to end my ability to focus, hold it together, and drive towards my shattered dreams. I was so broken-hearted and hurt from the last 18 years I had dedicated towards this sport when the meet ended and our winning streak ended as we placed second to Richard's new team Stanford. Everything ended. I started crying uncontrollably—I couldn't hold it in any longer. Especially since I justified it being a senior. I came to know the loss of our streak of wins for the school that I loved and for the teammates that I cherished. Every tear that I had held back wanted to be let free in that moment: There was no gate, no stopper, like there was no gate and no stopper from a coach moving into my inner space while unknown to those around me. That is what we train our athletes to do—to remove all barriers to their inner selves. Mine was completely gone in that moment.

When I returned to school from NCAA, I wanted to take the rest of the semester off. I needed a break from swimming. I knew in my heart I didn't have it in me. I really wanted to drink for three weeks to drown my sorrow, I was in so much internal pain. I asked Mark for a few weeks off till the end of the semester. I stated that I wanted to focus on school.

We had a meeting in the classroom outside of the pool, where I pleaded my case to Mark to get some time off. This conversation started out with my demands, but quickly escalated into a fuck-you conversation when Mark responded with a no. All the disappointment that I had from my coaches was being projected onto Mark, the one coach who I thought cared about me. If he cared about me he would have given me what I wanted because that is what the definition of caring was to me at the time.

As I perceived Mark's lack of caring, I raised my voice and showed true anger like I had never done before. The last time I cracked like this was with Fred after swimming in the dark alone. I had found myself at that place again. After all the battles with Paul, and the other coaches along the way, I had managed to not crack like that. Over all the years, I had managed to stay poised and controlled with my actions despite the intensity of my challenges that I endured. But not this time; it was like the Hoover Dam had just broken. I was even shocked to be experiencing this myself.

I was so angry that I wasn't getting my way. I was really angry that I wasn't being seen. I was so done with not being heard or understood. I was so over it. Mark confronted my yelling and screaming by not backing down. I walked out of the classroom saying, "Fuck you. I quit." I turned around and left and never looked back. I couldn't take it anymore. I got my way and quit and drank myself right out of school.

My parents weren't ready for me to be done with my swimming career and I wasn't ready or willing to return to my parents. Neither of us wanted the other really. I decided to move to Florida without a clear plan other than to take a break and keep training. I needed to swim to stay on the parents' payroll if you will. I moved in with my friend Wendy whom I had met at the Olympics. Wendy won a bronze medal in platform diving, dove for the University of Miami, and we saw each other on the collegiate circuit as well. We carried on our friendship after the Olympics. I also had other friends in Florida from swimming there the previous summer, like my friend Michele, who missed her second Olympic Team after winning a silver medal in 1984, being the youngest American to win a medal in those Games. I didn't have a coach there, but I had friends, and Wendy had found this great art deco apartment for us in South Miami Beach.

When I arrived in Miami, Wendy was still in the throes of her diving career. I was around someone who was capitalizing off her success as an athlete with commercials and endorsement deals while also competing for her next Games. There was something infectious about that. I also liked being around a team of people. I started going to the University of Miami pool and working out when the divers were training. I was trying to find my way back, sort of. I couldn't give up the idea of being a swimmer. I had nowhere else to go or anything to do. It was all I knew. I wanted to be an Olympian again. The cycle started right back inside of me.

I reached out to my friend Michele's coach, Charlie, who had trained Michele to her Olympic silver medal in 1984. I asked him if he would train me. He agreed. At the time he was coaching at Gulliver School in Miami, where Jeb Bush's kids attended. I would often run into the Secret Service that hung around when I was training at the pool with a small group of swimmers. I started training with no connection to my heart or myself. I was on total autopilot. I could do all the training and sets—I knew how to do that—but it was the performing that I took for granted. I never wanted to be hurt performing again was where I really was in my heart.

While I was trying to find the rhythm of the Olympic cycle, so was Wendy. Wendy was having the in-between success of her recent accomplishment of a bronze medal, as well as being a NCAA championship diver with endorsement deals while she pursued her next Olympic Games. Even if I had wanted to, I wouldn't have been able to have done the endorsement deals in the previous Games due to the amateur status requirements for the Olympics and the NCAA. I was now free from all those rules and requirements and could make money from my success. One of the deals that came through for Wendy was to be the model for USA Diving that was sponsored by Phillips 66, as was USA Swimming at the time. Wendy asked me if I wanted to be the model for the USA Swimming ad campaign. Of course I said yes.

We did the photoshoot at the Mission Bay Aquatic Center pool in Boca Raton where I trained the previous summer. The photographer, Walter Iooss Jr., worked for Sports Illustrated and was famous for how he captured Michael Jordan. Here I was feeling like a fraud having not excelled at the level I knew that I was capable of, doing a model shoot with a photographer for one of the best athletes of all time. Adding irony to irony was that having competed for Great Britain I was about to be the model for USA Swimming. That ad with my image would end up being run in every major magazine and newspaper for close to 20 years.

My life in Miami started becoming a story out of Miami Vice; I was surrounded by drug use, drinking, and partying. My lifestyle and choices created a wedge between me and Wendy, as she was trying to train for her next Olympics, while I couldn't bring myself to go in the same direction. My swimming career started to fade as I focused on drinking. I had no one to hold me accountable—no coach, no parents, and I certainly wasn't capable of holding myself accountable for anything. At some point Wendy had to distance herself from me and protect herself from my destructive behavior.

When Wendy moved out it was about the same time that the first print of my ad went national. While it was in every magazine, it was also regularly on the inside cover of the TV Guide. As my disconnect from life increased and my world became smaller and smaller, I would find myself staring at me on the inside cover of TV Guide. Yes, we used those back then.

While I was in the midst of my partying lifestyle, I got a call from my brother wanting to know if I was doing drugs. It's a long story on why he wanted to know that, but the net-net was that he was demanding that I get a drug test right there and then, he was so mad and upset. No one had been upset with me for this behavior so it was a bit of a wake-up call. I didn't know enough to stop, but it was enough to maybe think about going to therapy. I started to see this therapist and share some of my stories around my swimming. All I heard from the therapist was that maybe I should go to Alcoholics Anonymous. I was a good soldier and people pleaser; I had that in me. I would do something that someone said—maybe that was actually the problem at this point. I wasn't making decisions of substance for me; it was always what someone else wanted me to do, when really I just needed someone to hear me, to really hear my dream and help me get there. I was so lost and so far down the rabbit hole at this point that it felt like there was no getting out.

I showed up at this AA meeting in Miami and listened to a guy from New York share, just as you read about and see on TV, and it was not my story. I raised my hand and shared at the end about drinking the night before my most important event in my life. I could feel the destruction and just wanted someone else to feel it too and help me. Someone did come up to me and I'm sure they gave me their number and even called me. But I was so deeply lost to all that was good that I had no ability to connect to anything other than the misery inside of me.

During the course of that summer, I missed qualifying for Nationals. The ad that I did was now literally the poster for the event—the beautiful shot of me diving in the water for all to see and admire and I wasn't even there. I don't know that I really tried, but when I did swim I wasn't swimming fast enough to go anywhere or do anything. I was battling with my internal pattern of wanting to be an Olympian again. It was like a clock inside of me that said that I needed to train. Yet my outside version of me wasn't having any of it. All I wanted was the dream, but as my swimming faded, my presence did not.

In order to appease my craving to be an Olympian, I thought moving and trying to train with Mark again might be a good idea. So I packed up and left Miami to head back to Austin. I rented an apartment, registered for school, and was ready to go. I hadn't even spoken to Mark about this plan; I was going to just show up with the hope that he would take me back.

When it became known that I was back in town ready to pick up where I left off like it was no big deal, I got a letter from the athletic director, Donna Lopiano, that my scholarship had been revoked. I was so mad. I felt so rejected and hurt. I was furious if you really want the full description. I felt so betrayed that they could do this to me, especially since it was completely lacking in integrity given that the letter I received was backdated. They cheated me on a technicality. I was holding them to account where I wasn't holding myself to account; that didn't matter to me when I could clearly see others' faults.

All of this threatened my pursuit not just for the Olympics, but for the idea that my dad might love me again. Maybe if he would see me competing and swimming then I truly had the talent he saw when I was a little girl. I wanted my dad to love me desperately. I had made no effort to speak of with me basically being checked out when I was in Miami, but I still hung onto the idea that this was my only chance to get him to love me again. The sadness was overwhelming to think that I was being denied that. This lead to me impulsively renting a U-Haul truck and packing up all my furniture by myself, including the couch. I moved it from the second floor, struggling, but moved it by myself, I was so determined. That was the strength that I had in life; when I was focused I could move mountains. And just like that I moved myself out to LA.

When I got to LA I moved into another coach's home and started to train again. However, within a month or so of training my shoulder started to shut down. It wasn't really my shoulder that was shut down; it was me that was torn apart. I got my shoulder scoped as a quick repair so maybe I could swim again. But my heart wasn't in it. My parents were pretty much out of my life. I had become very distant from my family. They weren't helping me at all. When I called them in tears that I was going to have to get my shoulder reconstructed, there wasn't any family there to support me, my sole support was Chris. A couple days before Christmas I went into surgery. The surgery required a couple of nights in the hospital and to wake up with your shoulder completely reconstructed without a soul, I felt so unwanted. The only way I could find a moment of relief was to push the button to pump more morphine into my body. I wasn't sure what I was medicating, the pain from the surgery or the broken heart; either way there wasn't enough morphine to heal that pain.

The 1992 Summer Olympics came around with the Dream Team and the usual fanfare. This time I was on other side of the dream. There was no innocence of that little girl wanting to connect to her dad. There was only the broken-hearted woman wondering if her dad would ever love her again. I watched my friends compete and saw new swimmers rise up. All I knew was how lost I was in life and wondered, how did I get here? I was never supposed to be on this path as I looked down at the latest magazine with a stunning picture of me that I could only hate for being a fraud and not good enough.

As the Olympics came to a close, my internal clock and cravings went unfulfilled. The only way I knew how to deal with life was to drink and now to smoke, as it seemed like that was a good thing to do to suppress my feelings and destroy everything inside of me. What also ended was parental financial support. I had maxed out all my credit cards at this point and needed to figure out what to do. My parents had a spare house, where one of my brothers and sister and her future husband lived in Minneapolis, and they offered it to me as a place to go. My sister was getting married later that year and she had asked me to be her maid of honor. At this point in my life I had spent maybe thirty days with my sister over the past ten years since I had left at age 11 for my swimming career. I thought I could get to know her before the wedding.

Shortly after I arrived in Minneapolis, the Olympics had passed and even though I hadn't competed, that didn't stop the post games cycle of depression and sadness. In late September 1992, just as I was starting to recover from the post-Olympic blues and could marginally function, I got word from England that Paul Hickson had been arrested for sexual abuse of a minor. It was front page news all over Britain.

It was my friend and teammate, Bettina from Coventry, that brought the charges forward. Bettina was Paul's prior victim before my sexual abuse started. As I learned of this abuse I didn't know how to respond. Part of me wanted to ignore it and move on. Another part wanted someone to speak up for me that I was abused too. I wanted someone to solve my problem and release me from my pain. What I didn't know was how to do that help myself.

While this was front page news across every newspaper in Britain, the internet wasn't a thing at the time. As this was happening, my sister's future in-laws were coming to the States to prepare for the wedding. When they arrived they had saved all the articles from the papers in Britain for me to read about it. As they handed me the articles they would ask, "Did this happen to you?" My mother was usually standing right there in the conversation and it left me frozen and not able to answer. I wasn't sure what to say, so I didn't respond or say anything. Later, I would take the time to thumb through the articles to see what the headlines said and who was reporting on this. I would see Pat the journalist's byline. I would see her name and wanted to talk to her. I knew she would understand; I knew she knew all along. But it didn't end my silence.

My mother was curious as to what the newspapers were actually reporting. I would come to learn of my mother's strong opinion that Paul was innocent and that the girls wanted sex from him. I couldn't help but recall the day walking out of my room at the World Championship Trials as Paul walked out of her room. I couldn't help but wonder what happened that day. As my mother pressed on with these opinions about these women it made my experience seem like it was my fault. The idea that they wanted the harm and harassment was essentially what my mother was conveying to me.

During this time I was also traveling back to England regularly for various family functions or official Olympic gatherings. Due to the high profile arrest and it being the first of its kind in Britain, everyone was talking about the case. Every person who knew me, the first question they asked was always, "Did this happen to you?" I never had the courage to just say yes. I didn't understand what would happen or what could be done. I was so disappointed in humanity that I trusted no one and saw no solution for me other than continued silence.

Over the next several years, my sisters-in-law and everyone coming to England that was going to cross my path thought I would be interested in the case. My mother was especially interested in this case. She had a habit of writing letters to her friends over the years as her way to stay connected. One of those people at the time was Paul. As I was learning about her loyalty to Paul, I also was witnessing the loyalty of Paul's wife. They had moved to a small village in France to avoid the criminal charges against him. All of Paul's actions and the ways that he was continually escaping the law became known to me through these articles and conversations. I couldn't get away from the subject.

One night at my parents' house, all of my siblings were there which was a rare event. We had not really seen each other for the past ten or fifteen years or so, but my dad would get up and leave the table when he was done, sometimes in mid-conversation. This was one of those nights. The conversation was around me and that my parents shouldn't have put as much focus on my swimming as they did. How that messed me up. I was blamed for my swimming failures as well as my constant weight gain. Then my dad just got up and left to go read his book.

As he got up from the table, I followed him wanting some kind of reassurance or something that my dad still loved me in some way. I wanted something, anything that would reconfirm my existence as a person. We could no longer talk about my times in practice or something that I did well. I had no way to have a conversation with him unless it involved my weight. There was never a "Hello" or a "How are you?" It was always, "You are fat," "Your face is puffy." I never heard an "I love you" once. If I did try to say something, he would say, "Make it quick, I'm busy." I wasn't a slow person, but when it came to speaking up for myself or exposing an emotion, it was met with fear and intimidation. My father was abrupt in his demeanor with me. He lifted his head from his book and told me that I was a loser and the rest of the words became a knife in my heart. I could no longer hear the words, only the anger and his disgust for me. I had disappointed him so much that I wasn't of value to him anymore. He was no longer Annabelle's father. I was just an embarrassment to him.

My mother would try and console me with excuses about my dad while at the same time she would gossip about the next actions that Paul had taken in the course of the progression of the case. I was bombarded with nothing but pain and disappointment from every corner of my life. At the same time, I had faith in Pat continuing to cover the story in support of all the women who were now coming forward to speak out about their abuse. I was wondering if Pat or anyone else would think to contact me or question me. The media had been interested in me when I was swimming, but why weren't they interested now? Did anyone even know where I was? I didn't know where I was.

As the story of Paul was going on in the background, I was fading on the inside and growing on the outside. My connection to my swimming friends had all but disappeared. The last friend I saw was in town for a swim meet, and that night ended in me getting a DUI and another trip to jail. This time there was no one waiting to pick me up when I got out. I had to figure it out alone—a state of being that I knew only too well.

I disconnected from life at this point, and found my way into working in travel. I wanted to stay connected with all the people that I had met all over the world during my swimming career despite the fact that when I got to that country I wouldn't look anybody up or try to connect with them. I pretty much let everyone drift away. I struggled daily with trying to understand the purpose of life and why I was here. It all seemed like a waste of time and there was no point to my life. I had no skills, no real direction, and I felt I was never going to be that good at anything ever again.

I watched as my next brother found himself a great wife while my sister started to have children and a family. My siblings were moving along the life spectrum as it was designed. I would be happy for them and at the same time feel so broken and nonfunctioning. I would walk around staring at my feet all day, barely looking up to miss a lamppost—and this was pre-texting behavior. The intensity of the loneliness felt like I had run into the iceberg that sank the Titanic leaving me to swim around in the ice cold water praying to be saved from the world that I found myself in.

Meanwhile, my ad continued to pop up in random places like Sports Illustrated, People magazine, Smithsonian magazine, and The Wall Street Journal. It just appeared when I couldn't have hated myself more. This was coupled with the drama of my coach in his court case where the rules didn't seem to apply to him.

Around this time I was in London with my parents. I'm not sure who else was there, but Paul had evaded his court appearance and had just been captured in France and was being brought back for trial. I was eating a meal with my mother and her dear friend, Janet, who was like a second mother to me, when she asked about Paul's guilt. My mother went into the story that I had heard one too many times about Paul's innocence and that it was the girls that wanted sex, like my mother was there or even understood anything about the relationship with a coach. It was the same person who let Fred coach me in the pitch dark, the same person who had no mechanism of protection for me ever. The same barriers that I didn't have she didn't have either and those were now being projected onto other people unfairly and meanly. How could this person ever come to my rescue if I did say something? It was always going to be my fault. That is what I was left to think about and believe as I listened in disdain to the conversation.

When my nephew was born his parents decided to have the baptism in England at my brother in-laws' church in Newcastle over the Christmas holidays, which was also around the same time as their anniversary. When I arrived in England I was welcomed with more articles about Paul's trial. At first I looked at the articles and there was Pat's name front and center following along and capturing the story; she had stayed with it throughout all the drama. The headlines read that Paul was given 18 years in prison, the longest rape sentence given to anyone ever in Britain. I had regretted not making the effort to reach out to her, but I also felt that I wasn't enough and my story didn't matter, or more truthfully I didn't have the words to tell my story. I was telling it through my actions but no one was listening.

One of the ways that I was managing was with fighting with my siblings. Just before the baptism, I drove into town with my siblings and on the way back, we got in a fight and I refused to drive with my brother in the car. From my perspective he was being an asshole. From his perspective, while they knew nothing of my pain or what was going on with me, they just wanted me to stop being a bitch to them. The problem with this situation was that I was the only one who could see and drive a stick shift on what was, for my siblings, the wrong side of the road. My sister could drive a stick shift but didn't have her glasses, so my brother navigated the car home for them, while I walked back to their house. I really wanted to run away.

My mother continued to feel that Paul was wronged with this sentence. Sitting through her conversations pushed my desire to live about as far away from her as possible. Why I didn't float away, why I was rescued and swam into shore—all these whys started to circle in my mind. I had no answers for them. I felt so unwanted for everything and everyone around me.

As life became more bleak, I don't know that it could get any worse. The trial was over, the swimming was over, and my dad was a person with no love for me. It was painful to watch how he showed so much glee and joy for my brothers now, and especially for one of my brothers who had stepped into being his favorite as his career was rapidly excelling. They shared their love of golf. I didn't have anything to share anymore.

As my thirtieth birthday neared the reasons to drink became plentiful. I was also working hard at the time as I learned how to live two lives: the hardworking, people-pleasing worker who shows up and the drinker. It was no different from my swimming days. I was given a project by a major client who needed a meeting planned for 600 people in three weeks. It was the kind of rush and adrenaline that I desired, and reminiscent of my addiction to praise. I had found a way in my work life to seek and find it there.

After pulling off this meeting planning feat, I had called in sick to recover after being up for 24 hours making all this happen. I was laying on the couch drinking a beer because I was sick when the phone rang and it was my mother. I answered with my usual "I'm-irritated-to-talk-to-you" voice that was coming regardless of the conversation. My mother in her happy chirpy voice shared that she "received a letter from Paul in prison." I responded with something so simple as "Really?" in shock and awe that I was even getting this call and that my mother was happy that he contacted her. Then she went on to say that he was innocent and that he wanted her help to get him out of prison. Before I could utter anything out of my mouth, she started down the path of how innocent he was. I didn't know what came over me in that moment, but I cut her off and said, "You know that he raped me, don't you?" Her tone and response changed to "Oh" and then there was silence on the phone as I waited for her to say something and nothing came. I hung up the phone and slammed the beer.

We have never spoken about it again, even to this day as I share my story. I was left with what I dreaded: no support, no comfort, and no place to go for someone to help me. I was unwanted by both my mother and myself at this point.

CHAPTER 15

Halted in my Tracks

Who knew so much weight and emotion could be behind two letters? "Oh." I was so devastated by my mother's reaction that any heart I had for her closed off, along with the rest of the world. I had every excuse in the book to make the choices I was making after my mother's cold and disconnected response to me. At least that was the story I was telling myself.

I knew that "oh" too well in other areas of my life. When someone would learn that I was an Olympian, there was a natural desire to know you, and learn what sport you competed in while trying to guess and visualize you from TV, like they had seen you there before and they knew you to some degree. It was always an interesting interactions. What I dreaded was the next question: "How did you do?" I would skirt around the question and want to explain my whole life story, justifying in most cases why I didn't win a medal. Almost inevitably when I would respond that my highest place was sixth place I heard this same silence that my mother gave me, followed by an "oh." Often the conversation ended abruptly there. I was left standing holding their bag of disappointment. At first they'd thought they won the lottery meeting an Olympian and then you'd see their disappointment that you didn't have a medal to show for it; it was like you somehow you cheated them.

As those conversations occurred over the years, often initiated by a friend who was proud of me, I became less inclined to share the facts about my life. You may imagine how it felt inside of me to get a hit from a cigarette and exhale as I shared about being an Olympian. Especially because being an Olympian came with the idea of sacrifice and dedication to greatness. Here I was destroying my body, my mind, and anything that I could manage to destroy with the notion that my body was the source of the problem.

After all the highs and lows in those years of swimming, my life had shrunk down so far to "oh." While I hated the idea of swimming and I wanted nothing to do with a pool, it didn't change the fact that wherever I went I always had my cap and goggles in my purse/backpack. Most people carried essential stuff, not me—it was swimming stuff. I left the idea of carrying around Bear, although I would have preferred and needed to have him with me at all times, especially on an airplane. I had swam for so long that I had lost all connection to God and this had become my replacement: cap and goggles.

As I drifted further and further away from a "normal" life, I started to wilt like a flower where the only place I looked when I walked was down at my feet. When I went to a store I would go through the process, say nothing, and have no interactions with the store clerk. I had nothing in me. Even if I tried I wasn't going to get anything out of me. I chalked this up to having social anxiety and that I was an introvert. I bought whatever I was selling to myself.

I don't even know how I managed to have a functional job, but I went to work every day besides my week-long episode when I was sick and needed to watch TV and drink beer during the day. I went to work, was on time, and performed at a high level. I also became accustomed to the challenge of having a disadvantage. In this case it was drinking at night, right after work until the bar closed. I'd go to sleep, wake up, and do the same thing over and over again.

I knew the monotonous cycle of life that brought me no joy, no love, no nothing. I was struggling with this life. Is this what it was all about? I had no real direction. I had bought a house, a car, and was living a life that I was supposed to live by the outside world's standards. I left all remnants of swimming, and my desires and dreams as a thing of the past. As thoughts of despair started to be more and more prevalent, the only way to deal with them was to drink to pass out, rinse and repeat. I started thinking strong thoughts about how desirable it would be to get hit by a bus. I didn't have the courage to do it myself; I wanted someone else to do it for me. I wanted it all to end. I'd get in a ball on the floor and yell to the world that I couldn't take it anymore.

Like every great decision that I had ever made about my life, I concluded that if I had a new career and a new life then all this pain would go away. I needed some excitement in my life. I had bought a high-end computer at the time the internet was starting to take off. You remember when you got the AOL free trial disk in the mail like every other week? I had always gravitated towards technology as my parents had an IBM computer in the early '80s. When I first went on the internet, I racked up a hefty phone bill from connecting our phone to the modem on this cradle that we had. Then in 1984 in the Olympic Village we had intranet and could connect with any of the athletes throughout their email system. Not to mention that my mother was one of the first female systems analysts for IBM in the 1960s before she met and married my dad. I had a long history of attraction towards new technology and started to spend all of my free time on the internet while drinking. As new sites would come up I was constantly engaging them, one of those being an employment site. I started to apply for jobs, just because I could. It was without any thought or direction. Besides, I had bought into the idea of changing something to fix my thought process.

I got a call a few weeks later from a company that I had submitted my resume to. Being that I am a curious person and didn't know how to say no, I carried on with the process and went in for an interview. The company was in an industry that I had never heard of or knew anything about. It was a German company that certified equipment and services for safety across all industries. The job was for business development—something that seemed interesting to me because I could talk to people, especially since I had stopped talking to people at this point. I pursued the company. It was like the feeling of rotating your boat in the dark hoping you still hit shore without having any idea where or why you were going in this direction, but it made sense at the time.

However, my new job didn't help with changing how I felt inside. It actually made it worse because I felt so much shame and now had to explain how I got here. Here I was an Olympian and now my life had evolved into stepping out the back door, hanging with the smokers at a job that was totally removed from what I did at my previous job. At least I traveled to interesting places that were almost as cool as where the Olympics and other international meets in which I had competed were held. Now I was visiting manufacturing plants and talking about production compliance. The only saving grace in all of this was that there was a tech group that I had an interest in and knew a lot about, but that office was located in the Bay Area in California. I got to know that group and wanted to join their team when an opportunity became available.

Then someone from the tech group called me and asked if I would join them in Atlanta for an annual big mobile conference. They needed staff to help them with the booth. The one thing I was good at was saying yes and I liked to be traveling and moving. Off I went to Atlanta.

If there was anything I had learned about myself by now was that wherever I go, here I am. I could not get rid of my desire to kill myself. The broken and hurt me was walking around like an open wound with nowhere or no one to help me. I was so incredibly lost. I also knew and learned over the years to hide me and hide all the hurt and pain.

When I arrived in Atlanta, the leftover Olympic presence was still strong, with the various statues, parks and other memorabilia left behind. That in itself was hard to look at. The rings of broken dreams and few successes. I also had a tattoo of those Olympic rings on my hips that had stretched over the years to imperfection, the same way that I thought about myself.

The conference that I was attending was huge, with 100,000 in attendance; it was one of the biggest mobile and tech conferences at the time. It was located in downtown Atlanta and I was staying out in Buckhead, not in the same place as my co-workers. I was also the designated driver for the company.

One of the nights after the conference my co-workers wanted to eat in Buckhead despite the fact that they were staying downtown. Being that I was a yes person, who had the car and didn't feel like I had a voice or opinion, I went along with what they wanted. During the 20-minute ride from downtown we were trying to figure out what we wanted to eat for dinner. One of my co-workers would point at an approaching restaurant and ask, "What about there?" Just silence as no one even made even a grunt leaving me as the driver with no clear or concise decision. I carried on down the street as one of my co-workers pointed out a restaurant and was making a decision for all of us, "Let's go here." But I looked at the restaurant and kept driving. I didn't flinch, didn't slow down—nothing. Then I saw a restaurant out of the corner of my eye, and I didn't even ask my co-workers. I cut across all lanes of traffic and went flying into the valet parking of the restaurant. My co-workers didn't say anything in disagreement; they got out of the car and were like, "Let's eat here."

We sat down at a table on their outside patio and ordered drinks. As the drinks arrived, someone approached the table and asked me if I was Annabelle Cripps. I looked up to see Mary Wayte. I hadn't seen Mary since the closing ceremonies of the 1988 Olympic Games. Now here I was having a random chance crossing of paths with the very person who was the bearer of my dreams in life. I was so tormented and broken up inside and was now confronted with this chance interaction.

Mary ended up joining us at our table. I was taken aback by this chance and random connection and feeling confused. Atlanta is a large city, there were 100,000 people at that conference, restaurants were plentiful, and none of us said we wanted to even go to this particular restaurant; I just cut across traffic and pulled in. Thoughts of my own demise and my loss of hope had been very strong as of late. I was so beaten up inside that the last thing I wanted was to talk to someone from my past; the shame, the embarrassment for how my life had turned out was beyond words. I was working for a company that was fine for all intents and purposes, but it was not my dream job or my dream life; rather it was a dull and boring existence as that was all I could allow myself to have.

What was so interesting about this encounter with Mary was I remembered her as a fierce competitor. There was something different now. There was a light in her eyes and in her being that I had not witnessed before. There was a softness to her soul that I hadn't experienced when we played cards for hours. There was a presence within her that was glaring so loud that I wasn't sure what it was exactly, other than it gave me hope and desire to be curious for the first time. I became interested in the person and not the Olympian. There was something so special that it took my breath away, it made me forget about my pain and anguish for a moment. It was such a profound spiritual change from my prior time spent with her that it was almost blinding. Blinding to the soul.

My co-workers were also taken aback from this chance occurrence that they too couldn't believe the coincidence. The evening went on and my heart and being were starting to question everything that I knew to be true.

At the evening's end, I had so many questions and no answers. I was filled with pain and knew of only one solution of how to not feel it, and that was to drink. A solution that I was tired of but had no other options; I had worn down that road with no other path to follow. I knew that meeting with Mary was more than a random moment from the force as to which my car drove across traffic more or less in slow motion. I could feel myself in the car like it just happened.

During the course of our conversation, Mary shared with us her transformation when she became a born-again Christian. I could feel the presence of God in her that wasn't there before or at least it wasn't as clear and evident as God was showing me now. All I knew of God were the donuts in the hall after church and Ginny in Hawaii who would send me letters about Christ. Also, my teammates took me to church in college while I was hungover, wanting me to find Christ in my life. They were doing that because they cared about me and from the goodness in their hearts. I rejected all that was good and certainly rejected any notion of God. I especially rejected God with the life and the world that I had to endure. I never thought God cared about me. I wasn't worthy or had any value in God's world.

After we said our goodbyes we exchanged contact information knowing that a conversation was going to follow this rekindled friendship. I wanted the glow that Mary carried.

I could feel this deep sadness in my gut, so deep within, in a place that I couldn't reach. My mind was consumed with needing to numb this out of me or something; my whole world was just rocked. I couldn't wait to drop my co-workers off at their hotel and drown in my sorrow. One would have thought how happy I was to run into an old friend. Yes, I was happy to have had the encounter, but it was filled with so much shame and torment from my life that I couldn't bear to let anyone know about this pain that I was carrying. I couldn't get behind closed doors quick enough. You know when you have to go to the bathroom badly? That was what it was like; I needed to retreat to destroy myself.

From downtown I drove by Centennial Olympic Park, and the Olympic symbolism flamed the fire within me, leading me to the liquor store. My only intention was to just pass out and carry on with my next day, like none of this mattered. When I got back to the hotel I was in so much emotional pain the alcohol barely touched or numbed it. I got down on to my hands and knees and started rocking back and forth as I cried. I started to scream out to God begging for Him to take away this pain. I don't recall ever having a moment where I invited God into my world. The pain was so deep within the fabric of my being that I all wanted was relief, if I could just flip the off-switch for a moment, have something to disconnect from the constant pain.

Shortly after Atlanta, Mary and I talked on the phone. We were now without the shock of the random encounter, back as old friends who were competing against each other like it was yesterday. That was the thing with the Olympics: the feelings cycled through my mind and body every four years in the various stages, with the same thoughts and feelings before making the Team, and then, after you competed, they carried on. I had avoided watching the Olympics, or at least not taken in the results with too much degree, and didn't hang out with anyone who brought it up; I just couldn't take another "oh" moment. All those thoughts and feelings never left me.

Mary prayed over me and then we talked. I could finally speak with someone who spoke my language. I was so intrigued with the person Mary had become that I wanted to learn more about her relationship with God. I remember so clearly how she talked about her faith in language that I could understand. Mary shared about swimming. She said, "Sometimes when you race it hurts and it's painful and there are times where you feel nothing; some call it the zone, I feel it is more than that. I feel there is the zone and there is the zone with God in it. The moments that I swam and could feel like I was just there in the nothingness of life, the completely empty space of existence." That was how I imagined it being in my mind when Mary spoke about the difference between the races and she equated that to her relationship with faith. I could hear that and understand that.

After the call I was left with hope, yet I still had all my old coping habits. The idea of reconnecting to something from my childhood was starting to fester inside of me. I had learned how to guard myself from disappointment and this time it was no different. I hadn't let anyone else into my life, so how was I going to let in a rekindled friendship or God for that matter? It wasn't just the passion inside of me that was destroyed. I had lost all passion for life for anything. It was the spirit of how God was within Mary that touched my heart enough to cause it to melt. The conversation concluded, but my desire to be friends with Mary did not.

The idea of a friendship from my old life wasn't necessarily on my agenda of things to pursue. Well, in reality there was nothing on that agenda. Yet, I had this strong desire to connect with Mary in person. I couldn't help but pursue this random crossing of paths when everything inside of me said it wasn't random. There was something inside of me that wanted to believe that I mattered. I had never felt that I, as a whole human, mattered. It was always about my swimming and my body; it was never about the person inside of me. For an instant, I had felt seen on the inside.

Mary lived in California at the time and I was in Minneapolis. I had this sense that she would understand what I had experienced. I don't even know if I knew what I had experienced. I just knew I was in pain and that I desperately wanted to speak to another Olympian and a swimmer. It wasn't like I had any clarity in my thoughts at the time. My actions were my thoughts, but nobody knew how to read them but me.

As the summer passed by so did my life. Then the tech group that I joined in Atlanta asked if I wanted to come out and meet them at their office in the Bay Area to learn more about their business unit. I knew that that was perfect since I could go out and visit with Mary and connect with my best friend Chris, who was a diver at a high level and a fellow drinking buddy.

We agreed to meet at Half Moon Bay. Chris was there as a buffer and along for the co-dependent ride that the two of us were on. We met at a beach and started to walk casually around as we reminisced about our swimming days. We talked about our rival college programs, our post-Olympic life, the post-Olympic letdown and everything in between. My letdown, however, lingered a lot longer than Mary's. She had found her way to a career, marriage, and seemingly productive life. At some point after the conversation warmed up, if you will, it went much deeper and became more meaningful. I had dropped all resistance to keeping information inside of me as I started to talk about my coach and the abuse that I endured. I didn't even know the words or have the language to talk about my experience. All I had was a bellyful of pain.

It was like I woke up that day, and my heart opened for a moment as I started to share for the first time. I was listening to myself express these thoughts for the first time. It felt like I was having another out-of-body experience as I spilled my guts and Mary knew what I was talking about. She was so compassionate and kind as I shared. The only other person who had given me any kind of compassion or cared about me was Ginny when I was in Hawaii. Then, I was too young and in so much pain that I could not accept this kindness and compassion. Mary's compassion was like a hot flame on a block of ice. This was not the heart that I had known from a fellow Olympic swimmer; this was more evidence to me that the presence of God was speaking through Mary. It was so strong that it was hard to ignore at this point.

At the same time, I couldn't believe that or digest that as truth. Why me? Why was I being heard now? I had no self-esteem whatsoever—it had been completely sucked out of me. I didn't even know a person who could be that kind and thoughtful. It was never something that I witnessed from my family, the families I stayed with, or the coaches. After several hours of pouring out my dark secrets my swimming career and abuse, one would think that I walked about feeling heard and cared about—I did feel that. Yet, what I didn't expect and know what to do with was the intensity of the pain. It was like Pandora's box. What I realized in that day was that it hurt more to be loved than hated.

After we left Mary, Chris and I went back to our hotel room. It wasn't anything fancy by any stretch. Frankly I'm pretty sure it was subpar in the way that I was used to. There was no pride here. Something below a Motel 6, it was that place where you didn't want to touch anything and pull the curtains closed so no one could see you there; the reality was because you didn't want to see yourself there. That room was a representation of where I was on the inside of my life.

My insides were going crazy. I felt the kind heart of the very person who realized the dream I had for myself as a little girl, the same dream that broke my heart gave Mary hers. Don't get me wrong, I'm a believer in that the Olympics are about the best person competing on that day, and it's any given person. That day it was Mary's day and it was her rightful accomplishment. I never felt owed or denied that spot, but I was sad that I never got to find out what the truth of my talents were had I followed a different path to get there.

As the pain inside of me festered, I had one solution to the problem and that was to drink, smoke, and do whatever Chris brought with him in the way of drugs. We stopped by the liquor store and I loaded up as if the world was going to end. As far as I was concerned, it just did. I could feel the pain of compassion and the pain of my life at the same time, something had to give. Next was going to be me numbing it all out. It was the first time in my life that I couldn't get it all to stop: all the chatter, the voices that wanted to kill me became even louder, and the desire to end it all was a drink away, at least that is what I thought. Chris and I stayed in that hotel room and drank for the next 48 hours, never seeing daylight or any transition from night to day, day to night, nothing. It was nothing but a blackout for which I was completely awake.

In good well-trained fashion I still had my commitments that I would honor. But this time I had gone overboard and was on the path of no return. I needed a direction to go; mine was to death, but my spirit was asking maybe there was a God. I was literally battling the good and evil inside of me. The way that battle won was me canceling the work meeting and wanting to get home to Minneapolis. I wanted to be in my own bed, like that was going help all this go away. Actually, I wanted to completely step out of myself and be in a state of being, but the only way I knew how to do that was drinking, but now I wanted to reverse the effect with the same solution and therefore had no pathway forward. I was so lost in every aspect of my life.

I rescheduled my flights to take the next flight out as I hightailed it out of town looking for the off-switch inside of me. When I got to the airport, I decided to call a friend on the payphone—yes, more old school technology. I called a co-worker who had introduced me to her husband who was sober. I mainly wanted to call for sympathy or have someone to agree with my choices or something. Then I started to say that I was an alcoholic and that I needed to get help. I was sharing while this screaming baby was wailing in the background. I can still feel the screech of that voice as I write this now. I was listening to myself shocked that I was even asking for help.

All the pride of suffering by myself in my own world was being dismantled in that moment. All that I wanted to say and do when I was swimming in the dark, or when I was being raped, or when I couldn't take living in the garden shed anymore, or when Paul was touching me. All I wanted was for someone to know what to do and help me. I needed a person with compassion to open up and touch my heart so I could know who the other people in my life were who could help me get on the path to healing.

My friend called Hazelden and they didn't have a bed right away, but they could help me in a couple of weeks. It was enough to rethink and possibly get the notion that I needed to reconsider this rash decision of getting sober. How was I going to relate to my family? How was I going to connect with my family if I didn't drink? After all, I'm British and we are drinkers. I started to back-pedal out of this decision.

Before I could go to Hazelden they needed to figure out if I was actually an alcoholic. The intake person called me and we went through these questions, and they said, "Yes, you've got a problem with drinking." In my distrusting and paranoid way, I was convinced that they just needed my money. I was sure they'd heard that before. Then my paranoia was met with, "We actually get a lot of folks that have depression and not a problem with alcohol. We have found you are suffering from both." They didn't have a bed right away and I would need to wait about ten days or so before I could go there.

I was relieved to hear that about myself and concerned at the same time. I knew that to find my pathway to my friends I needed help. I knew that if I wanted a friendship with anyone of substance I needed help. I was also concerned with how I was going to get this help. I had a heavy travel schedule where I visited clients every few weeks. What was I going to say? I had a million questions and no answers.

I had a conversation with Mary about this and she decided to pray over me to get guidance and that God's hand would be at play with getting the healing that I needed. I listened in wonder with wanting to believe that God cared for me. Intellectually I could feel it; having faith in God was what I was seeking and I wanted it desperately. As the time neared I wasn't sure what I was going to do. I was committed to getting sober, but didn't know how I was going to deal with the work situation. Then can you believe it, the airlines went on strike the day I was to start rehab. The path had opened for me. The miracle of this situation was that the airlines went off strike the day I was done. I was able to get the help I needed without the guilt of not showing up for my work commitment. That feeling of the obligation to my commitments never left me.

I look back and wonder about that fateful cut across traffic in Atlanta—if that was a power greater than myself who drove that car or who took over the steering that day when I ran into Mary. I found myself on a new path that I had never thought or dreamed about.

During this time, the headlines were filled with the latest sexual abuse case in the Catholic Church as it was becoming evident that it was rampant and happening across the world. At the same time, I was starting to believe in God. That in itself is what would send me down another rabbit hole. The idea that I had now just opened my heart up to the idea of God, well, the idea that God loved me enough to intervene in my life the way He did.

CHAPTER 16

The Search

After Mary showed up in my life it changed everything for me. I saw it with my own eyes and felt it in my being the change within Mary—it was so profound and loving to me. I knew God was present in Mary. I wanted that, but at the same time, I was so broken and hurt that I couldn't see how God could heal all that was hurt within me. It had started with being hurt by religion and the nuns from the Catholic school I went to as a child.

I had such strong memories of my passion to swim while also feeling out of place and unwelcomed by the nuns because of my size and inability to fit in with the other kids. I still felt burned from that feeling of someone robbing me of the very innocence of love that I had for myself. The idea that I was bad because I was tall or that I couldn't fit under the desk—those feelings lingered inside of me. It was the idea of an authority over me that took me off the path and not the authority within me. Coupled with my physical strength, the will and desire to excel became my own god along the way. The Olympian in me had rejected the need to be connected to a source of love and compassion while at the same time seeking it for comfort.

My struggles would go deeper than all of this. I was so traumatized that as I began to melt, my anger and internal traumas started. I knew this battle from the days of fighting with Paul, but only this time there was no one there for me to fight with. It was just me now. I had nowhere to direct this anger, while at the same time I carried on with my pleasant personality hoping that if I was nice someone would come to my rescue.

I knew that Pandora's box had opened in one direction and there was no going back in that direction. All I had left of my devices was my smoking, at least that was all that I thought I had. As I stopped drinking, the smoking carried on. I still felt the anguish about being a fraud while wanting to hide the fact that I was an Olympian.

As I got sober, some things changed in my life, like my ability to show up for work and actually apply myself. I hadn't lost the need to be recognized; if anything that became even stronger in me. I had a job that provided that kind of feedback as I was in sales/business development. The rewards were very clear, and immediate. I got to please the company and they in return provided praise to me. I managed to get the "most improved" award from really just showing up to work and actually applying myself a little. The high of recognition was light. Then six months later I was rewarded with a move out to our Rhode Island office to work in the sports department.

I hadn't spent much time on the East Coast. I had an affinity for the West Coast as I loved the Pacific Ocean despite its much cooler temperature. When I got all settled in Providence, I found myself wanting to go to the beach on the weekends. I had quickly made some friends with the same interests. I started to feel this desire to be swimming, yet I could still feel the hurt and anger that I carried. I would go to the beach but couldn't get in the water. Putting on my swimsuit was so painful, yet I couldn't go anywhere without my swimsuit, cap, and goggles. I needed them in my life but then rejected them all at the same time.

I had a business trip to San Francisco, with my swimsuit, cap, and goggles in my hand luggage. During this trip I visited Mary and met her husband who were gracious hosts and wanted to share the beautiful California coastline with me. We found a beach near Half Moon Bay. It was one of those days where we drove along and looked to see which beach we should stop at and then we eventually stopped at one. The energy and the feeling was a lot like the evening in Atlanta when I drove into the restaurant to run into Mary. We eventually stopped at a beach.

On this particular beach we stepped over a dead sea lion and continued on without a thought as we placed our stuff down in the sand. If I could make a point of reference, Mary's husband Jim has a PhD in biochemical engineering and was a patent agent. One would argue that he was very intelligent. We settled in on the beach and Jim and I decided to go in the ocean. Mary had the post-Olympic-no-need-to-swim issue that we all had, so she decided to stay on the shore and let us get to know each other and bond. Jim and I got in the water and we talked as we bobbed over the waves. It wasn't the kind of beach that you would necessarily surf or body surf the waves—these were shore-breaking waves. The water was also very murky and you couldn't see anything at all. As Jim and I were talking in mid-sentence I felt a shock in my heart, and I bolted out of the water. Following right behind me was Jim. There was a silence between us as we packed up our stuff and left the beach without a word.

After I checked in for my flight, I picked up a paper and read that there was a shark attack at the same beach where we were yesterday and that a person died. The thought of stepping over the dead sea lion might have been a clue, but it was that feeling I had in my body and my knee-jerk reaction to get out of the water. Why I was being protected was starting to weigh on my mind and I asked myself, "why wasn't I the one who ended up dead?" I would have been happy to exit out the backdoor if you will. It would have been an accident and sort of a graceful way to go.

Returning to Providence was hard. I was going back to more loneliness, hiding from the world the pain I was carrying around inside. The only person who really knew to what extent was Mary. I didn't know when our paths would cross again. It was the after-a-swim-meet let down feeling that I didn't like. It was all the unresolved goodbyes that I missed as a child over the years of swimming. While that was the least of my issues, it was a real issue of the life of a high-level athlete who gets attached to so many people.

At the same time, I was willing to try and do anything that would take away the pain that was so crippling to me. Then a sober friend wanted to quit smoking, well, her husband was pressuring her to quit smoking. He found a person in Boston called the Mad Russian. She asked me if I would go with her for support and maybe I would quit as well. We drove up to Boston on September 11, 1999, to meet the Mad Russian, who charged a grand total of $65, guaranteed to last a lifetime. I wanted to stop feeling like a fraud, being an Olympian and a smoker. I felt it was a really small investment and a reason to hang out in Boston for the day—this worked for me.

When we arrived at his home in Cambridge, there were about 25 people sitting around the room, as he talked to us in a very thick, heavy Russian accent. It was hard to catch everything he was saying. The few things that I heard were, "We didn't come out of the womb smoking." It wasn't a natural thought. He also talked about the oral fixation and that we needed to stop chewing gum, mints, etc. as well. I listened without any real thought about it, as it was hard to follow along with the heavy accent. When he was done talking we all left the room and one by one we went to meet with him, as he would erase the thought of wanting to smoke from us. I arrived in the room, sat down, and then he asked me to think of a time I was smoking and then raise my hands. I did that and that was it. He then went on to touch my head and shared with me that I was special and had a special path ahead of me. I wasn't sure what he meant by that, but his face was beaming with happiness. I hadn't seen that look from someone since I was a child and started to show my gifts as a swimmer. It was something that baffled me and opened my spirit to what life was awaiting for me.

I left Boston that day on a high from that engagement, mostly because I came across a stranger who saw me and wanted to pass along this message of my soul journey. I stayed on that high for several weeks, and quit smoking for good.

After the high of the Mad Russian faded, my feelings started to rise to the top again with nowhere to go; there was no drinking and no smoking now. I had taken away all the coping skills that I'd developed over the years. The hardest times were when I was alone. I lived in this three-bedroom apartment by myself. The anger and torment started to bubble up inside of me. I had no coping skills whatsoever other than to suck it up. There was no room in that inn, meaning inside of me, to stuff anything else in there. While I write this I wish to apologize to the neighbor above me who was studying for law school while I was so insensitive and played my music on full blast wanting to disconnect from my head and my feelings and not wanting to hear any of it.

After feeling the compassion of a few souls, I really wondered what was my purpose and path. I had no resolve or understanding for why I had the life I was having. As these thoughts permeated my being, the rage got so bad that one night I pulled out every medal, ribbon, and trophy that I had ever won and threw them all in the trash. This included all the copies of the USA Swimming ad and any articles where I was featured, and burned them in the fireplace. I watched as I saw Pat go up in smoke along with everything else that was written about me, good or bad. All the times that I had cracked before this was nothing compared to this time. The only difference was that it was not directed towards anyone but me. I was so upset and mad that my life turned out the way it did. I had no reason to live. Everything that I cared about was taken from me. I couldn't bear the pain. I also couldn't bear to tell anyone about the pain. I said to myself that I was weak for feeling this way. *I'm an Olympian.* No one would understand this was a favorite line of mine that I liked to repeat. I rocked back and forth in a fetal position on the floor, asking God to just take me. I couldn't take it anymore. The intensity that I felt within was beyond measure. A hard swimming workout was so easy compared to what I was feeling inside. It was like a sharp knife was slowly cutting out my heart and I was wide awake for it. I couldn't let the tears out fast enough to let go of all the emotional psychic pain that was consuming me.

No one knew what I had done, as I shared this with no one. I needed help and I knew that, but I didn't know how or who to ask for help. I was functioning in life. I had a job that I was showing up for. I had friends that I would hang out with. I had all the things that life was supposed to be about, but none of it was helping me be in life. One night I got a call from Mary saying that she and her husband had been praying for me and they felt guided to help me. Mary recommended a 40-day retreat that really helped her called the Ark. They offered for me to come out to California and live with them before I started the Ark program with the intention I'd find a job out there after completing it.

The Ark was a 40-day program started by Bill, a Jewish gentlemen, who witnessed his mother being raped by the Nazis in Germany when he was three years old. He designed this 40-day retreat of primal therapy along with other modalities of therapy and meditation. The retreat took place in a huge house in the middle of the Poconos in Pennsylvania. It happened every two years in January and February and during that retreat there was to be no contact with the outside world. It was 24/7 therapy for 40 days.

Before I could be accepted, I had to write a letter about my life and why I wanted to partake in this program. The way the program worked was there were leaders, therapists, and therapists-in-training. I was essentially applying to be a therapist-in-training, despite the fact that I didn't have any intention of becoming a therapist. I wrote the letter and then had a call set up with Bill.

I remember that call so vividly. Bill read my letter and all that I had written about my sexual abuse. He wanted to help me and I was thankful that I had found my way to him. He expressed so much love and kindness on that call; I could feel his love while we were on the phone. He also shared about his trauma and why he started the Ark. We bonded over our pain. I had yearned to have a moment like this with my father. We ended the call with Bill convincing, or more like accepting, that I was ready to take this next step towards my healing. Much to my surprise and sadness, I would never get to meet Bill as he died a few days later. I was touched to have had the call and sad that we were to never meet in person. I was the last person that he accepted into the program.

I packed up from Providence and headed out to California and lived with Jim and Mary for a few months prior to going to Ark. It was strange to be around people who were kind and caring towards each other. Most of my interactions up to this point were formed based on dysfunction of some sort or another. The dynamics that I would create in my previous personal relationships had some sort of emotional abusive element to them. I was witnessing this loving and caring marriage they had for each other and they extended the same kindness towards me. This was so foreign.

After I settled in with Jim and Mary, I had old feelings of my time with families growing up. I started to learn how to communicate with others. On the inside I was still the eleven-year-girl who left home and who had very few words to say. At some point during the course of my time with my friends, I had the courage to ask Jim about the fateful day in the water with him—mostly I was concerned that I'd abandoned him in the water. I shared about my experience as it was weighing heavy on me as I was trying to understand how I have been protected all along. It was much to my surprise that Jim shared that he too had the same experience: a jolt in our hearts and an instinctual response to get out of the water. It was then that I could grasp the idea of the spirit of God and how it lives within us even in the darkest of places.

After a few months of healing with Jim and Mary, I returned to the East Coast to go on this retreat. I arrived at this house—a nice-size house with a huge living room area, communal dining, and sleeping quarters that were a large dorm-like area for the therapists-in-training. The structure of the program was that the therapists-in-training had to do all the house chores which rotated among us. During the course of the day we had a schedule of some group therapy-type work. We learned different therapeutic techniques, and we learned how to give and receive therapy. The therapy sessions were an hour and half; Bill wanted them longer so there was enough time to go deep. He also felt that it was important to learn how to go deep into therapy and then come right out and be present and available for the next person.

The Ark was based on primal therapy and sandbox work. There was a padded room with a punching bag and many things to hit it with. The sandbox room was filled with trinkets and things from every garage sale on the East Coast, I'm pretty sure. It was full floor-to-ceiling with stuff ranging from jewelry, to stuffed animals, to kitchenware, to just about every imaginable object that could possibly trigger a memory of sorts. There wasn't an item missing and the energy of the room itself was so stimulating with the intensity of the memories that were in there.

It took me a few days to settle in and get the hang of the flow of the retreat. I was mostly numb and not connected with me. I was literally going through the motions. I went to the primal therapy room and it seemed more like a workout than anything else. I couldn't access any emotion. But I was trying. I was so well-trained through my swimming to suppress all these emotions combined with my physical strength that it was close to impossible for me to easily connect to myself like that. This was something that was always completely foreign to me. At the same time, I desperately wanted to release all that rage that I knew was in there. Then one day when I was in the sandbox room, I started to fill the sandbox with toys. I placed them all in the box from their waist down. I felt something come over me, almost like being in a trance of sorts. I walked around the room looking for what to put in this box. I reached for a wooden cross. I placed it the box as I started to feel the grief and pressure on my chest. I then found some plastic flowers and placed them in the box as if to say goodbye. As I placed these flowers in the box, I got what felt like an electric charge go right up my arm and through my heart. You know that moment in Caddyshack when they are playing golf in the thunderstorm and the priest is holding up the golf club as it conducts the lightning and it sends a shock right through him? That was what happened to me. I literally felt and heard this crack across my chest. I had cracked my heart wide open and with that came uncontrollable tears.

There it was, a crack of the armor that I had carried on my body to protect myself. I was like the Tin Man from The Wizard of Oz who was getting his heart back. I would like to say it was great and I was healed, but all this did was open me up or really wake me up. I could feel the hurt from that lack of love and compassion from my family that I grew up in.

As the time went by at the Ark, I continued to find my way into the sandbox room and the primal therapy room. Most of what the world knows about primal therapy is from the movie Primal Scream. While that was part of it, there was a physical aspect as well. Hence the padded walls. I would go there for hours and it would feel like a workout and I was still not tired after it. I would be taking the bat and hitting the bag. My voice was so weak, I squeaked out like a mouse; I was so mild-mannered like I had been my whole life. Yet the voice inside of me was so deep that there was no projection whatsoever. I had this British politeness that I was hiding behind, combined with this resonant suppressed voice that I had trained to be afraid to come up for fear of consequences. One could say that it had been years since I trained. I had trained for close to twenty years, all in my formative youth where I formed significant patterns in my life. As a well-trained athlete I learned to be a yes person when it came to physical response to activity, despite the combative dynamic that I shared with Paul. When I was asked to do a set it was with acceptance and no resistance. It was the sexual advances, harassment, and the bullying that I responded to. My behavior outside of the pool as a way to communicate is what killed my swimming career because I didn't know how else to communicate. When it came time to express myself with a primal scream, the connection to the depth of me was weak at first.

One of the driving principles of the Ark was that if you had an issue with anyone in the program, that issue came from someone else in your life because you had just met this person. All the issues and the irritation with people at the Ark was that of my own making. As the time passed, the people around me started to build up the emotions of who they reminded me of in my life. At the same time, I gravitated towards one of the female leaders from whom I sought solace and connection and who was comforting and protecting me. One could say she showed favoritism towards me. I was the youngest person there by ten years, with most of the participants in their fifties and sixties, and I turned 32 during the retreat. It didn't take long for that favoritism dynamic to start playing out with one of the men there, Jake. He started to try and separate me from spending so much time with the leader with whom I was connected. My world was starting to rock right after I started down the path of feeling that I could trust someone again. Now I had to defend myself while at the same time Jake was trying to isolate me from the help I needed. It was similar to my experience with Paul—it was playing out live like I was in it again.

After a while I no longer had the safety and comfort of having a solid and stable connection. I was then rotated into having to give therapy to Jake and then receive therapy from him as well. I of course had a huge resentment with how he had affected me. When I would bring it up, I was told that I needed to use one of the therapy modalities to address the issue. After a few sessions my world was disrupted and I was no longer able to keep the comfort of the one leader. Jake started to ask for sexual favors in our therapy sessions. At first I glossed over it; I wasn't sure what to do. Then it kept happening when we had to be together. When I wanted to connect with the leader, Jake would request time or find a way to intervene before I was able to say anything. When I did share about it, it was met with doubt and resistance that it was even happening to me. I started to experience this same situation that I had with my mother. I felt so powerless and at the same time was told that I needed to use the therapy to deal with my emotions of this situation. I had every dynamic going on at once here, from my relationship with my father, my mother, and my coach issues. The sexual harassment never stopped combined with the lying. I didn't have a solution to get around all of this. I was living this in real time after all that I had experienced and wanted to heal from.

As the time went on, my heart, while open, was caught in this all too familiar world to me. A place that I never thought I would find my way back from. At the same time, I was being shown how this happens, how the lie was staying in the system. Yet I was torn with where to turn other than using the tools that I was provided. There was so much doubt about what I was sharing and experiencing with no action being taken. I actually told someone and yet nothing was being resolved or addressed.

After thirty days of dealing with this issue and the craziness that came with it, Jake decided to leave early. Apparently, no one had ever left early before. Literally when the door closed on him I started to beat the crap out of the boxing bag as I let out a primal scream. I put Nirvana on full blast, which disturbed the entire house while I beat that boxing bag for three hours non-stop. While everyone else in the house could hear my screams, they were told to deal with their own stuff. They let me go and go and go. I did not let up on the intensity for the entire three-plus hours; there was so much anger in me that it took that long for me to have a moment to crack through the suppressed emotions.

As I fell to the ground on the padded floor, I started to see a time when I was about four or five years old when I was being sexually molested by the drunk raging father of a friend. It was like a movie was starting to play in my mind in black and white—it was so vivid and clear. Then what preceded that was a visual of how I formed my relationships with my best friends, lovers, and significant people because my life was based on the secret that my friend and I had agreed to in a childlike way. It was an unspoken spiritual agreement of sorts. In that moment it came undone and the flood gates opened.

It all made sense what was behind my drive for swimming, my love for the sport: it was my need to find praise, and it was all powered by this core pain; it gave me the freedom in myself that I sought and had lost as a child. When Paul raped me, he took away the passion that I had for swimming, my love for my dad and everything that was keeping me alive and disconnected from the pain. I had lost the passion for life—all of life—when swimming was taken away from me.

After having that awareness about myself and that realization, everything started to become clearer in my mind about the pain of my past. This started to free me up to stand tall again. I had been hunched over for most of life staring at my feet, and that gave me the strength, superwoman strength, like I ripped all my back muscles to stand up tall and look you in the eye. I could actually look you in the eye again. I could take on the world.

I would like to tell you that was the moment of truth for me and that everything was smooth sailing for the rest of the time. I was awakened in the middle of the night with the instruction to make a sandbox. The idea was to be in a dream state and not have any inhibitions with what we were drawn to in the room. The leader who woke me was met with the stubborn me not willing to get up and do that. I didn't want to go. I didn't want to do this exercise. I knew I was going to win this battle and after much time they gave up. I was also informed that I would still have to participate in the ritual of sharing my sandbox story and that I would need to share why in fact I didn't have a sandbox. I was good with that.

When it came time to share our sandbox, we sat around in a circle. Everyone went around the room sharing what was meaningful, often about the loss of a loved one or in some cases the future joy that they were open to exploring upon leaving or the growth of self that they had found along the way. When everyone had gone it was time for me to say something. I had an instinctual moment as I wasn't sure what I planned to do. I knew how I felt inside but didn't know how to express it in plain English or in a voice that could barely speak up. I stood up and stripped down to my swimsuit and clipped my cap and goggles under my swimsuit one on each side. Then I climbed right into the sandbox, get into the fetal position, and started to feel what I wanted to feel all my life. I was just a swimmer. I was never just Annabelle. People have wanted something from me all my life. My coach wanted power and control of my mind, body, and soul. My dad wanted glory from me and my mother wanted whatever my dad wanted, to get what she wanted from him. My life was never about me; it was always about what everyone else wanted from me. I don't recall there being a moment in time that I was considered as a human; my value was only what I could bring to the table for someone else. I was flooded with tears and purging these hurt feelings that I carried with me and felt all my life but had nowhere to take them or heal from them. It took all of this time to access the hurt—to just touch a small part of my soul that I wasn't able to connect to in 50 minutes of time over the 30 days of non-stop therapy. I was allowed to cry and express my tears without a tissue, without any interruptions. I just expressed myself and everyone listened as they gave me the floor. People ask me if telling my story was cathartic—this was cathartic in a way that allowed me to start down a path of truly healing the broken and disappointed heart that I have.

After letting go of years of hurt and pain, I felt this shift, or at least I finally felt a connection to myself that I had lost along the way. I don't know that I ever knew anything other than that little girl who loved to swim. It was how my life started in a strong focused direction with so much innocence and passion for the gift that I came in with and developed at such a young age. There are so many blessings with being defined so clearly, and there is also opportunity to be taken advantage of by those around you. That started so young for me, when I had no voice, at a time when I didn't have the intellectual knowledge or capacity to form clear thoughts about it—I only had feelings. I took in how the world responded to me both good and bad. I knew early on that praise felt good and that it was something that I wanted. I had become dependent on praise feeding me from one event to the next. I lost all connection to the praise dynamic in my life when I realized that I was accepting praise in exchange for conditional love, thinking it was the same thing. When it ended so did I.

I left the Ark feeling like I cleared a lot from my system and was ready to go back to the world; the only problem was that the way I was taught how to process—a padded room, sandbox, and constant attention and love from the therapists—were not available in the world that I was returning to. After a few years, the effects of my experience started to wilt again as the despair started to creep back into my life. I was on a mission to heal from my past, but more importantly I was so confused spiritually as to why I suffered as much as I did. My siblings didn't have the same experience; they had different school structures, and they weren't in the praise-rewards system. I didn't have the words or the understanding. This was my dynamic at the time; all I knew was that I had an unusual life and that had to have meaning and purpose at some point, but I didn't know what it was. I felt all I was doing would be revealed to me at some point. My entire focus was healing from my sexual abuse and knowing that it was preventing me from participating in life in a meaningful way.

CHAPTER 17

Another Me

At some point, I wanted to go back to school and graduate as I had a nagging desire to go to law school. I knew I couldn't do that until I went back and finished just over a semester that I needed to graduate. I started traveling back and forth from San Francisco to Austin for the summer and the fall semester. After the fall semester I had one class left in my major of sociology, I had already delved into understanding homelessness and suicide as they were both of interest to me. I was surprised to learn that the lowest suicide rate was with the homeless community even though it was more challenging than the more structured "normal" life. It got me to wonder about sexual abuse and how it happens, more importantly how to heal from it. For my last class I designed my own independent study to explore the healing modalities for sexual abuse. I became obsessed with answering this question.

Then one day I was watching TV and the thought came to me about dolphins and the healing effects of their sonar. There was something intriguing about this thought so I followed it. I decided to write about the dolphins and their potential healing effects from being sexually abused. The way that the study was designed was based on personal experience and supported by literature, symbology, and ideology depicted in storytelling. Now I needed to find the right place for the personal experience part of the study. Naturally I found my way back to Hawaii, only this time I was on the Big Island.

I only planned on being on the island for a week while I pursued this study, but my week turned into a months-long stay. I was determined to get answers to my questions, and heal from the wounds of my past. I had this strong belief that God was unconditional love, compassion, and kindness. If I believed that then I could heal. I wanted to find the purity of my spirit from which I came.

When I got to Hawaii, I found one of the most popular spots to swim with dolphins is Kealakekua Bay. It was a place to rent kayaks or swim from the shore and you often came across dolphins in the bay which was a protected area from fishing. It was surrounded by mountains, a stunning place to swim, and an even more beautiful place to come face-to-face with the dolphins. I started to go there every morning. It was the first time I was drawn back to the water, a place that I had resisted all these years despite my need to always have my cap and goggles; getting wet and being in the water was something that I never wanted to do again. Here I was drawn in willingly.

I started this daily journey, recording my experiences that were profound and subtle all at the same time. I had an intuitive connection to the dolphins. I would dive down and dance with them underwater as they jumped and played right next to me.

It wasn't until one day that I truly understood their healing power when a couple of kayakers were headed towards the Captain Cook Monument; a father and the mother and their 13-year-old son. The son, who seemed to be on the autism spectrum, was sitting out in front of Mom's kayak and looked so excited to witness the dolphins. I had never seen a smile so grand in my life. It was the same joy and adulation that I sought. As the spirit moved me, I asked the boy if he would like to join me in the water with them. There was the moment of hesitation and then I shared with him and his parents that I was an Olympic swimmer and I promised that I would take good care of him. They felt confident and could see my water abilities. Their son jumped right in the water with me. It was this moment that I truly understood the healing effects of the dolphins. As this boy got in the water, it was like a calling for all the dolphins in the area to come and shower their love upon him. The dolphins started circling us and formed this protective circle as they one by one started jumping over this boy's head. Then in their upright position they formed and danced around us. I had never seen this; it was not orchestrated in anyway. It was a pure response to the joy of this young man. The smile that started with this boy had now lifted him off to heaven. I could feel my heart melt with joy watching and partaking in this incredible display of affection.

This led me to wanting to explore swimming with the dolphins on a daily basis—could this heal me? I became curious after witnessing the transformation in this young man; the joy in his heart was something that I sought for myself. I started going out in the same spot every morning in search of something, not knowing what I was going to find. One day I was out in the ocean swimming by myself in search of the dolphins to come by and then this woman showed up. Within a couple minutes into this conversation I learned that her good friend was Wendy who I lived with in Miami and the reason for me even being in the ad for USA Swimming. My relationship with Wendy hadn't healed at this point in my life and she was one of the people that I still needed to make amends with but didn't know how to find her. Here I was in the middle of the ocean over a continent away and someone shows up with that information, another moment of God working in mysterious ways.

After that swim, I got her email, but Wendy wasn't willing to share her phone number with me. Yeah, I had some wreckage to clean up. I wrote an email expressing my apologies and got a response something to effect of, "I'm happy to hear you're sober and good luck with your life." It was not the response I expected after having this amazing random connection. That in itself left me wondering about how this healing really works.

For the past five years I had prayed in agony to have God remove my suicidal thoughts as I rocked myself in the fetal position, begging Him to either take me or stop my mental and emotional torment from me. It paralyzed me in every aspect of my life. I wanted to be free but I had no idea how to do that. I noticed a change in my spirit after I left the Big Island. I wasn't gravitating towards the floor at night to scream to release the pain that was plaguing me.

There is something special about Hawaii to me. I felt so connected to God in the water there; I felt like I was being held in His grace, in the palm of His hands when I laid my head on the water. As He held me, my spirit was cleansed back to the state of grace. It wasn't just the water—it was the people I crossed paths with as well, like meeting Ginny and having her share her faith. I know that it was because she had a heart for humanity and could see the hurt from within. I know that was the seed that opened my heart when I crossed paths with Mary all those years later with the same message. It seemed as if God was always on my trail leading me back to Him. Then there was my moment of being saved out at the North Shore. Were my thoughts magnified through the water? Were my cries really heard? My experiences in Hawaii made me question this, especially after having so many mystical engagements with people in the middle of the ocean. However, all of that was clouded as I continued to struggle with the trauma and harm that lived inside of me for no one to see and only for me to hear.

I couldn't leave the idea of wanting to heal from sexual abuse; whatever that meant or whatever I could do, I wanted to do that for myself. I was so hurt on the inside and disconnected from the world that I knew that I needed something drastic or significant to happen. An idea came over me on the island that I needed to change my name; it was like a gnawing thought that if I didn't change my name I knew it would be so hard to get out of bed in the morning and be me. I was done with the pain of my past. I saw a new name as a way to invite a new future. It felt healing and spiritually guided. Yet I had no idea what that name would be.

As I acclimated back on the mainland after spending several months in Hawaii, I had this notion that maybe one day I could tell my story with a pseudo name. I only knew I wanted a name that felt strong and, more importantly, felt feminine. I wanted to feel the true beauty and power of being a woman; something I felt had been taken from me. I wanted a name that also embodied my personality and what I liked about me. The name Annabelle, while pretty and lovely, didn't feel like it was strong enough or connected to the warrior that I felt inside me.

I went about my life, which was really a search for my truth, which would become my mission even though I didn't recognize that mission.

As I opened to the idea of my spiritual self, it was also coupled with the idea of exploring and being open to experiences that would enhance my curiosity. As my mind kept busy in the background, I kept hearing that I wanted to be a writer, yet I felt hesitant, as I listened to voices of failure that were making out to be my friend, albeit not a nice friend. As I leaned into this idea about writing, my ideas of grandiosity always superseded and intervened in understanding the purpose of even going down this path. Although it got me thinking about characters and people as a way to construct these stories.

The idea of turning these stories into a screenplay interested me and like all aspiring screenwriters, a trip to LA from San Francisco, where I lived at the time, was necessary. After I flew down there as I was driving around the city, I heard the name Katherine Starr. I was to become Katherine Starr. I was wondering if it was the name of one of characters that I had been developing, a young girl who was a genius that brought peace to the world using her intuitive abilities to sense danger in human behavior from her connection to the animal kingdom. I knew it wasn't meant for my writing; it was meant for me. It was like I swallowed this idea and became Katherine Starr in that instant.

It wasn't like I ran out and told anyone about it—I just sat with it. I wasn't sure how all of this was going to go. I had decided to join a silent retreat in New York in a few weeks with a friend I had met in Hawaii who suggested I meet her guru. I was open to just about anything at this point to find myself, if you will. It would be a great place to sit and contemplate about what was next.

When I arrived in New York for the retreat I was still Annabelle filled with fear, shame, and remorse. Yet when I connected with Katherine I could feel a different path and trajectory for my life. I hadn't mentioned anything to anyone at this point, I was still trying to understand this path. My idea was that this was going to help me write my story, yet I wasn't really writing my story. It felt too heavy and too much and I wanted to distance myself from that life. If I erased my path and took this new name then all would be right in the world. That didn't quite sit right either. I knew that I had more questions, and no answers and a lot of fear. I wanted answers. I was already convinced that I was going to become Katherine Starr, but I just didn't know how the transition was going to happen.

At the end of the retreat I learned that there was a trip to India to explore the temples and the ashrams. Having disconnected myself from embracing a community, I now felt that childlike connection that I had when I first started swimming. The compassion in the group brought that feeling back while doing what I love to do: travel the world connecting with culture and people while also going on a mission to find the truth. This time I didn't need a cap and goggles to rediscover that feeling. I wanted to understand why I continued to experience all this hurt and pain. I knew there was a reason, but I couldn't figure out what it was all for. I couldn't believe that I came here just to suffer and be in pain for my entire life—it had to be for a purpose. So far I was coming up empty as to what that was.

Before I went to India, I attended my other brother's wedding. After sitting with the name Katherine Starr for a few months, I felt it was time to mention it to my sister. I thought I would run it by her, well, really drop the information. It wasn't something that was open to discussion or comment. However, in good sibling fashion, my sister felt inclined to comment on the name choice in a derogatory way. It seemed like I had received enough family feedback to end discussing it any further with anyone. Although this didn't deter me, it might have confused me and activated my uncertainty of how was I going to do this. There was a moment of doubt, yet I knew that the train had left the station. I was to become Katherine Starr. I could feel the force of the name start to permeate.

As the India trip approached, I felt a calling to LA and felt that I should be in LA when I returned from India. The desire to be in LA started long before this move; it was ingrained in me as a small child that LA was where I was destined to live since the day the Olympics were announced, if not before then. My tormented heart sought the light and the dark; Los Angeles seemed to be me in my spiritual mind. There was such a strong spiritual force for me to be here. It came in my thoughts and in my drive in the pool. This need to move here was like an avoidance that I skirted my whole life only to know that this was home. I also had a strong connection to the ocean and needed to be near it, see it, feel it, but not necessarily always be in it. It soothed my soul just knowing that it was there. A force from within led me to pick up and move to LA without much planning or thought. It was a similar force like when I drove across traffic in Atlanta, left the garden shed, and picked up and moved to LA for the first time. There was a force that I am not strong enough to resist and must go where my next spiritual lesson is to be. I don't always have the explanation, but I have the knowing that it's what's meant to be.

I arrived in LA without a place to stay and well before the birth of Airbnb. What I know about me is that I'm resourceful. I have self confidence that I just know that I will figure things out. It took me a couple of weeks to find a temporary place a few blocks from the beach within walking distance to all the shops and restaurants. As I settled into my new neighborhood, I was also preparing for a few weeks' long trip to India. I didn't have time to think about how Katherine Starr was going to come alive—it was no longer in the forefront of my mind. It was a lingering thought I hadn't acted on or knew what to do about. Yet that didn't mean the pain of my life wasn't still lingering. I wanted to become Katherine—that wasn't the issue. I just had no idea exactly how to do so or the courage to take the first step.

I thought about India, a country that I had not yet visited, a place in my mind that came with a spiritual intrigue. I didn't have any expectations about what I was going to experience other than meet some new friends and follow a guru around. I was attracted to the culture of the adventure. I was an explorer by nature and curious about life and especially curious about faith, God, the meaning of life, and why we are here. Of course, the most prevailing question remained why was my life so painful. The idea of being in India brought the illusion that something magical was going to happen. I think it says that on any brochure describing India: come for the magical illusions and the sacred cows.

As we traveled around India moving from one ashram to the next, there was a lot of time to just stare out of the bus window and observe the people and their way of life. People were everywhere, even in places where you would not expect anyone to live—they were there too. I started to observe their visible emotions, especially the young children. What excitement they had just to see a bus go by. They would stop what they were doing and run across the field to make sure that they waved as we passed. They came with such open hearts and pure joy for the moment. These children didn't have Nikes, phones, or even anything that resembled a new piece of clothing, yet they showed me this joy that I wanted for myself. I was lost in the needing of "things" while the people of India, the poorest people of India, found "it" freely within themselves. They shared their hearts, beings, and souls with such freedom; it was that freedom that I sought for myself.

While I had some freedom from my past when I arrived, there was still much that was unresolved. As I carried Annabelle around, I yearned for what I believed, the idea of the freedom and joy that would come with being Katherine. I felt like I needed to blend in somehow with my peers and just be plain old me. Although I wasn't really just plain old me as blending into anything isn't something that I could do and India only exaggerated that to the ninth degree. I have often wondered what "it" was, as it wasn't my size or stature, but I seemed to always draw a crowd when it came to Indian children and just Indian people in general. Someone would come running over to me and give me a blessing; it was very odd and I wasn't sure what it was about when it happened. I would say that was how it was there, but they didn't respond that way to the others on the trip. I tried to hide in plain sight but didn't do a very good job.

One of the spiritual things that we could do was to get what they call your Nadi leaf read. It was a reading about what life you chose to live. I always had this theory, or visual, when trying to make sense about my sexual abuse, that there was a movie that played out the life lessons and then the soul had to choose the life that it was going to live. I had this vision of the souls all gathered in a circle as "they" laid out the life that I would choose. The souls did not speak up because of how challenging this particular life (mine) was going to be to live, but eventually the peer pressure was like, "okay, fine, I'll do it." Then here I was living this life, on this path, knowing that it was going to be a challenging and meaningful life. Understanding my purpose was still a big question mark. All I knew was the heartache from which I came.

We headed out from the hotel in one of those three-wheel taxis, called a tuk-tuk, to God knows where. There weren't any clear coherent street signs and it was hard to tell the difference between advertisements and directions as they were posted somewhere in the vicinity that must have made sense to someone but not me. The traffic was comprised of motorcycles usually riden by the entire family: mom, dad, children and babies; meandering cows, some cars, and the tuk-tuks. It was utter and complete mayhem. Although, It all seemed to make sense to everybody that was partaking in the craziness. After about thirty minutes of breathing in dust, cow farts, and tuk-tuk backfire, we arrived at a grass-roofed hut. A cow took up the best space in the home. Then we were met by a very old woman, in her late nineties with only a couple of teeth that matched the color of the smoke coming out of the tuk-tuks. She greeted us in her broken but understandable English. I can't say that I have ever been in such a place or willing to have such an experience. This did not meet my hygiene sniff test, well, all of India didn't, so it was time to just go with it.

The old lady led us around to the back of this grass hut where we met a man who was only wearing a loincloth and didn't speak a word of English. There were a lot of directions and rules about how and where we could be in relations to the cow and the various other animals, including several monkeys floating around in the trees. The cow was sacred—a pet cow of sorts.

I then had to follow the old lady and the old man in the loincloth upstairs where we sat down at a table with the old lady sitting next to me and the old man with only his loincloth sitting on the other side of the table. I sat there in awe and wonder, just fascinated by this whole chain of events.

At the table, the old man got up to grab something that looked like a wood paint stick that was blank to my naked eye, yet he was looking at it like it had something written on it clear as day. He asked me questions in Sanskrit which I do not speak or understand. Thankfully, we had the old lady who was there to translate. He started flipping through this stick, if you will, and asked me these yes or no questions. He asked a few questions like, "You are a politician?" I said, "No." "You are a movie star?" I said, "No," and a few other careers were added in this line of questioning. He continued to ask a few other questions that I said "no" to as well. He then got up and picked up another Nadi leaf and then returned to the table. We went through this a few times until he asked this next set of questions. "Were you born on a Friday?" I said, "Yes." "Do you have three siblings?" I said, "Yes." "Are all three of them married?" I said, "Yes." Then he asked if my brother had three children, and I said, "Yes." Then he asked if my sister had two children and I said "yes" to that. It was all starting to seem very odd, this round of questions as he was trying to find the path that I had chosen to live. I knew that we were on the right one after he asked about all my siblings being married. Then after we sorted out what life I had chosen, he said something in Sanskrit followed by, "Ka-trine Starr." My ears perked up—I sat up in the chair and leaned in. The old woman said, "You have two names." Before I could say anything, he said it again, "Katrine Starr. You are Ka-trine (phonetic) Starr." The old lady turned to me again and said, "Yes, you have two names. You are meant to be Katherine Starr."

I sat there in disbelief. I had only told one person that I was going to change my name and what it was going to be and that was my sister. Here I was in India, in a grass hut, now having a conversation with a guy in a loincloth about my new name. In the interest of full disclosure he did have a cellphone. But I do not believe that he and my sister had chatted. It was like the stars had aligned. Then he went on to state the life that I had chosen to live. There were a lot of careers that I was involved in and I seemed to be heading towards a big life. The rest of the information became a blur after I heard about my name. I knew in that moment I was to become Katherine Starr. And, when I left that grass hut I was Katherine Starr.

When I returned to the group, I started to say and be Katherine Starr. There was a change from the inside, I could feel the empowerment of the name. I also felt along the way that the name was me turning my head when you called. You needed something to call me to get my attention. With that thought, I felt like I could let go of the attention on Annabelle; I could give her a rest from the hard work that she put into my life so far. There was an immediate and welcoming connection to my new name. It was a soul connection to self and a connection to God on a deeper level. It allowed me to feel the power for which I was searching for. I wanted to feel the conviction and strength of the name. I wanted to experience all I thought I had lost.

I also knew that I would never truly let go of Annabelle; it was more like I was protecting her. Giving her a break from the hard path she walked. There was no secret or hiding the name change. But it also was me, which meant there was a heaviness inside brought on by fear and anxiety of speaking up and telling my family, my whole family, that I changed my name. I was committed from the moment I returned to the United States that I was going to make this official.

As I flowed with being Katherine Starr for the rest of the trip in India, I noticed a change in the way people interacted with me. I was sought out even more. I was mainly along for the experience and wonder of India in a more self-discovery mission. Then one day I was asked if I would meet with the leader of the group that everyone was constantly trying to get close to. I was really interested and honored to be asked, but it was also intriguing to wonder what it was that he was after with my presence. I accepted this formal invitation, which was meant to be akin to meeting a great spiritual leader of whom everyone seemed to be in awe. I already drank the Olympic Kool-Aid and knew this ideology and pattern. I had lived it my whole life.

We met with a formal acknowledgement of each other along with his security person or right-hand guy. I sat down feeling awkward with the engagement yet empowered and protected by my new persona. The leader wanted to meet me because I was going to do great things in the world. I really didn't know what that meant other than I felt that inside of me. I felt a sense of importance to my mission, not really knowing what it was. He was in a position of worshipping me (of sorts) for being a follower of his. He wanted to invite me to attend a ritual and ceremony (of sorts) at his ashram with a guru that read omens and paths of world leaders, politicians, and people with significant power. I was flattered with this offering and it seemed more tied to my Olympic accomplishments, but at the same time I am always interested in experiences that would increase my understanding of life.

After accepting this invitation, I extended my trip in India for another week to witness this event. I had witnessed a lot of things over the years and had embraced different cultures; however, this was strangely engaging all of my senses in a way that I hadn't experienced from all the people who had crossed my path including all the politicians, royal family, and other leaders of our world. While this guru had little more on than a loincloth and displayed a full set of teeth, he still spoke in Sanskrit unless he was speaking directly to me in which case he spoke in broken English. The ceremony occurred over the course of two days as he read the signs of the environment, how things showed up when they did, and the reaction that happened as a result. The leader wanted this guy to read my path or future. He too was fascinated with me. He was honored to have met me and saw me fighting a battle that others wouldn't fight. I had no idea what he was saying or talking about. I knew I was feisty in general and would be willing to call you out for your wrongdoing to me. What I was being guided towards was to right a wrong in the world and that was to be my path. A warrior of justice for myself and others. That general idea resonated with me, but I had no direction or understanding of what that path really looked like. I left that experience with fascination, wonder, and the same question as before: "Is that the reason people are gravitating towards me?"

India became special for me in how it touched me on the inside. It felt guided and purposeful to fulfill whatever it was that I was meant to do. It also led me to knowing that there was a purpose for my life. I wasn't clear on what that was, but there was one. It felt like I was given my purpose when I came here and then that part of my memory was erased—I was spending my whole life trying to recall that part of my being. The blank canvas inside me was starting to develop an outline.

Now knowing my purpose, I arrived back home with the confidence to become and live the rest of my life as Katherine. My first order of business was to change my voicemail. Since I was relatively new in LA, it was a perfect time to just say that I was Katherine Starr going forward. It was with family and lifelong friends that I needed a more substantial means of transitioning. That all happened with my brother getting my voicemail and wondering whether his sister was, well, crazy? I was pursuing a path outside of societal norms. I wasn't much for the societal norms anyway; if they were so great then we wouldn't have rampant sexual abuse around the world.

The day after I arrived home, I had gone to the Santa Monica courthouse and filed for a name change. It was going to take about six weeks for it to become official; they gave me a date of January 5, 2006. I had much to do before then, like finding a permanent apartment since I was renting part of a house and wanted my own space. I found a place that I could move into January 8th right after my name change became official. Before all of the events, I planned to meet my brother and his family at my parents' condo in Keystone, Colorado, between Christmas and New Year's. My brother was opinionated about this name change and not really willing to accept or acknowledge the decision that I had made. I however saw the visit as a way to formally transition to Katherine. Since my name wasn't going to be official until right after the New Year it made perfect sense. A formal goodbye and a welcoming to my new name.

I decided that I was going to drive out to Colorado from LA and stop along the way, making an adventure out of it. That winter it seemed like there was significant snow and challenging road conditions in the Rockies. I had experience with winter driving and knew that I could drive anywhere in the world on any side of the road; I had been my parents' designated driver in many foreign countries, including Greece and Turkey, not to mention the snowstorm with marginal visibility that I drove my mother in up this mountain. She was a nervous wreck the entire time, not because of my driving, but because that is the person that she is. Yes, that makes it even more challenging when you are already driving in challenging conditions. Needless to say, my confidence was high and I felt competent.

As the week progressed with the family, I was just Annabelle. I don't know that I even had a chance to say anything about becoming Katherine. Knowing how my brother would have likely responded. I knew that when I returned to LA I would be Katherine Starr. As the week ended, another storm was heading our way, so my brother and I both decided it was best to leave on December 31 and not stay for New Year's.

We left the mountain and headed our separate ways, my brother went east and I went west. I left around 7 a.m. as the sun was just starting to rise. Keystone is on the top of the mountain range as you head west towards Vail; they are all part of the same mountain resorts. Vail is about fifty miles along I-70, mostly down a steeply graded hill. I was driving with traffic, nothing crazy, cautious and mindful of the conditions; it was cold but the snowstorm hadn't come in yet. I was content leaving and ready to get back to LA. As I was thinking about that, there was a strong bend in the interstate which was still at a fairly steep incline. I hit black ice. I felt the back of my car come loose and completely spin me around in traffic so that I was staring at the cars coming towards me. I would like to tell you I know how the next moment happened, but it felt like I was being pulled from behind as if in reverse, out of the traffic as I slammed up against a large, 50-60-foot wall of mud, rock, snow, and sludge off the interstate. It was like being in a bumper car as I bounced right off that and my car started to roll along, parallel to the interstate. My car landed on the top corner of the driver side windshield as it crushed right up to my face. No airbags went off and I held on to the steering wheel as if I was rolling along in slow motion, my athletic body moving along and clenching at all the right moments as I intuitively went with the flow of it all. Somehow, I had collected a massive boulder which was rolling around with me on the inside of my SUV. Then my car abruptly stopped, wheels up, with the entire car looking like it had gone through the trash compactor with a cut-out shape perfectly surrounding me in on the driver's side. I couldn't see anything in the outside world with every window shattered or smashed. I slid out of the car shocked as I felt my body, patting it down in doubt as I took in that I was still alive and in one piece. Although rattled inside, I walked away from that crash with only a few pieces of glass in my face.

Then a calmness and sense of peace came over me as I looked around my car to see that with one more half roll my car would have gone over the cliff. I knew in that moment Annabelle was in a better place and it was time for Katherine to find her way. As I was standing there taking this all in, a couple of cars stopped. They had completely expected me to be dead having witnessed the crash and watched the car roll in such a dramatic fashion. One of the drivers was so awed after witnessing this, that he told me he was convinced that there must be something important that I am meant to do. It was similar to what the omen reader in India had to say about me. I knew that I had purpose in life—I just didn't know what that was yet.

Needless to say my car was totaled and I had to fly back to LA from Vail after I dropped the remains of my car off at a junkyard. I didn't go to the hospital or need any medical help other than experiencing a little shaking from the intensity of the crash. My only objective was getting back to LA.

I headed to the Vail airport for the one flight to LA that wasn't scheduled to leave for several hours. If you have been to the Vail airport you would know that it is rather small, about eight to ten gates, and security wasn't working all the time due to the infrequent flight schedule. They had these plush leather chairs, very nice may I add, in the airport prior to security. I found a place to sit down and just chill before my flight. I pulled out the book I was reading at the time, Life of Pi, and the moment I started to read a woman sat down in one of the other comfy chairs and started reading her book as well. I looked up and she was reading the same book—yes, I know it was a popular book at the time. I thought I was late to the game in reading it. Either way, it intrigued me after having a lesson in reading omens; I thought this was another sign that I needed to inquire about. I had to make a comment, pointing out that we were reading the same book. That quickly led to discussing the interesting story and where we were in our respective books. What was incredible to me was that she on the same page and paragraph as was I. For me, it was another omen that Annabelle had moved on to a better place and Katherine would be moving forward. Five days later, I officially became Katherine Starr.

CHAPTER 18

Two Hearts Beat As One

As I settled in as Katherine Starr in LA, where no one knew me as Annabelle, I could feel how I missed Annabelle. I missed all that she had been through and done. I also knew that it was time to give that part of me a break. While I was comfortable with this choice, it was not so for my father. It was actually quite offensive that I would want to distance myself from our family name. My father was strong in his views about carrying on our lineage and tradition, as was my mother. How I thought about it was that if I were married it wouldn't matter anyway. It wasn't so much about the last name; it was about changing the first the name my parents had chosen for me. I could no longer be "Little Annabelle" to my dad.

I was now faced with this challenge of knowing and committing to this new direction that I knew was the right choice for me. Being Katherine Starr didn't change the family that I came from or heal me from my past. I wanted my parents to see me, especially my dad. I wanted him to know what was hurting me, where his only interest in me after my career was how I was presenting myself on the outside—someone who was never good enough as I continued to struggle with my weight. It fluctuated a lot over the years, but mostly towards an upswing. The higher I went in my weight it seemed that the more my father voiced his disappointment with me.

As my weight increased, I created a wedge between myself and my connection to God. I wasn't maintaining any relationship with God and frankly couldn't understand and connect to God in my heart. I wanted the love and the compassion, but my continued need to suffer and cut myself off from the sunlight of the spirit was a way to punish myself and others around me. It was one big FU to the world that I couldn't let go of. It was stronger than me. I noticed that there was a separation between how I felt inside and what I presented to the outside world. As I became this person, this Katherine Starr, I also came across challenges concerning how I talked about myself; and who am I? What do I do? All those basic questions that people ask.

While I continued with the struggle to figure out who I was, my father never abandoned me financially. I freely accepted his gifts as he tried to make sure I didn't fail in life, albeit I was failing by the mere fact that I was allowing him to prevent me from failing. Neither of us knew that. He wanted me to be something and I wanted him to be something and we came at this from different places. I couldn't see beyond my hurt, when in reality all I wanted was a "sorry," or some sort of forgiveness from him. In my mind I thought that would make up for all the hurt that I had experienced from him over the years. I wanted my dad to drown in my sorrows with me and tell me that I would do better next time and that he still loved me. I was in the "not enough" cycle and he was in the "I need more" cycle, and neither of us could see each other for who we really were. My dad was always the life of the room with his charm and clever personality. I was that too, but you wouldn't know that when we were around each other. I was starting to see that spark fade away in him as he started to age.

I couldn't let go of the idea of needing and wanting to write a book as I had been advised from the moment I shared my story. But I struggled with what was I going to talk about. I didn't want to talk about misery without resolution, but I had no resolution or ending for the story. It was painful and even now I'm using words to convey a physical, emotional, and spiritual experience that is only as good as the choice of words that comes with that. It's a feeling and an experience after talking to me that you can have a truer understanding of the impact it had on my life. I also have a determination and drive that has emerged to heal myself and to lead others on a healing path of their own. Yet I didn't know how to actually go about this. All the messages that I have had on the way guided me in a vague but significant direction. My ego latched on to the idea of "big" and "significant" as a way to feed the need for more praise—like the vulture that I was when it came to be recognized—but I could not see that or understand that at the time.

Feeling defeated with my path and life, but no longer being tormented by suicidal ideations, I knew something was changing, but my ability to fend for myself was not there. I was getting some answers but no direction. Going back to work in the tech world made me feel trapped. The idea of that made no sense to me. Why did I have this life only to spend it in misery? I battled these thoughts and direction. What was the "important life" that I was to pursue?

In order to answer that question I knew that I needed to clean up my past more than I had already done. I had cleaned up most of my friendships and my relationships with anyone who was still important to me, but I had not truly embraced cleaning up my swimming past. I had so much sadness and remorse. I also carried around this dynamic of me being an athlete and feeling less than or, more accurately, submissive to life in general. It was a dynamic that plagued me in my relationships, whether a romantic relationship or a personal one. I took the submissive role because that was what I was trained to do. This role that I had taken in life was so ingrained in me that I never thought it was possible to break away from. I also was stuck on this idea that I had blown up my life with Mark, my former coach, and therefore there was no hope of reconciliation. Now here I was in the same part of the country as Mark and I wanted to resolve the conflict. It wasn't like I didn't keep in touch with Mark over the years; it wasn't frequent but he was always nice to me. I desperately wanted to break this pattern and dynamic that I had with Mark and all coaches in general.

I reached out to Mark and asked him if we could meet for breakfast. Mark graciously agreed—actually he was excited that I asked and welcomed the chance to catch up with me again. I, on the other hand, was filled with fear. I knew the purpose of wanting to meet was to share with Mark about my abuse while also resolving issues from our past relationship with the hopes that it would heal me. I hoped that, if I was healed, I could more clearly understand my purpose in life and find some direction as to how to begin to fulfill that purpose. It was a mystery that was providing me with what seemed like very few clues. Anyway, I was willing to play the game.

We arranged to meet at some busy trendy breakfast place. I had trouble with Mark during our weigh-ins, not that I wasn't making my weight—I was; he was actually mad at me because I was eating like crap and still weighing under my goal weight. I chalked it up to just having a great metabolism. Here I was now having to openly eat a meal with someone who had criticized my weight, not quite like my dad, but in the same vein, where the body was of more value than the person, at least that was what it felt like. As I let go of my fears about the food and body issues, I started to share with Mark about what happened to me during the course of my swimming career. He expressed his heartfelt apologies and said that he didn't know what had been going on with me, and that he would have made different choices with me if he had known. He was really sorry. We had the most beautiful caring conversation that one human can have with another. The coach/athlete relationship was changing in that moment to one that showed compassion and understanding. That was something that I wanted when I swam and I especially wanted to have this conversation with my dad with that same response of understanding and care. I could feel this shift in me like a seesaw that was finding its way to level again.

While I reconciled with Mark and began to resolve the issues surrounding how I ended my swimming career, I was still paralyzed by my biggest fear: losing my dad. I loved him so much. I wanted desperately to talk to him about what had happened; I wanted to have a conversation with my dad like I had with my coach. I wanted him to tell me he was sorry and that he should have protected me and cared for me better. I had a simple view of what forgiveness was at the time. I had this idea that if he asked for my forgiveness first then I could let go of whatever it was that I was holding onto inside of me. It was essentially the battle of our wills and they were both as strong, albeit I think I won the stubborn prize amongst the stubborn folks. Little did I know that I was not the only one suffering here.

During my dad's final years I started to travel with my parents on occasion as their driver just to help them do what they loved to do which was to travel. My father also wanted to continue his talks around the world. I started to spend more time with them. One of those trips was to Greece and Turkey. We flew into the Greek island of Ios and then took a ferry to Kusadasi in Turkey. When we got to Turkey we had to go through immigration. My parents had British passports and, as we know, I had two passports, a British one and an American one. They went through the European Union line, which was shorter and cheaper, may I add, while I wanted to be American and went through the other line. My parents were at my mercy as I was the driver and needed to rent the car in my name when we got into Turkey. They basically walked right through customs, which I could have done but I was committed to being an American. My dad's frustration with me making this choice brought to mind my long standing conflicts as to what I loved more. In other words, where was my loyalty? Was it to my nationality? My parents' nationality? It was the same conflict that I felt with my allegiance to swimming and then, who did I serve? My dad or my coach? I couldn't always serve both when there was a conflicting direction. I started to see how this conflict of identity and role was serving those around me but not me

I had found myself trapped in my own thoughts of destruction without even being aware of it. All while I wanted to just be in my relationship with my dad. I wanted to hear my dad call me "Little Annabelle" again. I wanted the innocence of our relationship that existed back when I loved to swim. The place where we stayed in Cesme was right on the sea, absolutely beautiful. The sea was the perfect temperature and calmness. All there was to do was swim, relax, and eat. The eating was the easy part: I felt comfort in the distraction and way that I managed my life and feelings at this point in my life. The swimming was the harder part. His whole life my dad swam just about every day because he loved it. I wanted to love it, but I resented him so much for how my swimming career turned out. I was mad at him and myself at the same time and I didn't know who to forgive first.

During our time in Cesme, I started to go to the sea and try and swim. Once I started swimming, everyone stopped in awe and amazement. There was that moment of feeling proud but I couldn't enjoy that feeling; I felt so undeserving, like this was the very gift that destroyed my life. I was holding myself and those around me hostage for having these feelings about it. My dad would usually watch me swim. He could see the joy it brought me, and I felt the joy that I got from it, but I didn't want to give him that. What I really experienced was this feeling of grace in the way that I slid through the water. It was so powerful. I wanted that same feeling on land but had never found it. I was stuck in the quandary of wanting something from this gift of mine while at the same time resenting it and everything and everyone around me.

I feared my dad's death as I watched his health decline. However, his mind, and a brilliant one it was, remained alert, I wanted to be that little girl/adult woman with those moments where I would lay on my dad's chest. My dad had several open heart surgeries over the years and the first one occurred when I was about four, around the same time that I started swimming. I remember when he came home from the hospital he had a fresh scar down the center of his chest, but it didn't stop me (or him) from crawling onto his chest and just being together. There was no rejection, disappointment, or anger for anything that I had done so far in life. He only loved me for me and the idea of what I was going to become for him. The innocence of that love was all I wanted back. The freedom to love each other without expectation of outcome.

I was still trapped in the approval, love-reward system with the desperate need to perform and receive praise of my actions. While I had worked out a part of that dynamic with Mark, there were coaches that still left me scarred, leaving me vulnerable to keeping this system alive. I could see it more clearly now. It would be in the smallest of things, really any act of doing triggered that need, as I saw it for example in my need to be a good driver in a strange country. I had the idea and the thought that recognition was going to heal me and take away the pain of life.

I had all of those thoughts and my only way to combat them at this point was to eat. I was no longer drinking, yet I needed some kind of vice to deal with the intensity of these emotions and thoughts that were coming at me a mile a minute. I also justified the eating because I was sexually abused and it was okay to eat those feelings. It is what sexual abuse survivors do and everyone felt sorry for me. While I didn't say those thoughts out loud, I know they were in me and at the core of my beliefs and justification for living life the way that I was.

After several of these trips with my parents over the next couple of years, I saw the window gradually closing with having any kind of resolution with my dad. I could possibly say the words, "I'm sorry," but that wasn't what I wanted. I wanted a moment of our hearts being open to each other. I wanted to be able to have an honest conversation like I did with Mark. Instead of opening my heart, I carried around my most dreaded fear: the fear of his death. I feared the death of the ones I loved more than my own death.

As that fear lingered in my thoughts, I got a call from someone who had found my information online and wanted me to know that our mutual friend Chris had died. He was the one with me and Mary that day in Half Moon Bay, and the one I was holed up with in the hotel room. He had died of a drug overdose. The person who was contacting me wanted to know if I could help get his ashes from his brother as Chris only ever spoke of a few people by name and I was one of them. My heart went out to my friend as for many years we loved each other's pain; we understood each other's misery that we might as well have celebrated it together, as we did. It couldn't have been more than five minutes after I hung up from that call that I got a call from my mother, from the cruise ship she was on with my dad, to tell me that my dad wasn't doing well and that she didn't know if he was going to make it.

I had finally received this dreaded call, the one that I feared since I was little girl. I was also the one in the family you would call because of the level-headed manner in which I would handle such emotions. My brother would have been a wreck; the other brother could handle it, but he suppresses his emotions more than me, and my little sister would want me to take the lead, while she supported me. We all had our role in the family and this was mine. I called all my siblings to let them know to be on guard for what was going to happen next.

When I got the news I felt that I needed to talk to my dad and heal our relationship. I felt forced given the circumstance and ready at the same time. I feared not being able to see him again. I started to pray and ask God to let me have a moment with my dad to heal our relationship. I didn't know how that was going to happen but I had turned desperation into determination.

I spent that night in quiet reflection of the unknown, I knew something wasn't right this time. My mother had manipulated us my whole life that my dad was going to die as a way to keep us close. She knew how much we all loved him and especially me; it was the wedge in my relationship with my mother: the love that my dad had for me. It was really our love of swimming; it was our passion for something that we bonded over.

The next morning I got a call from my mother. The cruise ship had just left Cabo, Mexico, and headed to LA. The doctors didn't think that my dad would make it and they needed to airlift him off the cruise ship to a hospital in the States. So the ship changed course to meet the Coast Guard who would take my father to a hospital in San Diego. My mother was calling me to coordinate which hospital to take him to. I was also directed to round up my siblings and let them know that they needed to get to San Diego if they wanted to see Dad and say goodbye.

I jumped in my car and sped down the freeway fast, yet calm at the same time, to San Diego to pick up my sister from the airport. All the while staying in contact with the Coast Guard on where they were taking my dad. I knew the best hospital there was the Scripps Hospital and I had to barter with the Coast Guard to take my dad there. I knew that was where he wanted to be. I had that connection of knowing with my dad. Our whole relationship was based on this intuitive knowing that one has with a parent and heightened in the athlete-child relationship that we had together. I could hear my dad speaking to me like he was directing traffic when I was driving them around the world; this time it was no different, he just wasn't in my physical presence.

After picking up my sister, the two of us met the helicopter at the emergency landing pad. I remember seeing my dad laying there lifeless with tubes, oxygen, and everything else connected to his body, while still having a pulse. I could see that I needed a miracle to have the much needed resolution with my dad. I had closed my heart too long. I also started to hear my dad talk to me. I could hear my dad comfort me with the words, "Little Annabelle, I'm going to be okay." I wanted to believe that, but knowing how fast my dad was losing blood—it wasn't looking promising.

My sister and I met with the doctors and they had to give my father a blood transfusion to combat the rate at which he was losing blood. My sister and I were left to make all the medical decisions. My sister wanted my mother to give me the power of attorney and let me take the lead until she arrived the next day. However, her "diplomacy" and inability to make decisions got in the way of that. It was no different than being left to swim in the dark alone. It didn't stop me, however, from showing up to make all the best decisions that I could in the moment because I knew that something had taken over me and the doctors to get whatever care my dad needed. After we got my dad on track with the doctors, both my brothers arrived. It was just us with our dad and I know that my dad felt all of our presence there in that moment. It was the love of his children that was starting to have an effect on him.

The next day, he went into a coma and was moved to the ICU unit from the Emergency Room. This particular ICU unit was next to the maternity ward. There was no waiting area other than some couches and chairs outside of the elevators. We would hang out there as only two people could be in the room at a time. By this time my mother had arrived and took one of those spots so we would rotate going in to see him.

We all sat with our phones and watched the comings and goings of the people on the elevators as we perused the internet and played games to pass the time between visits to my dad. Something came over me to look up Paul while I was sitting there only to learn that he had just died. He had actually died the moment that my dad arrived at the hospital. I was so jarred after reading that I felt even more conviction to be able to talk to my dad. My nemesis was dead. I was free to talk and express myself about him. The only problem now was that my dad was in a coma and no one knew when or if he would wake up.

What was also spiritually intriguing about all of this was that my dad's internal medicine doctor from home was lecturing at the Scripps hospital that morning and was able to take over some of the care. There was also one his "favorite" residents who had a practice at the hospital, and came by regularly to check on my dad's care. What I found the most profound moment about what was going on were the random people who were there to show up to say goodbye to my dad, all unplanned—or was it?

Over time the elevators opened and one of my brothers recognized the man in a happy couple that were clearly heading toward the maternity ward. My brother has one of those memories where he has not forgotten a face or name of anyone in his life. While I'm good, he takes that skill to a whole new level. My brother recognized the man from one of my father's work trips to Turkey, and so he introduced himself to this couple. I watched wondering who he was talking to, only to find out he was a Turkish doctor that my father had worked with for decades treating Turks who had developed skin deformities after ingesting toxic wheat given to them by Germans after World War II. This couple was randomly in town because his son and American wife were having their first child; now the ICU was on their agenda. It wasn't just this Turkish couple that my father adored that happened to come out of those elevators; there were others who just happened to be there who were coming by to see my dad and pay their respects.

While all these interesting coincidences continued, I couldn't help but wonder about the passing of Paul at the same time. I would watch the elevator and wonder who was coming out next: a happy family to witness the birth of their first child, or an addition to their family, or a family sad and worried for a loved one in the ICU. The intensity of these emotions had me moving about often so I created a ritual of visiting my dad, and then going to the gift shop to buy two Tootsie Rolls and a Diet Dr. Pepper. Then I'd walk around the grounds listening to my dad comfort "Little Annabelle" in my mind. As I connected to my dad's caring voice for that little girl, I prayed for a moment of reconciliation. I was lost in the little girl connection. I was lost in all the moments that I let slip by because of how hurt I was on the inside. I was lost about why my dad couldn't protect me. Why didn't he see me as well as he could see the gifts that I had as a human being? Why did he miss the gentle tender person that I really was on the inside? When did that change for us? I wondered about all this and had no answers for our relationship and feared that I would have to live my life never knowing this without any closure.

While I continued to contemplate and reflect, we waited patiently for something to change with my dad's status. A couple of days went by, and after going through my newfound routine, I arrived back to my oldest brother sharing with excitement that Dad had woken up and I should go in and see him. The younger of the two brothers and I went into Dad's room. When I walked into the room, I locked eyes with my dad. They were wide open. I moved closer to him with my brother over my left shoulder, and I locked in with a gaze as my dad clearly wanted to move as he displayed this intense excitement to see us. My brother placed his hand on my dad's leg as he comforted him with, "It's going to be okay." The whole time I was fixated and locked into my dad's eyes. I could see that he wanted to take out the breathing tube to say something to us, although for me, it felt like he was trying to speak to me directly. I had narrowed out my brother as I fixated on my dad's eyes. I could see this deep sadness. I could see and feel this forgiveness that he was trying desperately to express in that moment. I could see his remorse and sadness for not protecting me. He had protected me financially, but I could see that he was saddened that he never protected my heart, that little girl, that little Annabelle heart. It was his sadness for not caring for my soul, the gentle loving person that was torn out of me, and that he didn't try and know how to put that back together again. I didn't either. As this unspoken exchange happened through our connected knowingness, tears started to well in my dad's eyes. We spoke without words; both of our hearts started to melt into forgiveness for each other. I could feel that he truly wanted me to know how broken-hearted he was for the life that I had endured. It was the first time in my life that I truly felt free from my father's expectation of me and me of him. As my brother continued to comfort my dad, my dad had a tear wanting to escape his eyes that rolled out as his eyes closed. I watched that tear roll down his face. As I wiped away the tear, my dad slipped back into a coma only to never wake again. My heart was broken and my biggest fear realized.

It would be another nine torturous days of watching those elevators open and close as sadness and joy presented itself, not to mention being summoned into a conference room from the hospital executive staff to address our behavior of coming and going in the ICU and not following the rules of only two people at a time. To us it was two, not counting my mother as the constant fixture at my dad's bedside. If it makes any difference, it was my ability to see the dynamic of the head nurse and how he exercised his control while manipulating his position with the other nurses. I brought this to the executive staff's attention in a clear and concise way. They couldn't put their finger on the dynamics before, but I saw and articulated it in a way that allowed them to see another story to what was being communicated. That moment showed me a gift that I didn't know I had or one that had developed in me over the years. It was a dormant and silent aspect of my personality, in essence I learned something about myself that I didn't know: my ability to see people other than as they present themselves. I didn't know what to do with this gift, but it became apparent that it was in me.

After my dad's passing, I stayed behind to take care of my dad's cremation and pick up his ashes. It was a surreal moment to pick up the urn with my dad inside and be left with just memories and feelings that defined and shaped how I participated in life with and without him. The dynamic had changed in that I was carrying his memory with an open heart as he gave me that gift in his final moments. I connected with my dad as a dad who loved me unconditionally in that moment as I did him.

I was left with the loss of my dad, and more importantly, I lost the war that I was battling most of my life now that my opponent was dead—well actually, both of my opponents were taken out at about the same time. Who was I going to fight with now? There was only me left.

With his ashes in tow, I got on a plane to Madison to celebrate the life of my dad. The service was at the beautiful church we went to as children on the square across from the magnificent state capitol building. When I arrived at the church there was a section at the front of the church roped off for family. As people began to gather, the family section started to fill one by one as I was greeting, catching up, and accepting the various condolences of the guests coming to pay their respects. Some of the people I hadn't seen since I was little girl, some more regularly, and many of whom were very active in my life like my coach from the Hawaii days, Jack. I was poised and respectful to everyone who arrived, but I was curious and actually bothered by these people who were invading my family's area. They didn't look like anybody from my parents' fancy neighborhood and I couldn't understand what walk of life these people were from—certainly not my dad's. They looked scruffy, but well-put-together scruffy, like they got the best clothes they could find out of the trash and wore those. They brushed their greasy dirty hair so it looked more organized for the moment. They sat there staring at a picture of my dad with great respect. I watched them as they showed a deep sadness, one that I wished I could have within myself, but I wasn't ready for that. I could see how much they cared for my dad.

I finally asked someone who these people were that were sitting in the family section. I learned that they were from the homeless community that my dad treated. They would wait outside my dad's office every night whenever they needed medical attention and my father would treat whoever was there. He never turned someone away and always gave them the medicine and the care that they needed. They all knew where to go. My father was the father they always wanted and never had; they got to experience the father that I always wanted but never had. I saw my dad's beautiful heart when he was trying to connect with me in his final moments that day.

Leaving my father's memorial, I learned more about my dad's heart in that moment and how broken my own was. I didn't have the skills to reconcile with the pain of my past and with my father on my own. I got home and prayed to understand my life. I prayed for direction for my path. I had lost my opponent in battle, but now what was I to do?

I love you, Dad, and miss you with all my heart. I know that you have been on this path with me writing this book and I hear your voice of love and compassion over my shoulder.

Now I was left with a piece of my dad as my siblings and I shared his ashes. My birthday was a few weeks after he died and I wanted to celebrate him like I wanted to remember him. I thought of a private beach in Malibu that I often go to with a dear friend.. It is one of the most beautiful beaches in the world. I wanted to leave him in the ocean and put my dad back where I know both of us belong.

On the day of my birthday there was a huge storm and the waters were rough. My dad loved a good storm. I also didn't shy away from rough waters. I put on my wetsuit and tucked my dad's ashes under my wetsuit so I could swim out and scatter his ashes. I was smart enough to wear fins for this adventure as it was extremely rough this particular day. I was determined to have this moment. I knew the joy that it would bring my dad, and besides, he was watching over me now. I swam out in the huge swell, not quite like the one in Hawaii when I got rescued, but close to it. I found a spot where I could tread water over the rolling waves and pull out the ashes. I took the lid off and let him go. I watched the wind swirl and carry my dad off with the elements back to where he belonged. I felt that moment of freedom from me, from him, from everyone.

CHAPTER 19

Drifting to Shore

After my dad left us and I returned him to the ocean, I too found my way back to wanting to spend more time there. I now have so much more clarity and solace when I get in the ocean—there is something so healing of the mind and the emotions when it is cleared with the saltwater washing over your thoughts. It was a quick and efficient way to reset my emotions, thinking, and clarity about life. I formed this dependence on that connection to the ocean; it was like my only outlet where I felt like myself and where my soul found a deep sense of peace. It didn't feel like training—there was nothing that confined me in the ocean like I found in the pool. I was free to be me and that is all I have wanted to find and be in all of this.

While I found my way back to being in the ocean, it didn't bring back the passion for swimming that I had as a child. I knew I felt comforted in the water. I would eagerly want to swim from shore when I saw dolphins go by and join them on their journey like I was one of their pod. I couldn't let go of the idea that either swimming was going to be part of my life or the story of abuse was going to be part of my life. I would press in my connection with God to reveal why I was on this path and what was I supposed to do? I was just as lost now that my dad was gone. I desperately wanted direction with my life.

Even as I was in search of the next path, my sister would always say that she wasn't worried about me and that I always landed on my feet, all the while aware of the extent of my struggles. I also believe that to be true about me. I had watched myself go through life with resilience. I wanted to believe in my direction with conviction. I yearned to be lost in water as these thoughts distracted me from the overwhelming grief of losing my dad; it would take me away to where I wanted to be—just away. Then one day I was flicking through the channels and something about water perked my interest. It was ESPN's *30 For 30* about Hawaii and of course the big surf of Pipeline on the North Shore featuring Eddie Aikau who was a lifeguard and surfer at the North Shore. As I was watching this show, I started to feel goose bumps as I realized who saved me that day out at the North Shore. I started shouting at the TV, "That was the guy! That was the guy that saved me!" I wanted Eddie to respond back like he was there and could hear me. I knew that it was him. I wanted to reach out to him to share my story with him. Only to learn that he died on the first night he set out to sail on a mission and his body was never found. I felt this gratitude for life and purpose for me being here. It was like when I crashed my car and someone said that I had a purpose. This was the icing on the cake of confirmation that there was a purpose for my life that led to Eddie being there that day to guide me back into shore.

My curiosity led me to wanting to learn more about Eddie's life and when he died. All I wanted to do was drift off to my next life and not carry on with this one. He interjected in that trajectory. As I began my research, I couldn't believe what I was learning. Eddie had been dead for over four years when we had our encounter. He was known as "Eddie Would Go" and had saved over 500 people in those treacherous waters. I was one of them.

As I recall that day, I was laying in the water thinking about wanting to die when I heard this voice, *Do you need help?* As I look back on my life, I was always so proud to not ask for help, only to find it has always been there. I had never seen until that moment how I have been supported all along. The idea that I was saved once again and that maybe there is someone and something always looking over me. I had so many signs and hints along the way but wasn't always able to understand them in the moment—now it gave me the inspiration to engage in life in a meaningful way.

Once again I was on my mission of trying to figure out my path with some clues to guide me. I decided that I would try coaching swimming. Maybe it wasn't where I was meant to be, but coaching was something that I was willing to try. I had always felt comfortable and confident in my abilities in the pool and wanted to rebuild that confidence. I thought that all I really knew was swimming despite having worked in technology and other industries. It was the only skill I knew I had at a high level.

So, I found a job on the Westside in LA and started coaching a team. Shortly after I started coaching these kids, a twelve-year-old boy joined the team and my group. He wanted to swim because was being bullied in school for doing ballet, which he was very good at. I started coaching this young man, and he started to improve so fast with his reps and times in training. As he started to swim faster, his confidence grew and he became proud of himself. He developed a sense of self that allowed him to be strong in who he was as a person. His friends changed, his schooling changed, and the way that he engaged with life changed. He was living his current dream-filled life, but it was based on my perceived value as his coach. As I watched and witnessed this change in this boy, what I realized was how susceptible he was to being abused. The power and the credit for the change was freely accredited to me. It all became clear as day to me how sexual abuse resided in the system. The role of the coach, and the dynamics that are naturally developed, as well as the age of separation from the parent all aligned. It wasn't just that I had played an integral part in developing him as a swimmer—that wasn't what made him vulnerable—it was an outside source that was credited and praised for giving the person this gift. This dynamic that started to develop was the reward-recognition cycle and the need for praise that we all yearn for in sports and performance-based dynamics. The need for recognition is what creates the cycle and vulnerability to being abused in any form.

As I started to watch this develop in front of me, I knew that was how the problem was created in the system, combined with the lack of policies to address these issues. I could see the silence in the athletes unable to speak their truth while gaining something they sought in return in the way of benefits that we all sought in sports. All this did was create more questions for me than answers. What I knew about myself was that I had all those questions about sexual abuse, such as, "why did this happen to me?" There had to be a reason that I had that experience. There must have been a reason that Eddie appeared and directed me back to shore. There must have been a reason that Mary and I crossed paths that day. It was all starting to make sense as to where I was meant to go in life. I had wanted the answer to this question: why did it happen and how did it happen? As I continued to coach, I continued to see the issue in plain sight. That to which I once could not see, feel or touch had become the wisdom which would guide me.

Then it started to make sense to me how I saw Eddie that day. When I reflect back, he offered me help in the way of direction and gave me a guide and a way home. He said that he would swim right by me, which he did. At some point the splash that I thought was Eddie started to fade into the background. I made up a story about that situation that day. Like I made up a story based on my perception of the events in my life separate from what was real. The abuse was real, and I scared myself with the stories along the way based on my perception of events. When Eddie came back to me by revealing himself through this documentary, I had a strong feeling that he was guiding me through my life to put me back on track to find the path that I was meant to be on.

At the same time that I was opening my eyes to this dynamic, I had found myself in a very abusive personal relationship. If and when you meet me you will learn that I am a direct, strong, and powerful woman. Yet I lost my voice in vulnerable romantic situations that left me paralyzed with my voice and my ability to speak up. It was no different than sitting in silence and suffering throughout my swimming career. I had continued to recreate that dynamic personally. While I spoke back with Paul over the years, I never went and told someone what was going on. I wanted others to see and rescue me and no one did. As no one came to my rescue, I built up this story about everyone around me that I believed to be true based on their lack of action. How come you can't read my actions because I don't have a voice? As I was waking up and the veil of blindness was removed, I started to witness how it resided in the sports world. I was also able to see how my relationships were formed on a personal level that recreated this idea that I had about myself and the voice that I had for myself as well.

As I started to wake up and see that addressing the issue of sexual abuse in sports was to become my path and interest, it felt spiritually driven in that I was committed to doing something to help others and I knew there were many that had suffered the same fate as I. I wanted to help others heal from their past and change the trajectory for a new generation going forward. So I started to research the topic only to find there wasn't much in the way of research going on in the United States, not as I saw and experienced in sport. I did, however, learn that my former athletic director, Donna Lopiano, after leaving Texas, went on to be the President of the Women's Sports Foundation for over thirty years until she started her own sports management firm. I knew that I needed to clean up all the old hurt feelings from my past on this journey; Donna stayed the course when it came to my academic performance. You know your basic troubled kid that everyone wants to help but no one knows what's wrong or how to help? That was me.

The day that my partner moved out and we broke up for good, I had the courage and desire to finally ask for help. I felt directed to write to Donna. I knew that I needed to explain to her what had happened to me as an athlete and apologize for any trouble I had caused her and the athletic department. I wanted to ask Donna for help in starting an organization to address these issues. It took two seconds for Donna to respond back and say, "yes" she would.

We started by having several conversations about what it was that I would have needed to have prevented this from happening to me. As I started to work with Donna, she suggested we jointly write a paper on the topic to address the issues. That meant I needed to do research on a more meaningful level which brought me to one of the leaders on the topic, Celia Brackenridge. Celia had started her academics on this topic while researching and writing about Paul as he was the first coach with a public profile and a criminal charge against him which lead her to writing her first book on the topic. She had followed the case and its surrounding drama. This led me to reach out to her. Celia was just as receptive as Donna in that she too was quick to engage with me via email and hop on a Skype call to talk about my experience. After gathering our information and figuring out what had been developed in the area, prevention wasn't something much considered in the States. Donna, after publishing our paper online, began to create our organization's policies and procedures. With Donna's vast administrative and policy knowledge and my deep understanding about my experience, we created a comprehensive set of policies to address the issue at the local level which is where the problem exists.

As we were developing the organization from a structural standpoint, the news of Jerry Sandusky being arrested for pedophilia broke on November 11, 2011. Yes, we live in a matrix (11-11-11). I was so concerned that we had missed the boat with launching the organization knowing the shock and awe that was about to move through this country. I was almost defeated that we weren't ready to capture the wave. When I spoke to Donna about that she was calm as calm could be and said, "No worry, somebody else will have screwed up." When she said that I knew that too. I knew how deep the problem was and how prevalent it was from all my friends at an elite level. I knew there were many others and that it was rampant in the system.

A few weeks later Safe4Athletes was officially born in January of 2012. There was immediate interest and connection into the gymnastics community when I first started the organization. I was excited about this new venture. I was excited to show up for myself for once. It was certainly challenging with personalities and my own flaws at that time with communication and my inability to truly articulate what was going on. I also didn't expect or could really say that I was prepared for the newfound emotional intensity that I was experiencing. I had this deep shame about my experience with the significance of it that I said, "Fuck it, I'm doing this for the next generation." It was a constant struggle to expose and talk about my sexual abuse. It wasn't just with a friend anymore; it was now getting published and printed across the country and in fact, around the world. The one thing that I knew about myself was that I had the keys to the kingdom in my ability and intuition to understand sexual abuse so intimately from all the work that I had done on myself over the years.

When I first started Safe4Athletes, Annabelle had several swimming records across the country that were still standing. Katherine took on her proud role and was going to defend the honor of that little girl who loved swimming so much that it saved her life. This was where I truly stepped into the name of Katherine Starr. I understood the two names and the path that I was now on. I had that confidence that I knew was always there but could not access. I also felt that all that time in the ocean and swimming with the dolphins was a slow and constant change of my being working in the background. It wasn't like an immediate noticeable event. All of this was a collection of experiences that allowed me to see through the veil and on the other side of abuse.

At the same time that I was going public with my abuse, I also started to reconnect with my teammates from college; my swimming friends from around the world, as well as new friends that had a similar story as mine. All those goodbyes that I didn't get to have thirty years ago were here; people came back into my life to fill the void that I had created over the years. As I reconnected, there was some minor cleanup of relationships along the way. I had cleaned up most of my relationships from my past at this point in my life with sobriety or had at least made an effort. People reached out to me expressing the empathy for my experience wishing they would have known at the time and been there for me. The love was overwhelming and heartfelt.

Then one day I got an email from Wendy, who had now changed her name to Chaya. She wrote me to ask if I still had that email I sent her. Chaya wanted to reply properly. At this point, I was clearly well into Katherine's life and no longer had an email from her from about eight years before. I wrote back to apologize and she said that it was okay—she could respond without it.

When I received the email from Chaya/Wendy, she wanted to heal from our past in a meaningful way. She wanted to clear out all the hurt that had affected our friendship. I welcomed this and needed this as she did too. Our friendship had formed and bonded so quickly at the Olympics and then fell apart from my inability to talk, to communicate, to really be a friend with integrity. I had none of that and know that my selfishness hurt my friend deeply. This led to a series of emails of sharing raw and clear communication about our friendship in a meaningful and loving way. I was able to truly speak my truth as was she. I knew from all that work that I had done over the years that I had finally found the voice that I thought had left me. The one that I thought was never there during the course of my swimming career or with my dad. The voice that had always wanted to talk, but I wouldn't let it out of my own fear of the stories that I would scare myself with. I had trapped lies in my mind like a beehive buzzing with bees and now it was finally ready to be broken and set free. We spent the summer leading up to the London Olympics writing back and forth letting out the truth and letting go of the falsehoods that had plagued our friendship.

The same Olympic cycle was still in me as it was with my now grown Olympic friends. The time of year was like flu season for athletes where the old hurts and pains would start to cycle around again. This cycle was no different; it just came with a different hurt and pain for us to talk about, now that my abuse was going public. The lead-up to the Olympics brought light to the harm done to athletes, with sexual abuse being the next issue that was ready to be made public and get airtime. The rampant performance-enhancing drug use had long been in the headlines, and it was time to reveal the rest of the dark side of sport. The press and the interest quickly took off to share my story and address the issue from a global perspective.

During this time I stayed close to Celia and we started to develop a friendship as we talked about my abuse. I learned about the academic side of all the research that she had done on the topic. It was like we got to learn from each other and deepen our respective knowledge. I was able to take my experience and ability to talk about my coach abuse with such a clear understanding about the dynamics that happen between a coach and athlete while adding the formal language to it as I started to develop myself into an expert on the topic. As my expertise grew, so did my relationships with athletes from all sports across the globe.

As the issue started to become a more mainstream issue, athletes, parents, and coaches would contact me for help and direction on how to deal with their concerns about abuse. What I came to learn from speaking with athletes from all sports and all ages was that they all had the same problem as me: they didn't have the ability to communicate or talk about what was happening directly. I started to hear similar patterns in how one talked about abuse. It was often in regards to their love of their sport or about something unrelated, like another coach doing something that bothered them. It wasn't direct at all. I had this way of finding the truth, only knowing from my own experience about how I protected the secret of the abuse out of fear that someone would also take away my passion, only to learn that it was me that had taken away nurturing my passion as a result.

I also knew from my own experience as an athlete of how deep I pushed those voices down so I could hear nothing. If I heard nothing then no one, including me, would know. Going with this premise, I knew that I wanted to create a relationship with the women in gymnastics. I wanted them to know that I was fighting for them and that my help was available. It was much easier for a swimmer who is a foot taller than anyone in that sport to be their advocate than for them to feel like they are turning on their own kind. For me it helped that I was no longer active in the world of competitive swimming. I was free to step on toes.. It was clear in my mind that one day I would get a call that would pull the abuse right out of the system.

As my voice started to develop, so did my influence. I was contacted by senators to write for senate hearings on the topic, and was asked to support and help change age of consent laws and laws on statutes of limitation across the states. At the same time I was starting to work on legal cases that were complicated in nature and needed an expert to address the coach-athlete relationship. It was here that I truly found my voice where I could dig right into the case and apply my personal experience with clarity backed up by academia to bring clarity to the issue in the courts. My ability to understand complex coach-athlete behavior and discuss it clearly was turning out to be my calling and purpose in life.

I spent all that time being stuck in my life and resisting my pain from my past. I knew in concept that our pain is our biggest asset but I didn't have the tools to understand how that applied to my life. I was perfectly designed to lead this path. It was a hard pill to swallow to accept that those life events were going to be used for good. I was in constant demand by every side of this issue, and was invited to join the USOC Advisory Board For The Center of Safe Sport and the International Olympic Committee to write the latest consensus statements on harassment and abuse with the other recognized leaders on the topic. At this point I was now connected to this issue throughout the sports world, and witnessed where the issues reside in the system—many are still there today.

It was painful to see the hopelessness of the abuse floating around these sports and their programming. Sexual abuse happens because of the leadership of the organization. The purpose of Safe4athletes is to break the chain of abuse that exists in the system and give the power back to the athletes, combined with some communication tools to express themselves and actually be heard. Despite knowing that the power of influence and leadership is what allows abuse to exist in the system, I kept addressing this issue and continue to speak the truth and help others in the process.

I didn't keep going in this direction because it was a money maker, as it was not; I kept going in this direction and didn't give up because I felt I couldn't walk away from what I had come to see as the problem. I couldn't walk away from the silent screams of an athlete that I knew too well. It was like in Dr. Seuss's *Horton Hears a Who,* when the Wickersham gang want to cage and beat up Horton for fighting for the voices that only he can hear. It needed a call to the Mayor to say that every voice must speak up in order to be heard and so Horton says, "Don't give up! I believe in you all! A person (an athlete) is a person (an athlete) no matter how small and you very small persons will not have to die (be sexually abused). If you make yourselves heard! So come on, now, and TRY!" I took that to be fighting for the issue while also wanting to be a leading voice to help others speak about their experience.

As the book continues, Horton needs everyone to speak up so he says, "I can hear you just fine. But the kangaroos' ears aren't as strong, quite, as mine." I felt like that was me. I could hear the sounds of sexual abuse and see it in athletes who didn't speak up or say anything. I could see it in their body, demeanor, and in the way that they carried themselves. Horton then asks for everyone to speak up, as the Mayor in the story says, "Everyone seemed to be yapping or yipping! Everyone seemed to be beeping or bipping!" It seemed like in the athletic community that it had started to happen, but it still wasn't enough. I could see the silent suffering that was still not being seen or heard.

When the Mayor finds Jo-Jo in apartment 12-J, "Not making a sound! Not a yipp! Not a chirp!" what I felt was that everyone's voice was equally important in addressing abuse—you didn't have to be an Olympian, although the media seemed to think that was important. It was everyone in sport, no matter how small, you needed to speak your truth so everyone can hear the issues that plague sport at its deepest level. As the Mayor yells back to Horton with every voice speaking up, he finishes his speech with, "So, open your mouth, lad! For every voice counts!" It was, *"That one last small, extra Yopp put it over!"* where I could see how this story is about the silent suffering of abuse and that all voices matter for the issue to be truly heard. This story inspired me to find even the quietest voices in the darkest of places.

As Safe4Athletes continued its work addressing athlete abuse, Safe4Athletes and Katherine Starr became known as advocates for this issue. It was the crack in the system that opened the pathways for athletes to speak up and speak their truth. It truly did give an athlete a voice. Then one day the call came from Dominique Moceanu, 1996 Olympic gold medalist in gymnastics, with whom I had developed and maintained a relationship. She reached out to ask if I would speak with one of her Olympian friends about a coach issue that she was aware of. I of course said, "Sure." This was about a week before the 2016 Rio Olympics. I was sitting in LAX waiting for my flight to London to meet my siblings for a trip around Europe for my brother's fiftieth birthday. I was sitting in the American Airlines lounge when I made the call to Jamie Dantzscher to learn of her issue. I would like to tell you that it was a two-second call of "I was sexually abused, and will you help me?" but that was not it at all. The conversation was completely unrelated about something else that she wanted to talk to me about that was happening at a gym at the time. During our conversation I could sense something else that was plaguing her. That was where I was like Horton; I could hear what was going on, which gave me the gift of directing that conversation to find out what was truly afflicting her. I could hear all the statements, the excuses, the concerns, the resistance—all of it was a pattern that I had once known for me. I took that conversation to a place where we could start talking about the sexual abuse that was causing concern in this other area. It was so subtle within her; it hadn't been classified in her as being thought of as sexual abuse at this point. It was so rampant and common among her teammates that Jamie had normalized the behavior as had so many of her teammates who had experienced the same "medical treatment," if you will, by Larry Nassar. I knew otherwise. I knew that language of denying yourself what is to be true. It was our way of protecting ourselves, protecting our passion, and our sport. That was the lie in the system. It was so strong and the voices so quiet that it needed someone to speak up for until they could heal to the point of letting their own voices speak out.

I ended that conversation with Jamie saying that I would contact a lawyer and set up a meeting for us to evaluate potential legal action. I knew who to call: John Manly. I had sent cases his way before. Since I was going to be in Europe for two weeks I wasn't going to be able do anything until I got back, but I had set the wheels in motion.

When I was in Europe, the Olympics had started and in good dramatic fashion and timing The Indianapolis Star ran a damning story on the latest gymnastics sexual abuse case that showed the continued blatant disregard of protecting the athletes and the sport from the harm of abuse. The leadership was looking the other way. My phone was blowing up with requests for interviews, the news outlets were looking for studios wherever I was so I could be available to comment on the latest story. I made myself available the best I could while also trying to enjoy my family. At the same time I knew there was a looming case that was going to follow Jamie's.

I had set up a meeting with John Manly and Jamie, for the week when I got home. John and I flew up to Oakland on John's private jet and met with Jamie in a conference room at the private airport. I sat in that room with John as we discussed what happened. It was all coming out in that moment. I knew that if I was patient the real story would be revealed at some point. I knew to stay close and that it would be pulled right out of the system.

We left that meeting not knowing how deep and wide the issue would turn out to be, but I knew it was big. During the course of that week when we were with Jamie, one of her teammates reported the issue to the police in Indianapolis; she is often referred to as the Athlete A, or the first person that came forward. I, however, knew a different story based on the events that I was involved in, knowing it was my conversation with Jamie and the ability to hear the quietest of pain in the back of the soul of an athlete, that opened the floodgates of what was to become commonly known as the Nassar case.

After the case started to take shape, John took the lead as the numerous gymnasts started to come forward, making this situation the biggest sexual abuse case in the history of gymnastics. I can proudly say that I had a hand in righting a wrong. I felt like my work was done, like it was all worth it.

A few weeks later I was at my alumni weekend in Texas for our annual Hall of Fame induction, also known as the Frank Erwin Award taking place over a Texas football weekend. I had started to attend these regularly in the past years as I stopped hiding from my past and welcomed and cherished my friends from Texas. Looking back, it was really the happiest time in my life among beloved friends. During that weekend I was sitting up in the stadium by myself in that moment as my friends had stepped away as the Texas Longhorn band started playing the song that they wrote and dedicated to Eddie Aikau, "Are You Going to Rescue Me?"

I couldn't believe what I was hearing. I had goose bumps all over me as I saw my life flash before my eyes, not unlike the experience that I had at the Ark when I broke free of the dynamic that I had formed with people and how I created relationships. I had broken free again. It was in that moment that I knew that Eddie was one of my guardian angels and had been watching over me and saved me when I was needed in the world—I have a place and a purpose. Left to my own thoughts I would have just drifted off that day. Instead, my life had drifted to shore to follow my path and purpose in life.

CHAPTER 20

Journey to Freedom

After realizing that Eddie came into my life to redirect my course of action, it woke me up internally at a whole new level. I had so many people cross my path to love me, nurture me, and guide me towards my purpose and path in life. People were looking out for me, but I wasn't looking out for me with the same determination and peace of mind with which I had dedicated my life to helping athletes protect their passion and pursue their sport. I had started addressing the issue with an FU attitude that I didn't care what harm came to me—you aren't going to harm another generation. While that seems noble in theory, it was also harmful to my soul in the way that I left myself unprotected from attacks.

Now it was time for me to be as brave for myself as I was for others. I also didn't want to let anyone know that I was hurting inside. I felt that the awareness that I got for my work was both filling my cup and healing. I was ready to finally let go of any and all baggage that was holding me back from living a truly vibrant life. That led me to wanting to revisit the night of my rape; I was finally ready to watch the episode to the end. I was finally ready to see what I had missed and had never gone back to find out.

I decided to order the final episode of *Fame* and go through that day with a different story and memory attached to the show. I started watching the show and couldn't believe my ears and eyes as to what I was really watching that night. Besides truly digesting the theme song, "You got big dreams, you want fame, well fame costs, and right here is where you start paying." This struck me in the one area where I went wrong with all of this. What had I been pursuing? Was it to be the best in the world? Or was it a pursuit of fame? I needed to really consider what was my underlying motive and did that play into the path on which I found myself.

What was even more shocking to me about the episode is that it was actually all about sexual harassment and standing up for yourself. I never got to see that part of the story. All I got to see was the sexual harassment starting—I was left with no conclusion, as the TV was blared in the background that night fateful night, it was shouting about standing up for yourself. The teacher, Ms. Sherwood, was an advocate for herself when she reported it the office. I missed the lesson on who and where to go to speak up for myself. I didn't have the skills or knowledge to do that and no one told me it was even wrong at the time. I knew how I felt and that I was stuck in a battle with Paul, but I didn't know that anyone would or could do anything about it.

I opened up myself to have a different story that also confirmed the path that I was on. I would be the one who stood up against sexual abuse in sport. There was something pleasing and apropos about it when you realize that you're walking on the path that was designed for your life. I took away the lifelong hurt and pain of my experience and turned it into a purpose and a purposeful life for me. I know that the only reason that I could understand abuse so clearly is because of my experience. I really was perfectly designed by life events that were painful and now I can say that I am grateful to have been sexually abused so I can help others. I went from hurting with such intense pain to joy and was honored to be used in this way to serve the greater good.

When I was able to truly take all this in on a spiritual level, I figured out what was missing in me, and that was *me.* I started down the path of addressing an issue that was important to my heart, but the same heart didn't know how to love myself and show up for myself.

What all this did was block this idea of joy, reaffirming that I couldn't experience it in my life. If I did, did it mean that I had lost the battle of owning this misery that I was carrying around with me? I couldn't lose because winning is something that I prided myself on, especially with my need to be praised. I had no idea what I was missing in life.

Yet I knew that I wanted to rid myself of any and all pain for good. I didn't know how I was going to do that but I knew I was committed to it, whatever it was. Then one day, I was in yoga class and we were opening and closing our hands. I could feel this cord attached to my ring finger that went all the way up my arm to my heart. I couldn't tell if it was a spiritual blockage that was preventing me from connecting to my heart or if it was related to my shoulder. I kept on pushing my hands to open wider and wider with all my might to see if it would break or unravel itself. Then I felt a pop (I had no idea what made that pop), and I could feel the cord break away.

Like a good little athlete at heart I didn't think anything of it, and so I carried on with the day only to wake up the next morning with the most intense physical pain I ever felt in life, I could barely move my arm. What I had done was broken my reconstructive shoulder surgery that had been holding my shoulder in place—there was a band on the front of shoulder that kept the joint secure. I had an aversion to taking pain pills so Advil became my drug of choice to take the edge off. When I went to the doctor there wasn't much hope for me other than some physical therapy; there was nothing that they could do. They also quickly misdiagnosed me and I knew that. I left that doctor's office feeling completely defeated knowing that I would never be able to swim again. When it was my choice not to swim it was okay, but now it wasn't my choice. I was told that I would not be able to have a full recovery and would only be able to get partial use of my shoulder. My shoulders were where my true gift resided in my body. I was incredibly strong and now that was never going to be my identity again.

The loss of my arm's mobility was like losing my best friend. What made this especially hard was that my dad, the doctor, was also not here to help me connect to the right people to get the care I needed. I shared at a meeting about the pain of not being able to swim. It was the one place where I could connect with the grace that was in me and that was now gone. The powerful glide was my signature stroke and that was gone, just like that. I know I'm getting old, but the water was my place of peace. As I was sharing this with a friend, she wanted me to know about her journey through her injuries and wanted me to meet all the people that she believed could put me back together again, like Humpty Dumpty. I was so grateful for the introductions to various folks and one was to her trainer, Peter Park.

When I met Peter I learned that he had written a book called, *Rebound: Regain Strength, Move Effortlessly, Live without Limits—At Any Age* for athletes like me to come back to themselves later in life and in their career. I thought all of this was not possible with me and that all I really wanted was to just have my shoulder back and I would be good again. The first day that I met with Peter he gave me a weight for my arm and I couldn't even move it. I immediately felt a loss, that my Rolls-Royce engine was now completely gone—there was no engine at all.

What was even more painful was that I was being awarded The Frank Erwin Award at the University of Texas that fall. It's the equivalent of the Texas Swimming Hall of Fame. This recognition brought up all the old feelings from the dynamics of my family where my siblings resented any success that I had in swimming. This was no different and was an extension of our childhood feelings that we had for each other. What made this recognition harder was that this was the very reason that my dad and I were at odds with each other over the years and it was all for being recognized for my greatness and he wasn't there to celebrate it with me. It was why he drove me to practice in the mornings, and it was why he was mad at me when I didn't rise to the occasion. All the hurt and disappointment was about to be wiped clean in this moment.

When I arrived at the Texas stadium for the celebration, I was welcomed by the class of women that I swam with. The last time we were all together was on the night of NCAA's when we placed second and ended the five year National Championship winning streak. I was blessed to be on three of those, but the pain of losing and being in the class that failed to extend the streak was unsettling and hard to accept, especially since the amazing women in my class were called the "No Name Class." I was the only one who broke free from that label because of the path that I had found myself on. It was the irony of the situation.

It was so beautiful to see my teammates and reconnect with them. My entire class had stayed away from our reunions over the years and had made a special trip to celebrate me. I felt so loved. I realized then that all the hours and all the swimming up and down, staring at the black line, was for this kind of love, this kind of friendship. It wasn't for the wins and the losses; it was for the love of the same thing: swimming. We all had respect for our passion and the gift of our talents. I had worked out with a friend that we swam over 100,000 miles just to be friends with each other. It was the tie that bonded us. It was like all that disappointment had washed over me, not because of the award, but because of the love of my friends and how rich it was. It made me proud to be part of such an amazing program and group of women. I needed that experience to be reminded that it wasn't all as bad as I made it out to be. I was proud of my time swimming at Texas.

I also knew how proud my dad would have been for me. This award wasn't only for my swimming greatness; being recognized for the work and contributions I had been doing in the world made it a worthy honor. That was more important to my heart at the end of the day; I was changing the trajectory of someone's life for good without them knowing it. It was how I felt about Eddie that day in the ocean—that interaction changed the course of my life. It brought me to a much needed peace for which I had been searching.

I wasn't done with healing. I was seeking out ways to develop returning to that untethered spirit, if you will. I know it was hard to see and seemingly impossible to imagine or pursue, but I believed in my vision and desire for myself. It wasn't just for me; it was for all of you too, that was the way I saw it anyway.

Back home in LA, I started to train with Peter who trains professional athletes, and celebrities. I would be at the gym with active athletes taking in their drive at the height of their career, and get to be in their presence as I could feel my way back to what it was like to train. I was so afraid to embrace any serious training, in the pool or in a gym. I never wanted to have another goal or dream again. I was done with my heart being broken. Though now that my shoulder was damaged I wanted it back, and the thought of never feeling that grace in the water again was painful to me. The parts of my personality that had been dormant were starting to come alive, like my ability to focus, my determination, and really how strong I am as a person. It didn't take long for my shoulder to start to strengthen and be on par with my other shoulder with the wisdom of Peter's foundation training and strength exercises.

Peter training regimen included cardio at the end of every workout. I hated raising my heart rate too high; the mental energy needed to prepare for that felt too much like swimming or training, and I just didn't want it to hurt anymore. I didn't think that I had the mental energy to take that on. The amazing person that Peter is he brings the best out of you without trying and there was no getting out of it. He had such a simple and kind way of coaching. I was healing a deep wound training with him, one that I never thought could be healed.

When I really found the athlete that was in me was when Peter started having me use the Ski-erg. It's a cross-country cardio machine, mostly arms with a full body pull down stroke. It was hard, but about as close to swimming without a pool and a bench to do it from. Peter started giving me sets on the machine, not unlike my swimming sets, managing time, pace and distance, something that I was once a master at. I managed my energy and delivered what he asked of me. He gave me goal times and I worked on hitting them every time. I had learned to be fearful of my talents. When I started this training I was starting to tap back into that Rolls-Royce engine of mine. I could feel the core of me wanting to come back to life and play. The desire and the passion to perform again was starting to wake up. All this time I was wanting to return to the purity of passion and spirit only to learn that it was through the very thing that I feared and dreaded: performing. Here I was loving the idea of this. The rebound that Peter spoke about was true. I was truly starting to rebound inside. I was able to turn my attention to perfecting my craft with this new machine. As I perfected my craft, the other athletes in the gym were also recognizing my talent on this machine. I was being seen by my peers again. I was being seen for the person that I truly am on the inside.

As I started to connected with my inner athlete I started to hear a different version of my story with deeper meaning and understanding. As I began to listen, my inner self began to whisper another version of my life that I hadn't been able to hear before. It wasn't like the events of my life didn't happen; all that is true and accurate. What was becoming clearer was asking myself, what was I seeking? Was it me all along? Yes, it was. I couldn't help but vacillate between not wanting to accept any aspect of my life as me being the problem and what choices I could have made differently. After all, somebody else did something to me that I didn't want to have to happen to me and therefore it couldn't be me. I wanted to run with that party line. Then the question was posed: why did I wait so long to speak up? I had reasons and some we could say were arguably valid. I was a child without parents around who was fending for myself. But I still had a choice. I might not have known or taken it, but I still had a choice to speak up at any point in my journey. The idea of that thought, if I wanted to accept it, was true. It meant to me that there was something deeper that I was trying to protect and as a result I didn't go to any lengths to speak up.

When I started to process I knew that I needed to find my way to this truth at some point. I knew the truth, but I never wanted to admit it to myself. I was in pursuit of praise. My whole journey and pursuit of being an Olympian and a gold medalist was for the praise and the accolades of being a gifted athlete. I had the idea that my father would love me more the better I performed and the more that I accomplished. If my father loved me the most then my mother and I would have a better, more loving relationship. I had this idea that if I performed and delivered something for you I would feel better as a person. I was trapped in this vicious cycle of my need for praise and attention. I had started at such a young age winning and breaking records that recognition was all I knew from my dad, my coach, friends, and everyone that I crossed paths with. As my success grew, the power of the people grew; so did my silence in a desperate need of the attention that went with that from you and others. I was in a dance that I didn't even know I was invited to.

I didn't need the rewards and the accolades in the same way as I needed them growing up. I was changing the dynamic that I once knew as I trained with Peter. I was able to feel inside of me the growth of spirit, the confidence of self, and the desire to be the best version of myself. I was no longer training to be an Olympian, yet I was wanting to feel the drive that took me in that direction. I would say now I was feeling it with integrity with myself. I started to listen to my thoughts when I performed and trained to hear what I was telling myself there. I finally found the joy in sport that I always wanted and knew was there. I didn't win a medal, perform in an event, or have anyone cheering me on; the gift was the joy. The internal flame that was starting to shine bright again.

When I looked back at my life I saw a clear pattern and dynamic of me wanting my father to love me and for my coach to coach me to get his love. All the while I had resented and hated myself and others for having my gift and talent in the first place, like that was the problem in my life. Since I knew that it was me, I know that I was to blame for the failures and successes in my life. It was me and my reactions that caused the pain and sadness to stay as long as it did. I am finally free of this cycle of reward, recognition, and praise. While it is still in my life, it is not what drives me to have integrity with myself as a person.

As I grew in my integrity as an athlete the pain of my heart started to melt away. As my heart started to open so did my awareness of my internal battle that I had with myself. I had spent all these years blaming myself for the losses, for being responsible for being sexually abused by my coach, and for not accomplishing my dreams. I stayed in this internal battle trying to figure out how to win it. It was like I carried on my competitive spirit and drive as an athlete and repurposed it to keep me suffering and stay stuck in that sadness. My unknown logic at the time was that I was a failure to have let this happen to me and therefore I am a failure. As I heard these lies that I was telling myself, I have been able to completely let go of the past while gaining a deeper understanding of how deep this wound really was.

I can finally say that I am no longer in battle with my father, my mother or Paul. I have relieved them of their duties and now I can love my father from the other side and let Paul go as an opponent and forgive my mother as I ask for her forgiveness of me for not being the daughter that I could be. I have stopped fighting everyone. That fateful episode of Fame, "A Special Place;" it truly is a special place when one can find their way back to their self with integrity.

While I found forgiveness in those around me, my life was still not complete. There was something missing. There was one person that I had yet to forgive and that was me. The forgiveness of self is the most difficult of all. I felt that I was ready to love again and explore my newfound passion for life, but I needed a little help in getting there. I could hear the child voice of Annabelle wanting a puppy, that little girl desire to feel love and give love was permeating through me. The lost innocence of self was awakening with the idea of getting a puppy just like that eight year old girl only this time I didn't have to perform or earn it.

I now had an eye on the prize as I went in search of the right puppy for me. I thought a lazy dog would be ideal for my apartment living lifestyle; it would just sit around and love me and I would have to do very little in return. It was the perfect plan. As I began this search for a puppy, I knew that a rescue was not right for me as I didn't feel like I had the confidence to train a rescue. In fact, I was the rescue in this situation.

So I began my search for this ideal lazy dog. This pursuit also opened the door for me to have a safe conversation with my mother, knowing that it wasn't just letting go of an opponent it was loving my mother for exactly who she was. I asked her advice on puppies; I was met with the usual disappointment and rebuke of you don't want that puppy or this puppy as she thought they didn't match my lifestyle. My old resentment that my mother doesn't know me also surfaced. At the same time, I trusted my mother's knowledge about puppies since over the years she had wisely replaced all her children with puppies. Ultimately, she suggested a Vizsla. I had never heard of this breed but based on my mother's relationship with the breeder I decided to investigate this further. In order to get the right dog for me, knowing the breeder was the most important part of this process. After all this was an exercise in learning to trust again, in me and others. I also felt like it was time to have a relationship with my mother.

As I learned more about this puppy, I was learning more about my mother and her new husband's family. As it turns out, she was suggesting this breed because the puppies were on the way and the breeder was the daughter of my mother's new husband. I didn't take the time to fully investigate about the breed because for some unknown reason I felt confident about the people in my mother's new life. Without hesitation I said yes, not knowing what I was getting into.

I used to have a saying that the only thing that I was willing to commit to was to not commit to anything. I had lived my life with detachment. Here I was making a commitment, to one of the most active dog breeds. I quickly learned about Vizsla's athleticism and high energy as well as being extremely loving, nicknamed a "velcro dog". It sounded a lot like me. I felt so confident in the breeder and the idea of this puppy that there was no going back, I knew in my heart that this puppy was for me. Then I started to get scared about the commitment and the exercise requirements that this puppy was going to need. Many articles often referenced the puppy stage lasts until they are least 6 years old. If these dogs don't get the exercise they need they have been known to eat drywall. How was I was going to live up to this commitment? I had struggled to take care of me and now there was another living thing coming into my world.

I began to reflect on this commitment and a thought came to me: this puppy needs to go to "practice" twice a day. I needed to go to practice twice a day. Wait, I was a high energy child that needed to exercise a lot or I too was going to be destructive. I also accepted that my parents were committed to my training and accomplishments. It was me who sailed off course. Their goal for me was to embrace and use the talent that I had, albeit groomed by the system. They provided everything for me to pursue my goals, our goals. When I accepted the gifts that my parents gave me, it released the pressure of the commitment. As I understood the needs of my very athletic puppy, I started to truly understand their sacrifice. They did what they thought was loving. They were trapped in a system that was susceptible to harm. They came from a place of admiration; the system is designed to manipulate the good hearted. Little Annabelle was a casualty of that.

This revelation cracked my heart wide open. I couldn't help but hear the whispers of my father talking to Little Annabelle again. I wanted to honor the true love that I have for my parents by naming my puppy with the name that I was given. It was time to give little Annabelle with the joy of love again, So I named my puppy Little Annabelle of Arlington House H.R.H and for short, Bella.

When I awoke the morning after our first night together, I found Bella snuggled right in over my heart. As my time with little Annabelle has grown, she has taught me love and forgiveness at a depth I never thought possible. I have let go of all the hurt and disappointment that I had with my mother. I'm sad that I spent most of my adult life being mad and hurt at the wrong person, my mother. I wanted her to rescue me from my pain so badly that, I projected that somehow she could have done something about it. In the end she did, she led me to the most amazing puppy that has loved me unconditionally and brought a zest for life that I never thought possible. I love you Little Annabelle for Rescuing Me in more ways than one, you truly are the love of my life. More importantly, I love you Mum and hope that you will forgive me for never saying it back. Well, I am now, I love you Mum.

Acknowledgements

This book is an actual book with words on a page and not just thoughts floating around in my head with only a desire to put them on paper because of Lauren, who did what I could not do for myself: She held me accountable to my dream of writing this book with love and grace, and challenged me when I wanted to stop, give up, and take a break. It was met with, "Well, what are you going to give up?" to "No quitting on the fly!" to "Sometimes it is hard." Lauren never gave up on me when I didn't believe in me and my voice. My heart is filled with so much love and gratitude for you. Thank you for being the wind at my back and pointing me in the right direction.

I gave up all desire and hope of ever finding my way to the athlete within until I met Peter—you are truly talented in bringing out the inner athlete and making one feel alive again on the inside. That athlete's drive and focus I had thought was lost was brought back to life because of you and I can't begin to express the gratitude for you taking me under your wing and seeing the true me when I thought I had tucked it away for no one to see. You shined the light on darkness. Thank you, Peter, for being an inspiration to me and countless others.

There are so many people who have been on my path and have supported me through struggles and success that have kept me in the game of life; one of those is James Leonard. Jim, thank you for never leaving my side, always supporting every request, need, question or negotiation, always with kindness, wit, and unconditional love. Thank you for never leaving my path and staying on the journey with me and seeing every project we do together through to the end.

When I had doubts about being a writer, I found someone to erase any doubt and stay on course with me. Alice, your patience, professionalism, and keeping up with my drive was impressive and quite frankly, saintly! We made a great team. I knew the story and you knew the tenses—thank you for editing this book and taking away my grammar shame that was preventing me from putting the story down on paper. A true blessing and thank you for that, Alice.

Hildie, I love you so much and am so blessed to have your coaching and support at every moment. Thank you for staying with me in the story as I wrote it. When I finished a chapter, I was so excited to share it with you; hitting send brought me so much joy and comfort knowing that your heart was right there in it with me. For that I am eternally grateful.

For all the people on my path who just picked me up and carried me when I didn't even know that I had given up on me, thank you. There are so many people that I wish to thank: I thank the ones that I know by name and the ones that I don't. Every smile and moment of grace when I was hurting so badly on the inside kept me going to believe that the story I wrote was meant to be told. Keep smiling! You never know when it fills another with believing in themselves and their dreams they didn't know they had.

My life wasn't quite complete when I first finished writing this book as there was still something missing in my life. While my heart was ready to soften, I still needed a little help in getting there. I never felt that I could take care of myself let alone another living thing. I was ready to welcome in a new version of me and puppy.

The biggest blessing of my life is Bella and I would like to thank all of Bella's friend, especially Pippa, Dexter, Bernie, Kobe, Kodak and all her friends from Rustic Canyon who helped this book cross the finish line. We couldn't have done it without you all.

About the Author

Katherine Starr is a two-time Olympian 1984 and 1988 (Great Britain). In 1986 she won two silver medals at the Commonwealth Games. Katherine also experienced success at the collegiate level in swimming for the University of Texas at Austin, participating on three NCAA championship teams and was a 14-time All-American.

Katherine founded **Safe4Athletes** in 2011 as a result of living for decades with pain and suffering from the tragic effects of coach-athlete sexual abuse. Since speaking out about abuse in sports, Katherine has developed a reputation for her expertise and eloquence on coach-athlete sexual abuse. This is evident by the rapid growth of traditional media and social media attention on the problem of coach-athlete sexual abuse since the inception of **Safe4Athletes** including features with ESPN (Outside the Lines), NBC Sports Radio, NPR, BBC Radio, *The New York Times,* the Takeaway, CBS Sports Radio, Take Part Five (PIVOT Channel), Aljazeera America, as well other nationally recognized media outlets.

After ten years of tirelessly addressing coach-athlete abuse she formed a new company **Team Athlete Integrity** (2021) (www.athleteintegrity.com) to address the greater issue that is plaguing sport; Integrity. **Team Athlete Integrity** works with all stakeholders in sport to find the path of Integrity. Katherine now spends her time inspiring teams and athletes to find their true north star through her coaching philosophy and team building programs designed to help athletes (retired and active) thrive in all aspects of life. Katherine's motto is to Win from Within.